Pioneer Voices

Pioneer

Cynthia
Peabody
Anderson

SUMMIT
BOOKS

Voices

From Plymouth to Breckenridge

The Peabody Family Over Eleven Generations

Library of Congress
Catalog Card Number:
98-61599

ISBN: 0-9666420-0-7

SUMMIT
BOOKS

3 Currier Court
Lexington, Massachusetts 02420
Tel: 781-862-8118
Fax: 781-862-3090
e-mail: summitbook@aol.com

Cover Design by Susan Hill
Book Design by Paulette Livers Lambert

Left: Peabody children, circa 1885

*To the memory of my grandparents, Elmer Clifton Peabody
and Victoria Rosedahl Peabody—who brought the world to me.*

*And to my husband, Ted; my children, Sandy, Scott, Karyn, and Brett;
and my grandchildren, Alex, Timmy, Dara,
Nathan and Kenny—who mean the world to me.*

Contents

Acknowledgments

This book is the product of a journey—a journey across eleven generations, starting from my home in Colorado and going back in time to the little villages in New England where the early pioneers of my family first settled. Over the span of a dozen years I traced the trail of my ancestors as it wound its way through old cemeteries, dusty attic trunks, libraries, museums, courthouses and historical societies. I am most appreciative of the many persons who shared the journey with me and offered their assistance and encouragement. Many thanks to those who made available to me old maps, photographs, early land patents, ship logs, early newspaper articles, diaries and journals.

I am deeply indebted to Mary Ellen Gilliland who served as my editor and prepared my manuscript for publication. Her wisdom and unwavering enthusiasm sharpened my skills and renewed my confidence along the way.

My sincere thanks to Tony Kelso, Duxbury historian and Director of the Plymouth Plantation Education Department, for his generous assistance and wealth of knowledge about early New England history.

Special thanks go to Bill Gateley, my second cousin and genealogical sidekick, who unearthed many historical treasures, tramped through old cemeteries with me and shared a fascination with our family's story.

To my parents, Elmer and Lenora, for their love and gift of life and my sister, Sally, the playmate of my childhood, I am deeply grateful.

And most of all, thanks to Ted, my husband and love of my life. He is my most steadfast supporter as well as my most constructive critic and has accompanied me from the beginning of the journey to the end.

Pioneer Voices

Pioneer Roots

My grandparents were pioneers of the West. In the early 1900's they homesteaded a small ranch in the high mountains of Colorado. Pags and Grama, as I affectionately called them (as a little girl I couldn't pronounce "grandpa" and "grandma"), were my dearly beloved. Their ranch provided for me a source of joy and wonder. I spent countless hours happily roaming the meadows, playing by the river and exploring the outbuildings. I made the barn and bunk house, the blacksmith shop, the coal and ice shed, the broken-down pig pen and chicken house into my playground. I even enjoyed sitting in the old outhouse and memorizing the 1920's calendars and newspapers which papered the walls.

But Grama's attic fascinated me most. Several old trunks were wedged between the eaves of the attic. With Grama by my side, I carefully opened their dusty, creaking lids and delved into the mysteries of the past. Such an assortment of family heirlooms—high buttoned shoes and feathered hats, antique gowns and a corset Grama had worn tightly laced as a young woman. Albums containing faded photographs of severe, unsmiling people; collections of early postcards; and packets of old family letters—were all carefully packed away. Grama and I sat for hours pouring over these links to the past. An air of mystery surrounded the relics and sparked my imagination. I wondered, "What was life really like in the old days?"

Grama would say, "You are related to the Peabodys of Boston," as if that meant something special. I had no idea what she was talking about, but her words carried a mystique. Actually I hated having Peabody as my last name. I suffered great embarrassment when the little boys teased me about it at school. I longed for the day when I would grow up, get married and be able to trade "Peabody" for something commonplace.

The years came and went. As a young woman, I moved away from Colorado. Ultimately I settled in Lexington, Massachusetts, with my husband and four children. In the back of my mind my grandmother's voice still echoed, "the Peabodys of Boston."

One day I found myself at the Boston Public Library's genealogical department. Seated at a long table, I surrounded myself with piles of books

Elmer Clifton Peabody, Sr. ("Pags")

found my beloved grandfather, Elmer Clifton Peabody! Going back in time, I found his father, and his father, and his father, and his father, for nine generations back to the original Peabody who came to this country. John Paybody (as the name was spelled then) came from England in 1635 and settled in Plymouth Colony.

What an exhilarating moment! Now I understood Grama's talk about the Peabodys. Eleven generations later I had made the complete circle, for I lived in Massachusetts, just a few miles from where it all began.

I was all the more eager to return to the ranch to continue my search. Over the years I had loved reading the old letters and journals, piecing together bits of history from scraps of paper, old postcards and albums. At first it was a crazy quilt—parts of the story all in bits and pieces, nothing that fit with anything. But gradually a picture began to emerge.

Eyewitness Chronicles

One day I stumbled upon a locked strong box tucked away on a back shelf. I don't know how it had eluded my inquisitive eyes before this. I was mystified. What secrets so precious—or shameful—needed to be protected under lock and key? (My grandmother, always a private person, had seemed reluctant to tell us about her personal life, almost as if it were a source of humiliation.) Now it took little effort to pry the box open. Inside I found a

on the Peabody family. I had spent a frustrating day, fruitlessly searching for some clue, some link back to my past. Before going home, I opened the last book, *Peabody Genealogy,* written by Selim Hobart Peabody in 1909. Old and dusty, its binding had come loose and only twine held its contents together. When I looked into the index, I could not believe my eyes. There I poignant account of her early life as an orphan on a Kansas farm.

Then I came across another fascinating story about Colorado's Big Snow written by my grandfather. Pags was just a 14-year-old boy during the winter of 1898. That year an historic snowfall buried the town of Breckenridge, Colorado, cutting it off from the world for 79 days.

Finally, I discovered with excitement the document that linked all the family vignettes together, an autobiographical account written by my great-grandfather's sister, Almeda Peabody Wagner. Almeda was born in 1844 in the wilderness of northern New York. In her memoirs Almeda reminisced about pioneer life in the "big woods," traveling west by stagecoach in the Colorado Gold Rush and working as a cook in a Summit County mining camp.

The discovery of these first-hand accounts inspired me to write this book. They were written by ordinary people who neither glorified their accomplishments nor minimized their struggles. They didn't consider their lives extraordinary not did they seek praise. Yet they did record their lives and for this we are grateful. These stories written by my pioneer ancestors provide us with a glimpse into the real lives of real people in America's early days.

Though I will begin with the earliest Peabody ancestors' arrival on the New World's shores, I will later rely on Almeda Peabody's account to form the

Victoria Rosedahl Peabody ("Grama")

skeleton of my story. Using her autobiography as the "bones" of my pioneer saga, I will flesh out Almeda's story with historical background, and cultural and social comments, including a sad portrait of the native peoples whom progress crushed.

Almeda's journal begins by referring briefly to the first Peabodys who arrived in the New World two hundred years before her. These Peabody ancestors came to Plymouth Colony, Massachusetts in 1635.

Word about these early people trickled down through the years from one generation to the next as Peabody folklore. As in the childhood game of "gossip," where the message undergoes some distortion from one message carrier to the next, we see both truth and distortion in Almeda's first sentence.

Some time in the earlier years two brothers came from England and after wandering around finally settled in the Green Mountain Country of Vermont...

In this one sentence Almeda condensed six generations of people and 200 years of history! Let's take a look at the two brothers she mentions and the tale of generations to follow.

Research confirms Almeda's oral history account, that Peabody forefathers emigrated from England. The two brothers Almeda mentions in her journal are the two sons of John Paybody. One son, William, settled with his father, mother and sister in Duxbury of Plymouth Colony. The other son, Francis, settled by himself in Ipswich of Massachusetts Bay Colony. Over the course of six generations the Peabody family migrated around Massachusetts, then to New Hampshire, Vermont and ultimately to northern New York, just as Almeda recorded.

The New England Pioneers

Just fifteen years after the Mayflower Pilgrims landed in Plymouth the Paybodys* undertook a similar voyage. Twenty-one year old Francis sailed on the ship the *Planter*, arriving in 1635. The rest of the family, his father and mother, John and Isabel, younger brother, William, and sister, Annis, sailed at about that same time but on another ship.

History books do not give the exact date they arrived nor the ship on which they sailed. It may be that the passage of Puritans and malcontents between England and New England was so brisk that Francis was not accorded a berth on the same ship as his father. Or perhaps Francis came in 1635 and John, hearing news of his older son's safe journey, was influenced to expose the younger children to such a risky venture the next year.

At any rate, Francis ended up in Agawam (or Ipswich) of Massachusetts Bay Colony, while John and the rest of the family settled in Duxbury of Plymouth Colony.

Mayflower Pilgrims

Upon arriving in the New World these early Paybodys heard vivid accounts of that historic first voyage— the *Mayflower* crossing. In 1620 a full boatload of 101 passengers had set sail across the vast ocean. About a third of these Pilgrims were Separatists unhappy with the Church of England. They felt the church was tainted and could not be reformed. So they migrated to the New World where they could be free to worship in their own way and create a "community of the godly." Economic pressures drove others from England. A string of bad harvests and several severe winters had left large numbers of the population struggling to survive. Regardless of their reasons for emigrating, they came with the intention of recreating in America the English culture they left behind.

The Pilgrims set sail from Leyden, Holland on July 21st on the first leg of their trip. They departed from England to cross the Atlantic on September 6, 1620.

---

*The name was spelled variously in England and in this country. In John's will it was spelled Paybody. Francis in his will spelled the name Pebody and then signed it Pabody. William used the spelling Pabodie. For consistency, I have used the Paybody spelling in this text until the present day spelling of Peabody came into practice in 1715.

Plymouth Plantation in the winter.

We wonder, why did they start off on such a perilous journey so late in the year? First, they had been delayed in securing the financing and in working out a contract with the Merchant Adventurers who sponsored their trip. Then, the second ship slated to sail with the *Mayflower*, the *Speedwell*, began to leak and had to stay behind. All her passengers crowded onto the *Mayflower*. The transfer consumed valuable time. By then the Pilgrim's financial state was precarious and would not allow them to spend the winter in England and wait for a spring departure.

So off across the vast expanse of water the Pilgrims sailed, despite fall weather challenges. They were headed for northern Virginia, which is now the New York-New Jersey area. After a harrowing, stormy 66 days at sea, they arrived at Cape Cod on November 9, 1620. Before anchoring and beginning their settlement, they had to spend several more weeks exploring the shoreline up and down the coast by longboat to determine the best location.

Several expeditions battled the freezing cold and engaged in skirmishes with the Indians as they explored Cape Cod. *Mourt's Relation* tells about one

Pilgrim who wrote in his journal: "Water froze on our 'cloths' and made them many times like coats of iron." The Pilgrims also considered another area 20 leagues to the north because of its reportedly excellent harbor and better soil and fishing. This was either the Boston or Ipswich area (or Agawam, as it was then called).

By now it was winter. The weather grew exceedingly cold and stormy and the sea raged. The Pilgrims faced imminent danger. They needed to make final anchor. With enormous relief and "unspeakable joy" on December 11, 1620, the Pilgrims finally discovered Plymouth harbor and determined it a suitable location to begin their settlement.

On Christmas Day, 1620, work on the settlement finally began. (Actually, the Separatists in the group didn't celebrate the Christmas holiday. It was

John Alden proposing to Priscilla Mullins.

just another cold, wintry day for them.) The harsh weather closed in. During that first winter the settlers still lived on the *Mayflower*, which had to be anchored a mile and a half off shore where the water was deep enough. Men who were able went ashore by shallops (long boats) to begin constructing a Common House which was to serve as a warehouse and fortress against possible Indian attacks. Then they built a half dozen rude huts.

The bitter cold, the wind, and gusts of snow made working an ordeal. The men spent much of their time in soaking wet clothing and freezing temperatures. When they came ashore in their shallops they had to jump into the water to pull their boats onto the beach. Although they built bonfires to warm their hands, they often worked all day in frozen shoes and clothing. One observer described how one man had his "shoes cut off his feet that were so swelled with cold and it was a long time ere he was able to go (walk)."

The miserable weather and wretched living conditions resulted in much suffering that first winter. As January and February passed, more and more were overcome by terrible illnesses (probably pneumonia, aggravated by scurvy). The death toll was staggering. More than half the Pilgrims who had arrived on the *Mayflower* died that first winter. Although only one person died on the crossing of the Atlantic, 54 people perished while anchored in Plymouth harbor. Out of 14 wives only four survived.

One of the young people orphaned was Priscilla Mullins. Eighteen-year-old Priscilla lost her mother, father, brother and the family man servant in the General Sickness that first winter. During the *Mayflower* voyage Priscilla came to know John Alden, a cooper (barrel maker) back in England. Twenty-one-year-old John came on board as a hired hand and was given the task of testing the *Mayflower*'s barrels of fresh water and beer during the voyage. Priscilla and John's friendship grew into a romance, and they were married the latter part of 1621, the second marriage in the New World. (Later their courtship was romanticized and fictionalized by Longfellow in the *Courtship of Myles Standish*.)

In addition to illness, fear of attacks by the Indians (or "savages" as the Pilgrims called them), created another source of anxiety for the immigrants. Plymouth, the area chosen for their settlement, was the site of a deserted Wampanoag Indian village. Just three years earlier a great plague had swept through the area and decimated a major portion of the Indian population along the entire coast of New England. The newly arrived English settlers interpreted this as a divine intervention by God.

The Paybodys were told the story about how, soon after arriving, the Pilgrims formed an unusual and fortuitous friendship. In March, 1621, an Indian brave named Samoset marched into the Plymouth settlement and met the newcomers, or First Comers, as they sometimes referred to themselves. (Actually, the Indians were the native Americans and the "first" comers. They had lived on this land for thousands of years before the English arrived. Around 15,000 years ago people from Asia entered North America from Siberia crossing the Bering Strait. This migra-

tion probably occurred at a time when the sea levels were lowered by glaciation. The formation of ice sheets locked up so much water that a land bridge, known as "Beringia", joined Siberia to Alaska. Over thousands of years these ancestors of the Indians spread southward to inhabit both continents.)

Samoset introduced the immigrants to other Indians, including Squanto, the last surviving member of the tribe which had lived on the site of Plymouth. Squanto befriended the colonists and played a vital role in the lives of the newcomers. He introduced them to Massasoit, who was the chief, or sachem, of the Wampanoag tribe which occupied the entire southeastern, Massachusetts area. In 1623 Massasoit became gravely ill. Edward Winslow visited him and produced what the Indians viewed as an almost miraculous cure. This laid the foundation for a long-lasting friendship between the Wampanoag Indian natives and the Pilgrims. Massasoit's willingness to befriend the English was based upon mutual protection. At that time the Wampanoags were at war with a potent adversary, the Narragansets. A peace treaty was negotiated; the Wampanoags and the English agreed not to make war on each other and to come to each other's aid. This treaty endured for more than 50 years.

The Paybodys heard stories about the Indians teaching the Pilgrims how to survive. It seems strange that in a land with an abundant supply of wild game, water teeming with fish and

The John Alden House on its present site. The original structure was moved and remodeled in 1650, 15 years after the Peabodys arrived in America.

shores strewn with oysters, clams and lobsters, the Pilgrims nearly starved. The Pilgrims basically were not farmers, or fishermen or hunters. Most of the immigrants had lived in English villages and earned their living as artisans or craftsmen—weavers, tailors, brewers and shoemakers. John Alden was a cooper (barrel maker), William Brewster a village postmaster and Myles Standish a professional soldier. Most had never put their hand to a plow. (Fortunately, the Paybodys, who arrived 15 years later, had been farmers back in Leicester and were more equipped for beginning life in New England.) The

Pilgrims arrived without knowing how to fish the oceans and streams or fire a gun to kill meat. John Smith put it, "Though there be fish in the sea, fowls in the air and beasts in the woods, they are so wild and we so weak and ignorant we cannot much trouble them." In the early days the natives showed the English immigrants where to fish for fat eels and Indian methods of trapping deer and other game.

The English, unfamiliar with Indian corn, learned to grow it from the natives. The Pilgrims considered corn less desirable, because it was coarser than wheat or rye which they were accustomed to eating in England. However, with survival at stake, they were willing to eat anything. The new settlers learned from Squanto how to plant corn "Indian style"—in small circles two feet across and two feet apart with each circle hilled toward the center. In the center of each circle the Indians planted a few seeds of corn, placing a small herring-like fish (called an alewife) with the seeds to help fertilize them. In later years they learned to sow a few bean seeds with the corn after it had begun to grow. The bean plants used the corn stalks to climb on. Also in these hills a few squash and pumpkin seeds were planted, their vines trailing across the uncultivated land between the hills. As a result of this new found knowledge, they harvested some food after their first summer and more easily survived their second winter.

Originally each family at Plymouth Plantation had its own garden plot nearby their home for growing traditional English vegetables. Each person was also required to work in the large fields laid out beyond the village. This produce went into a common storehouse. Many were unhappy with this communal arrangement. As historian Darrell Rutman writes: "There were those who idled while others labored." People showed a very human tendency to work less for the common good than for their own individual good. The lazy ones lived off the efforts of the industrious.

Survival was difficult. In fact, at the end of ten years the Plymouth families still only numbered 300 persons. But a momentous event occurred in 1626 when the English company which had financed their ventures in the new country agreed to sell all its interests to the Pilgrims. The Pilgrims then became owners of the colony. They had title to the land. This agreement marked a turning point in the colonists' lives. It made it possible for the Plymouth community to grant 20 acres of land to every man and 20 acres to every member of his household. In addition to these allocations of "great lots," cattle, swine and goats were also divided among the inhabitants. These land grants were to front on the bay as far as possible and to extend on each side of Plymouth as far as good land was available. The grants north of Plymouth ran to the Jones River and on around the bay, "some falling on the other side of the bay."

The end of communal agriculture brought about prosperity. "It made all hands very industrious," Governor Bradford recorded. "The women now willingly went into the fields and took their little ones with them." Personal incentive to work resulted. Individuals could now own land and make profits from their labor. This drew the settlers out of Plymouth village, and news of this opportunity brought more settlers across the Atlantic.

Meanwhile, back in England life under King Charles I had become increasingly harsh and repressive. When word was out that Charles had not only dissolved Parliament, but at the same time had granted a charter establishing Massachusetts Colony, a plan of escape became available. Opportunity for prosperity—land of their own—was now possible. Thousands of Puritans began making their plans to leave the strictures of the Old World and face the unknown dangers of the New World.

In the next five years thousands of Puritans fled England. John Paybody and his family were among them.

John and William Paybody — Duxbury, Plymouth Colony

When John and Isabel undertook the bold and perilous venture to move their family to the New World, their son, William, was just 16 and their daughter, Annis, was even younger. Their oldest son, Thomas, did not emigrate with the family. Perhaps he was married and had his life already established back in St. Albans in Hertfordshire, England. It is not clear why John chose to settle in Plymouth and not north of Boston nearer his older son, Francis. The record books fail to describe their relationship or to reveal what contact they kept with each other through the years. We do know that Francis was mentioned in his father's will. It is likely that John and Francis, and perhaps their families as well, visited each other from time to time since travel between Boston and Plymouth became increasingly feasible.

These first allocations of land expanded in both directions from Plymouth village. The grants north of Plymouth created the settlement of Ducksburrow (or Duxburrough, Duxburrow, or later, Duxbury). John Paybody joined Pilgrim leaders John Alden, Captain Myles Standish and Jonathan Brewster in homesteading farms in this new settlement.

Picture the Duxbury that greeted the Paybodys: along the shores of the bay and by the rivers and streams lay fields abandoned years earlier by the Wampanoag Indians. They had become overgrown, but not yet wooded. The Indians had come each summer from farther inland to grow their crops along these shores where shellfish provided an easy food supply. Because the Indians had abandoned these fields a few years earlier, the English settlers could use the clearings to begin their homesteads.

The Early History of Duxbury records: John Paybody, born in England; came to Plymouth N.E. as early as 1636, for his name is in the list of freemen of the colony dated March 7, 1636-7, and he was admitted and sworn with others whose names are in that list Jan 2, 1637-8. He received a grant of ten acres of land Jan 1, 1637-8 on Duxburrow side... The location was

lying betwixt the lands of William Tubbs on the north side and those of Experience Mitchell on the south and from the sea in the west and the Blew Fish River on the easte. *

The Paybodys arrived at the right time to receive one of these cleared acreages. Another tract, granted him on

---

* I believe that the original records transcriber mistakenly reversed the directions of the sea and the river. This was corroborated by Tony Kelso, historian of the Duxbury Historical Society. It should read that John Paybody's ten-acre land grant was located between the sea in the east and the river in the west. (See map of Duxbury.)

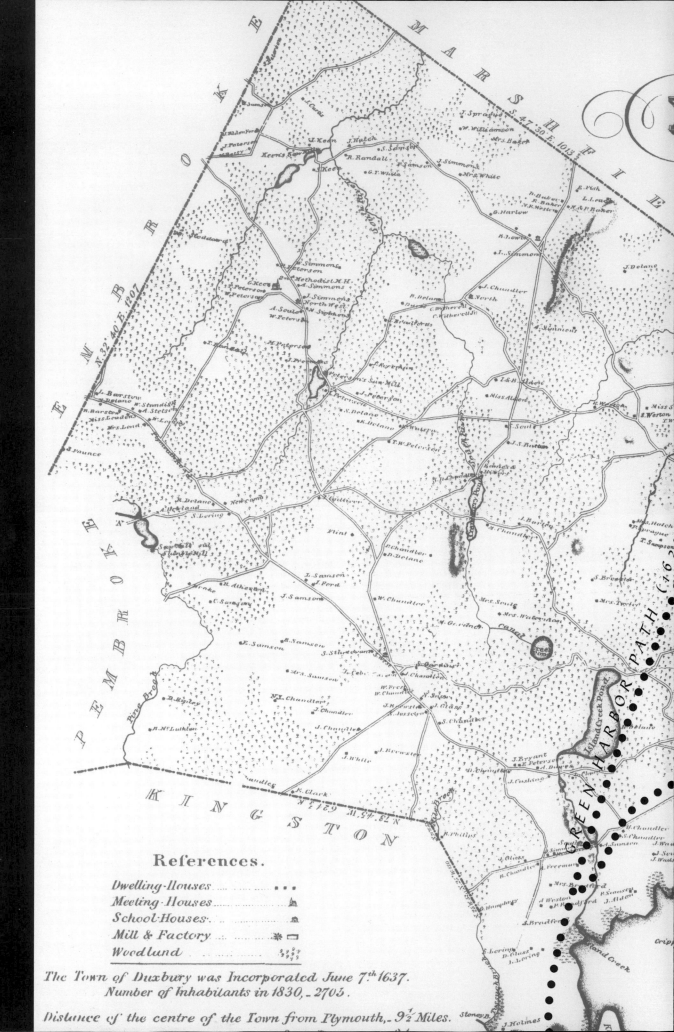

Duxbury Bay Area

References.

Dwelling-Houses .... • • •
Meeting-Houses ....
School-Houses ....
Mill & Factory ....
Woodland ....

The Town of Duxbury was Incorporated June 7th 1637.
Number of Inhabitants in 1830, – 2703.

Distance of the centre of the Town from Plymouth, – 9½ Miles.

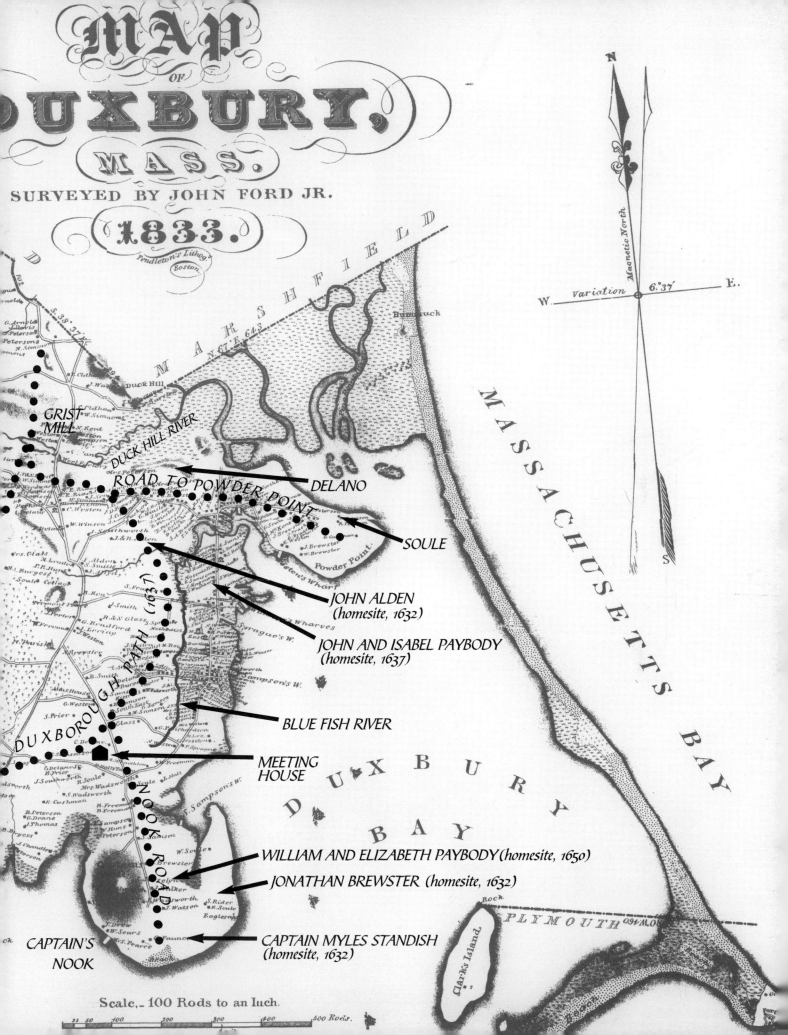

MAP
OF
DUXBURY,
MASS.

SURVEYED BY JOHN FORD JR.
1833.

Pendleton's Lithog. Boston

N

MASSACHUSETTS BAY

Variation 6°37' E.
W.

MARSHFIELD

GRIST MILL

DUCK HILL RIVER

ROAD TO POWDER POINT — DELANO

SOULE

Powder Point.

JOHN ALDEN (homesite, 1632)

JOHN AND ISABEL PAYBODY (homesite, 1637)

DUXBOROUGH PATH (1637)

BLUE FISH RIVER

DUXBOROUGH

MEETING HOUSE

DUXBURY BAY

NOOK ROAD

WILLIAM AND ELIZABETH PAYBODY (homesite, 1650)

JONATHAN BREWSTER (homesite, 1632)

CAPTAIN MYLES STANDISH (homesite, 1632)

CAPTAIN'S NOOK

PLYMOUTH

Clarks Island.

Scale, - 100 Rods to an Inch.

25 50   100   200   300   400   500 Rods.

Nov. 2, 1640, was 30 acres "with meadow to it at North River," according to Selim Hobart Peabody.

In these early years the settlers had few oxen, no horses, and no carriages. Draft animals were used only on the farm, never for travel. Even as late as 1685 the Paybodys walked to church on Sunday. In the early years not many of the footpaths were wide enough for a wagon, but before long, cart paths grew to accommodate traffic, especially to Boston.

Town activities centered on two places: the grist mill on Duxbury's north side, where farmers carried their grains for grinding, and the Meeting House at the community's southern end. All paths converged here. At the Meeting House all public meetings and church services assembled. Public notices—marriage intentions, lost or strayed animals, rewards—were posted on its door. Also, heads of animals that brought a bounty were nailed to the walls. Historian Wentworth, in *Settlement and Growth of Duxbury, 1628-1870*, writes that according to the law: "Ye heads of Wolves and Wild Cats shall be nailed to ye walls of Ye Meeting House before Ye bounty is payed." The stocks, whipping post, pillory and pound were nearby. Next to the Meeting House was the Old Burying Ground which became the final resting place of many of the early settlers.

On Sundays the Paybodys walked along Duxburrough Path to the Meeting House to hear Rev. Ralph Partridge preach. Since the Alden and Paybody farms were a distance from the center of town, they passed several homes along the way. They walked with their neighbors, the Aldens, Mitchells, Tubbs, Delanos and Soules. Perhaps they were joined by the Standishes and the Brewsters as they neared the Meeting House. The services were long but the Sunday gathering gave them one time in the week when they could meet and talk with each other.

These Sunday walks fostered friendships among the young folk as well. Sixteen-year-old William met twelve-year-old Elizabeth Alden who lived on a neighboring homestead. Elizabeth was the oldest daughter of John Alden and Priscilla Mullins who had been passengers together on the *Mayflower* and married their first year in the new country.

William Paybody and Elizabeth Alden became very good friends as they walked to Town Meeting, worked in the fields together and as their families helped each other build homesteads. In time their friendship turned to romance. In the early days marriages between neighbors' children was common. A young man had little time or means to travel far to win the affection of a young woman. Historian Dorothy Wentworth asserts, "no settler wasted shoe leather courting." At any rate, she reported, "The old Alden house had a happy event when on Dec. 26, 1644,

The Old Kitchen in John Alden house in Duxbury where William Paybody and Elizabeth Alden were wed.

Elizabeth Alden married William Pabodie, son of the Town Clerk."

Wentworth writes that after their marriage they lived on the Blue Fish River near the Alden farm for a few years before buying a farm of their own. Since John and Isabel Paybody lived on the Blue Fish River very near the Alden farm and had no children remaining at home (Annis had married in 1639), presumably the young couple lived with William's parents for their first six years of married life. Here their first five children were born. In 1650 William and Elizabeth had saved enough money to buy the Jonathan Brewster farm on the peninsula in southern Duxbury called the "Captain's Nook," or the "Nook." This area was also referred to as Eagle's Nest. William paid 70 pounds for these 90 acres of land that ran along the west side of Eagle's Nest Creek with the location of the house very near the Nook Gate. The sale included a good-sized dwelling, and "out-houses, Barnes, Stables, orchyards, gardens, meddowland and pastures." In 1657, he purchased half of Eagle's Nest Point across the creek from his farm.

For years William lived and prospered in Duxbury, gaining in land and stature. He became an important person in the town. William was a land surveyor and his name appears frequently in early town records regarding boundary lines he adjusted, farms he surveyed and various tracts of land he purchased. As a surveyor, he served a valuable function for the growing colony. His work laying out and surveying inland tracts, such as Bridgewater, consumed much of his time. Yet, he still found time to farm his land and serve as the Duxbury town clerk.

William became a town officer at Duxbury and a representative or deputy to the General Court of Plymouth colony. He was elected to the General Court which met at Plymouth, August 1, 1654, and re-elected each year until 1663; then again in 1668, and continuously from 1671 until 1682.

Ten of William and Elizabeth's twelve children were girls who grew up to marry prominent boys of Duxbury and settle on local farms. The older of the two boys, John, died tragically at the age of 24. Windsor, in the *History of the Town of Duxbury,* reports that an inquest found "that he ryding on the road, his horse carryed him underneath the bow of a young tree, and violently forcing his head into the body thereof brake his skull."

Historian Tony Kelso tells of two incidents in which William Paybody became entangled in disputes with his neighbors. In 1679, he brought suit against Sarah Brewster, wife of Love Brewster, for trespassing. William claimed that she "did pull up and deface the bound marks of the said Paybodyes land and make claim to said land." They settled the case out of court. Apparently, Sarah came out ahead, because later that year William sold his share of Eagle's Nest Point to her son, Deacon William Brewster.

Four years later William took elaborate precautions to avoid another bitter feud with his neighbor, Alexander Standish, son of Myles Standish. Alexander was married to Sarah Alden, so in addition to being neighbors, they were also brothers-in-law. Alexander owned a salt meadow which could only be reached by crossing over William's land. So William drew up a formal deed giving Alexander right-of-way over his land, provided that Alexander, plus his heirs and assigns, follow detailed stipulations for opening and shutting the gates and putting up the bars "so that the said Paybody nor any that succeed him be not damnified there-by."

In 1684, at age 64, William left Duxbury and settled in Little Compton, Rhode Island. One wonders why he resettled at this late age. Tony Kelso believes William and Elizabeth's house may have burned down in 1684 and that their daughter and her husband took over the farm. Possibly William knew that better farmland waited in Little Compton which was then on the western frontier of Plymouth Colony. Or perhaps, their neighborhood squabbles created such ill-will and animosity that he decided to remove himself and start over again somewhere else. Regardless of the reasons, William still lived another 20 years at Little Compton, before dying on December 13, 1707, at the age of 87.

William only had one son to survive him, marry and carry on the Pabodie name (as he spelled it). This branch of the family never changed its name to the Peabody spelling. (See the Family

Millstone—picture taken near the site of Francis Paybody's farm and mill in Topsfield, Massachusetts.

Foundations section for William's Last Will and Testament.)

Francis Paybody—Ipswich, Hampton and Topsfield

While John and William and their families established homesteads in Plymouth Colony, the other son, Francis, followed a similar endeavor just north of Boston.

In 1635 Francis arrived on the ship, the *Planter*. He became one of the early settlers in the little village of Ipswich, or Agawam, as the Indians called it. Only two years earlier John Winthrop and twelve others had first settled there.

After three years Francis moved northward with a dozen other families and founded the village of Hampton. Here he lived for about 10 years becoming a respected citizen holding responsible town offices. Francis received the honor of freemanship on May 18, 1642.

During these years Francis married Lydia and obtained a home site near

Isaac Perkins and William Cole. Neighbor problems soon erupted. An interesting entry in the Ipswich Court's oldest record book indicates friction between Lydia and her neighbor, Eunice Cole. Under the date of Nov. 4, 1645, it says,

> Eunice Cole is to sit in the stocks at Hampton and make acknowledgment of her slanderous speeches concerning Susan Perkings and lidia pebode and to pay to the witness Isaac Perkings 7d and feas of the court.

We don't know what slanderous comments divided these three neighboring women. Later Eunice Cole suffered more unhappiness and disgrace as one of the women accused in the Salem witchcraft trials. Eunice was found guilty and imprisoned. Her husband suffered great sorrow.

The records yield only spotty information about Lydia, her family or background. The couple had a number of children together and then at some point Lydia died, perhaps in childbirth. Francis, now a widower, married Mary Wood, in 1649, who became the mother of at least half of his 14 children.

When a determination in 1650 placed Hampton inside the colony of New Hampshire, Francis decided to move closer to Boston. He sold his house and 55 acres and moved to Topsfield, settling near the land he had first owned in Ipswich. Here Francis Paybody lived and prospered for the next 50 years.

Francis took an active part in Topsfield town affairs frequently serving on committees to establish boundary lines and lay out highways. He served as selectman much of the time between 1659 and 1682, town clerk from 1676 to 1681 and was selected lieutenant in the militia.

Author Walter Muir Whitehill writes:

There (in Topsfield) he bought 250 acres of land from Samuel Symonds soon after his arrival, and on 20 April 1666 bought from his near neighbor, William Evans, an acre of land by Pye Brook, on which he established the first gristmill in town, adding a sawmill in 1672. His house, which survived

---

Passengers to America

2 Aprilis, 1635.--Theis vnder written names are to be transported to New England imbarqued in the Planter Nic: Trarice Mr bound thither the p'rties have brought Certificate from the Minister of St Albans in Hertfordshire, and Attestacon from the Justices of peace according to the Lords Order.

Jo: Tuttell A Mercer	39	Mary Chittwood	24	
Joan Tuttell	42	Tho: Olney Shoemaker	35	
John Lawrence	17	Marie Olney	30	
Wm Lawrence	12	Tho Olney	3	
Marie Lawrence	9	Etenetus Olney		
Abigail Tuttell	6	Geo: Giddins Husbandman	25	
Symon Tuttell	4	Jane Giddins	20	
Sara Tuttell	2	Tho: Savage Taylor	27	
Jo: Tuttell	1	Richard Harvie A Taylor	22	
Joan Antrobuss	65	ffrances Pebody Husbandman	21***	
Marie Wrast	24	Wm Wilcockson Lynen wever	34	
Tho: Greene	15	Margaret Wilcockson	24	
Nathan Haford servant to		Jo: Wilcockson	2	
Jo: Tuttell	16	Ann Harvie	22	
Wm Beardsley A Mason	30	Willm ffelloe Shoemaker	24	
Marie Beadsley	26	ffrancis Baker A Taylor	24	
Marie Beadsely	4	Tho: Carter	25	servants
John Beadsely	2	Michell Willmson	30	to Geo:
Joseph Beadsley	6 mo	Elizabeth Morrison	12	Giddins
Allen Perley Husbandman	27			pred.

---

3 Aprill 1635

James weauer Statinor   23
Edmond weauer Husbandman 28 dwelling in Anckstrey in Herefordsher
& his wife Margarett aged 30 yers

[from Tapper, Michael. Passengers to America: A Consolidation...
Genealogical Publishing Co. 1978. p. 16, 17.]

until 1846, was on the bank of the brook, a short distance in the rear of the house. A little farther up the brook, Francis Peabody built in 1692 another two-story house that was destroyed by fire on 4 October 1914.

Historian Sidney A. Merriam adds:

He acquired more lands. He planted an orchard and it grew and increased. He built a mill for grain, powered by the river that ran through his property. He bought more lands adjoining his own and soon owned a pretty farm of meadows, brooks and upland. As the old man aged and his children grew, he acquired more lands, both adjoining his holdings and elsewhere. He bought large farms in Boxford, several hundred acres nearby, as well as other houses where he settled his sons and sons-in-law. He built up his own house until it was a manor with several cellars where provisions were stored over the cold winter and ice cut from the ponds was kept in sawdust during the hot summer. He grew corn, malt, rye, and wheat, and raised pigs, sheep and cattle for beef and milking. He kept a good stable and several carts. He had nothing so fine as a carriage, nor did his country neighbors; only in the cities were such luxuries available or useful on the roads. In the country both men and women rode astride and side saddle. Old Francis lived a long time; he was eighty four years old when he died and he outlived four of his fourteen children. He was perhaps the most prominent man in Topsfield at the hour of his death.

Francis arrived in the New World a simple immigrant. But within his lifetime he was able to acquire an estate large enough to give a good start to his ten surviving children and provide amply for the needs of his widow. Francis had 14 children, eight boys and six girls. Five of the boys survived to adulthood, married and had many children of their own. It is said that from these five patriarchs have come all the Peabodys in this country.

Francis did not pass his entire wealth to his firstborn son. Like most New England settlers, he broke from the custom of primogeniture which was still common in most of England (except an area called Kent). He bequeathed his land, as equally as possible, to his sons and sons-in-law. To each daughter he gave "five pounds besides what she hath already had of me." This was a common practice, giving daughters their share of the father's estate in the form of their dowry—kettles, cooking utensils, coverlets, cattle—at the time of their marriage. His wife received a comfortable maintenance. Francis specified a detailed plan for how her needs would be provided. As Ulrich corroborates, this was the familiar pattern: "land for sons, movables for daughters and for widows a carefully defined dependency." The other common practice was to leave the wife a third of the estate, as William did in his will. (See the Family Foundations section for Francis' Last Will and Testament.)

Topsfield

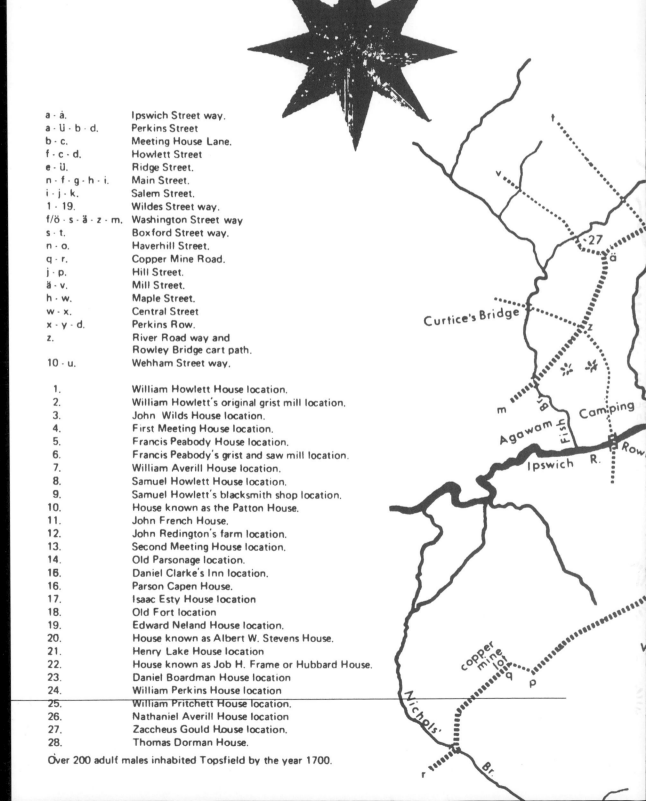

a - à.   Ipswich Street way.
a - ü - b - d.   Perkins Street
b - c.   Meeting House Lane.
f - c - d.   Howlett Street
e - ü.   Ridge Street.
n - f - g - h - i. Main Street.
i - j - k.   Salem Street.
1 - 19.   Wildes Street way.
f/ö - s - ä - z - m. Washington Street way
s - t.   Boxford Street way.
n - o.   Haverhill Street.
q - r.   Copper Mine Road.
j - p.   Hill Street.
ä - v.   Mill Street.
h - w.   Maple Street.
w - x.   Central Street
x - y - d.   Perkins Row.
z.   River Road way and
                Rowley Bridge cart path.
10 - u.   Wehham Street way.

1.   William Howlett House location.
2.   William Howlett's original grist mill location.
3.   John Wilds House location.
4.   First Meeting House location.
5.   Francis Peabody House location.
6.   Francis Peabody's grist and saw mill location.
7.   William Averill House location.
8.   Samuel Howlett House location.
9.   Samuel Howlett's blacksmith shop location.
10.   House known as the Patton House.
11.   John French House.
12.   John Redington's farm location.
13.   Second Meeting House location.
14.   Old Parsonage location.
16.   Daniel Clarke's Inn location.
16.   Parson Capen House.
17.   Isaac Esty House location
18.   Old Fort location
19.   Edward Neland House location.
20.   House known as Albert W. Stevens House.
21.   Henry Lake House location
22.   House known as Job H. Frame or Hubbard House.
23.   Daniel Boardman House location
24.   William Perkins House location
25.   William Pritchett House location.
26.   Nathaniel Averill House location
27.   Zaccheus Gould House location.
28.   Thomas Dorman House.

Over 200 adult males inhabited Topsfield by the year 1700.

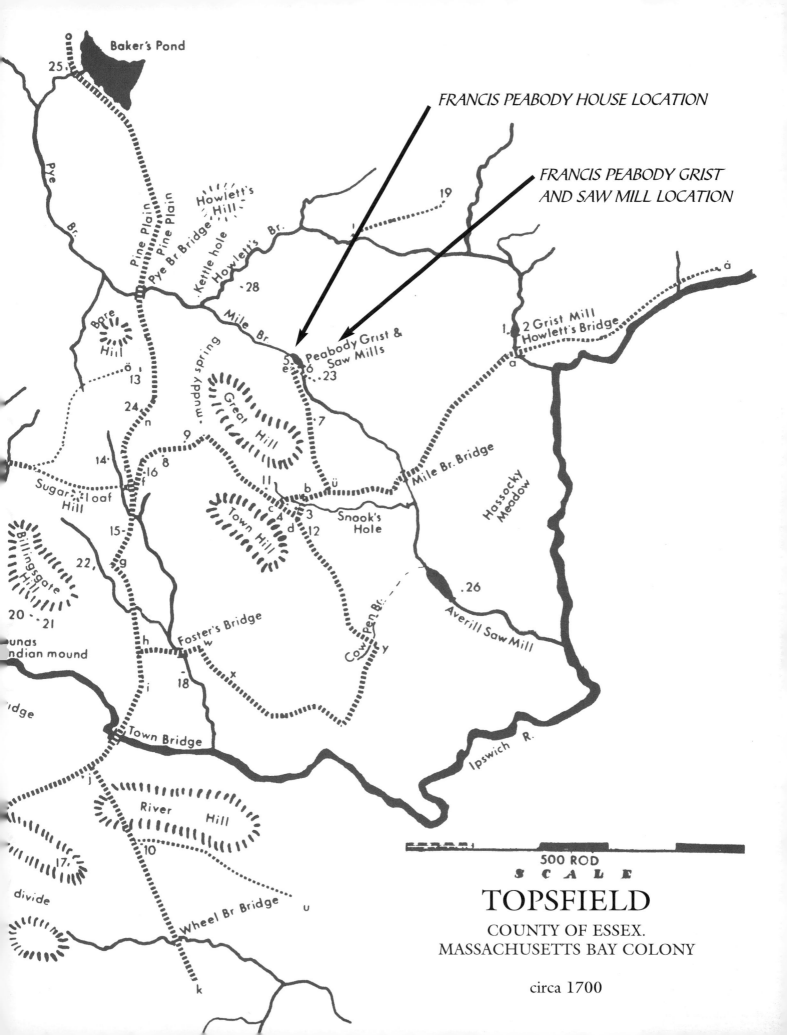

FRANCIS PEABODY HOUSE LOCATION

FRANCIS PEABODY GRIST
AND SAW MILL LOCATION

Baker's Pond

Pye Br.

Pine Plain
Pine Plain

Howlett's Hill
Pye Br. Bridge
Kettle hole
Howlett's Hill
Howlett's Br.

19

Bore Hill

Mile Br.

Grist Mill
Howlett's Bridge

muddy spring

Peabody Grist & Saw Mills

Great Hill

Sugar loaf Hill

Town Hill

Snook's Hole

Mile Br. Bridge

Hassocky Meadow

Billingsgate Hill

Foster's Bridge

Cow Pen Br.

Averill Saw Mill

ounas Indian mound

Town Bridge

Ipswich R.

River Hill

divide

Wheel Br Bridge

500 ROD
S C A L E

TOPSFIELD
COUNTY OF ESSEX.
MASSACHUSETTS BAY COLONY

circa 1700

Garden scene recreated at Plymouth Village

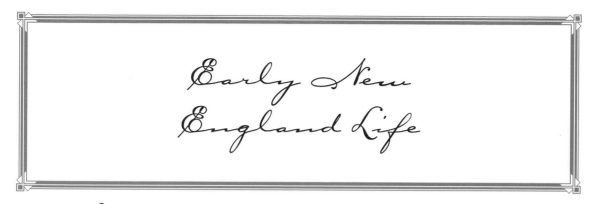

Early New England Life

In present day America we enjoy a heightened awareness of women's role in society and concern about female rights. As we look forward to the beginning of a new millennium, we are intrigued with looking back to women's lives 350 years ago. How does the colonial woman's life experience contrast with our own?

Women's Role

The archives contain no female diaries written in New England before 1750. Few letters written by women exist. Writing paper was extremely scarce in those days since England imposed such heavy taxes on paper entering the colonies. Although there were plenty of quills for pens made from goose and crow, neither steel pens nor graphite or clay pencils came into general use much before 1830.

Clues about women's personal lives lie buried in the inventories in last will and testaments, gravestones, embroideries, excavations of early homesites, court records, sermons and the papers of husbands and sons. Naturally these sources do not yield a complete picture of the private world of women.

If we were to wander through an old cemetery, we might come across epitaphs on certain gravestones. Author and historian, Laurel Ulrich, cites Hannah Moody's headstone (d. January 29, 1727) in the Old Burying Ground in York Village, Maine. "Eminent for Holiness, Prayerfulness, Watchfulness, Zeal, Prudence, Sincerity, Humility, Meekness, Patience, Weanedness from ye World, Self denial, Publick-Spiritedness, Diligence, Faithfulness and Charity." Whew! We smile and wonder, what would *she* have said about herself? We recognize that these words defined the virtuous qualities women aspired to achieve. They do not describe the real-life person who lay buried there. If anything, these adjectives obscure, rather than illuminate, an individual woman's day-to-day, inner life experience.

Learning how some authors have portrayed the lives of early New England women may also lead us to a simplistic or biased view. We often hear it told that in the 17th century a wife was considered to be her husband's personal property, his "chattel". The woman belonged to her man, just like his oxen and swine, his house and wagon. A wife must do as she was told. For example, she was told how to wear her clothing. James Thacher tells about a law that was passed in 1638 by the general court of Massachusetts regulating the length of her sleeves. "No garment shall be made with short sleeves; and such (women) as have short sleeves shall not wear the same, unless they cover the arm to the wrist..."

It is true that early New England women viewed submission to God and submission to one's husband as their religious and legal duty. Religion taught that God told Eve, "Thy desire shall be to thy husband and he shall rule over thee." Obedience to one's husband was also a legal requirement. William Blackstone stated this in his Commentaries on the laws of England:

> By marriage, the husband and wife are one person in law; that is, the very being or legal existence of the woman is suspended during the marriage, or at least is incorporated and consolidated into that of the husband; under whose wing, protection and cover, she performs everything.

This subordinate relationship of woman to man had long been embedded within the traditions and practices in England and continued in early America. A woman could not own property, sign documents or make a will. Although even today, the majority of women choose to give up their own last names and take their husband's as their own, the 17th century custom was more extreme. Ulrich illustrates this with the example of when Mary Jones married, she didn't simply become Mrs. Mary Brown, or even Mrs. John Brown. She was referred to as John Brown his wife.

Men and women's roles were clearly defined. For women, attending to their domestic duties was paramount. Men had the responsibility of providing for their family's economic needs. This influenced society's attitudes towards education. John Winthrop's opinion is often quoted: "A woman who had given her self wholly to reading and writing...had lost her understanding and reason...If she had kept her place and attended to household affairs and such things as belong to woman, and not gone out of her way and calling to meddle in such things as are proper for men, whose minds are stronger, she might have improved them usefully and honorably in the place God had set her." Some, like John Winthrop, thought that learning would bring a woman insanity.

Boys and girls both received instruction in reading, but, according to Ulrich, only the boys learned to "write a Ledgable hand and cypher as far as the 'Gouldin Rule.'" Sons would need to learn to do arithmetic and write in order to conduct business. Women had little need for this. According to Ulrich, "Women lagged far behind men in their ability to write, a discrepancy which actually increased over the 18th century."

To us, perhaps, this picture of apparent male supremacy sounds appalling. Modern feminists might be shocked to hear such examples of female subjection and "inferior" treatment. But it is too easy to judge 17th century New

England by today's standards. On a closer look we see that issues of power, dominance and human value are much more complex.

The hierarchical structure was essential to sustain the social order. Men and women's lives depended on it. The husband had both the right and *responsibility* to serve as head of the household. He was supreme in the external affairs of the family. The husband spoke for his wife, but his words incorporated her opinions and interests which she expressed to him privately. In return for a wife's obedience, her vowed commitment and service to her husband, she could count on a lifetime of protection and financial support.

From a legal, formal, and public vantage point the husband stood as the visible person and the one who dominated. However, a look at the informal, personal and daily lives of families reveals another side of the couple. As much variation characterized early New England marriages as exists today. At home a woman could be weak and servile, dominant and headstrong or a respected companion and partner who shared the decision-making with her husband. The domestic front was the woman's domain, and her husband relied on her for management of the household and children. Husband and

Pilgrim woman portrayed in domestic activity at restored Plymouth Village.

wife were reciprocally dependent upon each other for survival. Neither could have functioned independently. In fact, we frequently see that when either the husband or wife died, the remaining spouse soon re-married.

Within the neighborhood, women strongly influenced day-to-day life. Though excluded from formal affairs— voting, participating in town meeting, holding public office—women played a central role in the communication network linking people to each other. Neighborliness, then and now, expressed itself in many ways. It could mean borrowing a cup of molasses or a garden hoe, sharing in the sewing of a quilt, attending one another during childbirth, celebrating another's wedding, or sharing grief over a child's death. Singing and laughing, listening, confiding, comforting broke the isolation and bonded women together.

Community relationships also produced contentiousness and aggravation. Neighbor women served as an informal jury of their own peers, reinforcing values and standards of behavior. They might approve or disapprove as they passed along rumor, gossip and innuendo. When women talked, men, as well as other women, listened.

In the 1645 incident involving neighbors, Lydia Paybody, Eunice Cole and Susan Perkings, we heard how Eunice was fined and punished by sitting in the stocks for her "slanderous speeches" against Lydia and Susan. We'll never know the real-life story behind the official report of these human dramas, but we do know that the power women play in these clashes cannot be underestimated.

Within her various roles—mate, housewife, mother, nurse, mid-wife, neighbor and Christian— many women lived rich, fascinating and powerfully effective lives. Unfortunately, the ordinary, day-to-day, household experience is the invisible side of life. The inner life experiences of women remained obscure. The absence of letters and diaries made this especially true during colonial days. Although women functioned in strong behind-the-scenes roles, they received no public acknowledgment. They lacked visible status. But within the family and neighborhood they enjoyed great respect.

A woman's life achievement lay in getting married, producing healthy children and creating a family. Leaving mothers, sisters and female friends to come to New England or move to the next frontier frustrated their instinctive desire to create stable, nurturing homes for their youngsters. Primitive conditions made life harder. Yet colonial women, like the women who later pioneered the American West, wanted the chance for a better life for themselves and their families. They proudly resigned themselves to hard, monotonous work. Their shared hope gave husband and wife a unified vision despite their very different, and in some ways, unequal roles.

Everyday Life

How did John's family (and William's and Francis') live in their newly inherited lands and dwellings? We try to imagine the everyday life of these Paybody ancestors.

The housewife's domain included the family dwelling and the surrounding yard. The typical house, the kind the Paybodys would have lived in, was a crude affair—a long, narrow structure, about 40 feet long by 10 feet wide with four rooms, two upstairs and two on the ground level. Home builders sometimes applied unpainted clapboard to their home's exterior, frequently to the front or road side only. Shingles soon replaced the thatched roof of the earliest homes because wood was more plentiful than reeds and it reduced fire hazard. Often settlers tacked a lean-to on the back. Around the house were scattered one or more additional outbuildings—a chicken

Plymouth Pilgrims re-enact a 1621 scene.

coop, cowshed, barn or slaughterhouse, pig pen, an outdoor privy, and a vegetable and herb garden.

Inside the heavy wooden door at the entranceway, steps led down to a cellar, the coolest part of the house where John's wife, Isabel, stored root vegetables and other foods. On the ground floor was a large all-purpose kitchen, called the "hall", and another small bed chamber, sometimes called the borning room. Bunches of herbs and dried vegetables and fruits hung in Isabel's kitchen. A narrow staircase led upward to two bed chambers which also served as a storage room. Large bags of feathers taken from chickens and ducks, waiting to be stuffed into pillows and comforters, were stored in one bed chamber. In the other bed chamber, John and

Isabel packed away other produce needing shelter, such as baskets of wheat and barley and bags of grain.

A massive fireplace dominated the hall and provided warmth for all the rooms. Family life revolved around the huge hearth, the central feature of the house. The fireplace was equipped with a spit for roasting pigs, venison and chickens, hooks to hang heavy pots of stew and a wall oven for baking bread. The family gathered around its light for work and huddled around its warmth in the winter. In spite of its cavernous size, on a cold winter night the fireplace barely heated the small house. Much of its warmth went up the chimney. Sometimes at night the temperature inside the house would drop to freezing and ice would form on pots of water left on the hearth.

Furniture in the Paybody house was minimal—a few chests, a spinning wheel, a cupboard, a board table and a backless bench called a "form". And beds. Beds were everywhere, even in the kitchen. Cradles, cots, trundle (or "truckle") beds, a rope bed that was set against the wall by day and lowered every night, even makeshift beds made of hay strewn on the floor boards. William and Francis' families used every available space for places to sleep.

These small four-room dwellings often housed huge families. The norm in early New England was for one baby to follow the next in rapid succession until there were ten or more children in a family. John and Isabel Paybody had a rather small family with only four children and only two living with them in Duxbury. However, William and Elizabeth had 12 children and Francis with his two wives, Lydia and Mary, had 14, typical of the times.

The more children in the family, the more able bodies and extra hands to do the work. And there was plenty of work to be done. The Paybodys, like other families of that time, made many things they used or consumed. They made their furniture, candles, bedding, cider, ale, bread, butter, flour—all from scratch from materials at hand. They purchased only specialized items. They bought foods, such as sugar, tea, prunes, and spices, and they bought manufactured metal items, such as iron tools and utensils, guns, ax heads and silverware. These came across on the ship from England. Children worked alongside their parents. The boys and men worked in the fields, plowing, planting and harvesting the crops, chopping wood, hunting, fishing, and tending the animals. Daughters helped their mothers with the gardening and cooking, washing and cleaning, spinning wool and sewing.

Isabel and her daughters-in-law, Elizabeth, Lydia and Mary, maintained garden plots just outside their kitchens. Few indigenous Indian plants—corn, pumpkins and Indian beans—appeared in their gardens. These were still field crops. Vegetables from their garden supplied the cooking pot that simmered continuously over the fire. Though they grew the traditional English vegetables—leeks and onions, garlic, turnips, parsnips, cabbage and carrots—they brought from home an ingrained distaste for vegetables. The colonists were convinced that vegetables were unhealthy if eaten raw. So they cooked them to a tasteless pulp. Surprisingly, potatoes were absent from their diet. Colonist women looked askance on these "dangerous vegetables." Some even said if a man ate potatoes every day he would not live more than seven years. (Potatoes were not appreciated until the end of the 18th century nor were tomatoes accepted until the 19th century.)

The English settlers lived on a daily diet considered bland by today's standards. For breakfast—a plain porridge, diluted with milk and molasses, or perhaps some toasted bread and cheese, washed down with cider or beer in the winter or milk in the summer. Dinner, the main meal of the day, was served at midday. This one-pot meal consisted of a stew made up of a boiled meat with whatever ingredients the season provided. Supper, at the end of the day, usually repeated the breakfast fare. At the board table no individual place settings existed. Members of the family paired up sharing a "trencher"—a wooden bowl about ten inches square. The also drank from a shared wooden noggin. Spoons were the only utensil in the early days; forks did not appear until the 18th century.

At harvest celebrations, or when guests joined the family, Isabel or Lydia may have served their specialties. These meals were not only hearty, but creatively flavored. Herbs from the garden and spices imported from the East Indies seasoned the venison and other game from the forest, the poultry raised on their homesteads and the fish caught in the river. As in medieval England (where their recipes originated), women often mixed sweet and savory flavors combining chicken with fruit, cooking salmon in ale, and roasting pork with apples. A sauce for roast venison included wine, vinegar and nutmeg. Another was made with orange juice and lemon slices, according to historian Frances Hill. Everyone, including children, drank wine or beer or alcoholic cider with the meals. The colonists did not condemn alcohol although they heartily condemned drunkenness. Water, considered less

wholesome, appeared as a beverage only if beer was not available.

Herbs and flowers, which grew in great abundance, added flavor and color to pioneer life. And of course, Paybody families used herbs medicinally. Some herbs had more than one use. Dill seeds, in addition to flavoring pickles, were taken to Sabbath meetings by the children and nibbled on during the long sermons. They supposedly dulled the senses and kept the little ones from squirming.

Childhood ended early for the Paybody children. By the age of seven children were required to share fully in the household chores. After early childhood youngsters found little time for play. There were fewer toys than today. But children are children and some of the games they played are still popular—London Bridge, leap frog, hide and seek, blindman's bluff. Colonial toys were mostly handmade and included dolls, marbles, kites, rolling hoops and jump ropes.

Families considered the Bible their most important book. However, as seen in the inventories in both William and Francis' Last Will and Testaments, books were commonly found in the early colonists' homes. Most children did not go to school as few schools existed in those days. Schooling was thought unnecessary for girls because women's work could be done without knowing how to read or write. Boys needed some reading and arithmetic to negotiate farm business with the outside world.

Rhythms of Life

The rhythm of life for men and women differed greatly. Little variation existed for women from one season to the next. Summer and winter, day in and day out, the routine followed the same monotonous pattern—clothes to wash, gardens to tend, meals to cook, children to mind. (This may not sound altogether foreign to today's woman!) Women were tied to their house and garden, especially those who lived on a farm.

For men, the seasons provided variety—planting crops in the spring, tending them in the summer and harvesting in the fall, followed by winter, a time of projects and preparing for the next round of seasons. The men interspersed these activities with trips to the grist mill, the nearby tavern or town center for business as well as pleasure. Fishing and hunting also served this dual function of work and recreation.

This paints a rather dreary picture, for women especially, if we fail to appreciate the importance that community activities played in the early colonists' lives. People often gathered to perform some task together which gave them an opportunity to enjoy each other's company. At a barn or roof raising neighborhood men combined their strength and labor to help each other with hard physical work. Meanwhile women prepared and set out a feast This kind of activity gave the colonists a chance to share good things to eat and to exchange news and gossip. Like holiday rituals today they served to bring people together.

Men and boys took pleasure in competing in foot races, wrestling, plowing and corn husking contests. Women and girls enjoyed quilting bees, berrying, or sometimes spinning or cooking together.

The New England pioneers celebrated a three-day feast in honor of Governor William Bradford's wedding on July 30, 1623. This time of prayer and thanksgiving became a harvest celebration, held during times of good harvest or when a special occasion warranted it. In the early years only New Englanders celebrated Thanksgiving.

The Sabbath provided a welcome break in the daily routine. Walking to and from the Meeting House gave the settlers a chance to visit with their neighbors and share news of the day. In a land without a communication network of newspapers (let alone radio or television), the Meeting House served as a social and communication hub for the village. Two services were conducted, one in the morning and one in the afternoon. The length of these tedious three-hour hour sessions was offset by a picnic dinner between services and the socializing that took place. In the Meeting House itself, seating was by ranked order according to gender, wealth and age. Women and children sat on the opposite side of the room from the men.

More profoundly affecting women than the cycle of the seasons was the cycle of reproduction. A woman's life during the childbearing years revolved around pregnancy, delivery and lactation.

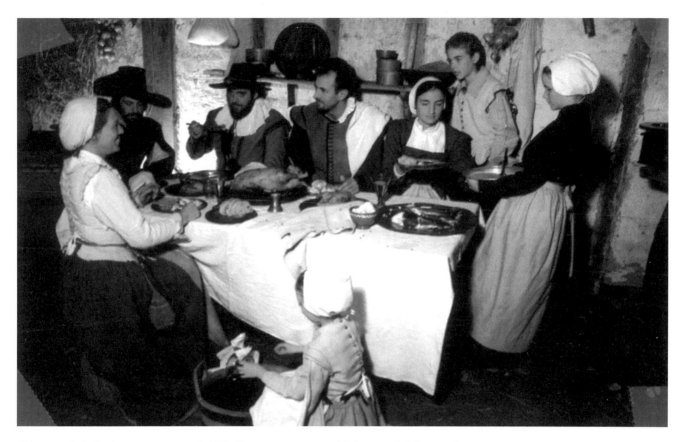

Plymouth Pilgrims portray a 1621 dinner at restored Plymouth Plantation.

In these colonial times when ten or twelve or more children were the norm, two year cycles stretched from the birth of one baby to the birth of the next. Almost no time existed between babies to free a woman from pregnancy or breast feeding. A woman's life was organized around reproduction. A bride came into marriage bringing her dowry of pots and kettles, furniture and a cow or two from her father and a set of "childbed" linens from her mother. These linens might be decorated with embroidery or lace, conveying the value she placed upon this aspect of her future life.

The reality of childbirth in women's lives testified not only to the subjection of women but also the mys-terious power of womankind. It is difficult for modern mothers with a couple of children to imagine giving birth to a dozen or more babies— all "naturally" of course, nursing them, *and* maintaining an active household, including mothering a handful of growing children. (Sounds daunting!) A woman could look forward to an endless cycle of discomfort during pregnancies, suffering during labor and delivery, and caring for the needs of others during all her childbearing years.

Yet, childbearing created a powerful intimacy. In early America control of childbirth lay in the hands of women. Except in a most peripheral way, men were not allowed to participate. In contrast to the present day where women undergo labor and delivery in the privacy of an antiseptic hospital setting, colonial women experienced childbirth as a semi-public, festive event. Only women were invited to the drama of delivery, and sometimes six or eight or a dozen women might be in attendance. For many women, the first stage of labor took on something of a party-like atmosphere. Historian Laurel Ulrich describes this phase:

> One of the mother's responsibilities was to provide refreshments for her attendants. The very names *groaning beer* and *groaning cakes* suggest that at least some of this food was consumed during labor itself. Midwifery manuals encouraged the mother to eat light but nourishing foods—broth, poached eggs, or toasted bread in wine—during labor and immediately after birth. They told her to walk about rather than lie down at this stage.

The importance of the women attending cannot be understated. Ulrich continues:

> In delivery there was physical as well as emotional intimacy among the women. A mother might give birth held in another woman's lap or leaning against her attendants as she squatted on the low, open-seated "midwife's stool." In cases of extreme difficulty a draught of another mother's milk was considered a sure remedy. The presence in the room of a lactating woman was useful for another reason as well. A

friend or neighbor was probably the baby's first nurse, since the mother's own milk (or colostrum) was presumed impure for several days owing to the "commotions" of birth.

Childbirth forged a primitive and powerful bond between women—one which mystified men. Momentarily, at least, childbirth reversed the position of the sexes, pushing women onto center stage, relegating men to supporting roles.

A Strict Religion

The Paybodys, like most of the colonists, were deeply religious. The church governed the early settlers' behavior in almost every sphere of life. These rules of conduct were particularly exacting in New England. Strict decorum was the order of the day.

New Englanders of the 1600's are known for their stern, austere demeanor. They left behind the roisterous Elizabethan England famed for its lusty enjoyment of life's pleasures. Sermons and other documents indicate that these Puritan settlers valued hard work, prayer and living simply. Impulses toward excessive enjoyment, pleasure and indulgence were inhibited and viewed warily as sinful distractions.

The Puritans outlawed Christmas, a day of revelry in England, considering it a pagan festival. Historian David Hawke, in *Everyday Life in Early America,* tells about Governor Bradford of Plymouth finding the settlers on Christmas Day, 1621, "in the street at play." He quickly ended their frolicking and was proud to say that as long as he ruled the colony, "nothing hath been attempted that way, at least openly."

Church law required the Paybodys, and their colonial neighbors, to strictly observe the Sabbath. From sundown on Saturday until sundown on Sunday it was a sin to engage in any non-religious activity. Tasks such as cooking, making beds, washing clothes, chopping wood, working in the fields were forbidden. Early settlers faced severe punishment for profaning the Lord's Day. Historian Francis Hill, in *Delusion of Satan,* cites examples of Puritan punishment: "In 1647 a man in New Haven who was tried for absence from public worship pleaded that he had fallen into the water late on Saturday, could not light a fire on Sunday to dry his only suit of clothes, and stayed in bed to keep warm. He was found guilty of slothfulness and whipped." In 1656 a man from Boston sat in the stocks for two hours because of "lewd and unseemly" behavior on the Sabbath—he kissed his wife in public after returning from three years at sea. "William Adey, for working on the Sabbath was severely whipt at the post."

Every town had its stocks and whipping posts which were positioned near the Meeting House so that the entire town could observe the guilty person. Punishment was intended to humiliate as well as cause physical pain. Onlookers often threw eggs at a person sitting in the stocks. Some offenders suffered public whipping or stoning. Whipping at a cart's tail while the cart was drawn through town was consid-ered a more severe punishment than whipping at the post.

Shame and terror were used to control even little children. According to Francis Hill, the prominent Boston minister, Cotton Mather, wrote in a preface to a children's book:

Do you to dare to run up and down upon the Lord's Day? Or do you keep in to read your book?...They which lie must go to their father the devil, into everlasting burning; and when they beg and pray in hell fire, God will not forgive them, but there (they) must lie forever. Are you willing to go to hell to be burnt with the devil...Oh, hell is a terrible place, that's worse a thousand times than whipping.

Officials dealt harshly with the use of tobacco, overindulgence in alcohol and sexual relations outside marriage. Thacher cites the following examples found in Plymouth records occurring between 1632 and 1640: "Frances Sprague, for drinking over much, fined ten shillings...John Phillip for drinking tobacco in the high way, twelve shillings." Similarly, profane swearing was punished by sitting in the stocks three hours a day and for telling lies the offender paid a fine of ten shillings or suffered the stocks for two hours for each offense. Historian Stratton cites an October 30, 1667, entry in which Thomas Delano was fined for "haveing carnall copulation" with his wife before marriage. His wife, Rebecca, was the daughter of John Alden.

Capital offenses were punishable by death. These included rebellion against the king, murder, or conversing with the devil by way of witchcraft.

The Salem witchcraft trials stand out as one of our darkest times in American history. The colonists brought many ancient superstitions with them from England; they found signs of the supernatural everywhere. These superstitions included the belief that certain women had evil powers given them by devils. During the 1600's in New England hundreds of women were accused of casting spells on their neighbors or practicing other forms of witchcraft. The witchcraft scare continued, reaching a climax with the Salem witchcraft trials in 1692. Many historians believe that Cotton Mather, the colonial preacher, did much to stir up public feeling against the supposed witches. In Salem, many were accused and imprisoned, 19 persons were hanged as witches on Gallows Hill and one was pressed to death. Meanwhile, back in Europe an almost hysterical fear of witchcraft swept the continent during the 1600's and 1700's. A bloodbath took place as thousands were burned as witches.

Many scholars agree with Arthur Miller's assertion that the witch trials exemplify an ugly, repressive side of the human character. Francis Hill, author of *A Delusion of Satan, The Full Story of the Salem Witch Trials,* writes about the roots of persecution. He asserted that the European immigrants, who fled religious persecution and sought the freedom to worship as they pleased, unwittingly brought persecution along with them. They came not only with their hopes and dreams, but with their fears and frustrations as well. Although they sought a new life, they imposed their definition of right. Their religious beliefs made them harsh and quick to condemn. Haunted by primitive terrors, they projected their fears outward upon others, and they judged as they had felt judged. This combination of superstition and repressive religion resulted in the Puritans choosing humiliating forms of punishment and, ultimately, in the witch trials.

At least one member of the Peabody family became caught up in the hysteria. Captain John Peabody (b. about 1642, d. July 5, 1720), the oldest son of Francis, served on a jury that convicted and sentenced men and women accused of witchcraft to imprisonment and death. Over time the witchcraft accusations escalated and more and more high ranking people were named. Even Captain John Alden, son of John Alden of Duxbury, stood among those accused. Fear swept through society's upper echelons. Prominent citizens began protesting the witchcraft proceedings. The growing dissent finally resulted in Governor Phipps dissolving the court, granting pardons to those still imprisoned and bringing an end to this horrible chapter of human atrocities. Enders Robinson, in *The Devil Discovered,* writes:

> Except for Justice Samuel Sewall none of the members of the old guard (Justices William Stoughton, John Hathorne, Reverends Cotton

Mather and Samuel Parris) ever acknowledged remorse or shame for the events that they had sponsored...The ministers either kept a convenient silence or tried to deflect their responsibility by appealing to abstruse theological arguments. It was left to the common people to step forward. And this they did. In a highly unusual act, twelve members of the witchcraft juries were moved to sign and circulate a declaration of regret. These ordinary citizens commanded the wisdom and moral integrity which their Puritan leaders so sadly lacked.

We do signify to all in general, and to the surviving sufferers in special, our deep sense of, and sorrow for, our errors in acting on such evidence to the condemning of any person; and do declare, that we justly fear that we were sadly deluded and mistaken; for which we are much disquieted and distressed in our minds. We do heartily ask forgiveness of you all, whom we have justly offended; and do declare, according to our present minds, we would none of us do such things again, on such grounds, for the whole world.

It was signed by Thomas Fisk, Foreman, William Fisk, John Bacheler, Thomas Fisk, Jr., John Dane, Joseph Evelith, Thomas Pearly, Sr., **John Peabody**, Thomas Perkins, Samuel Sayer, Andrew Elliot, and Henry Herrick, Sr.

To his credit, John Peabody had the courage to voice his remorse.

The witchcraft trials represent the extremes to which repression and condemnation can devolve. Puritan religion in early America also served a positive, even necessary, function. Their very rigidity of their beliefs may have given the colonists the grit, fortitude and resilience to survive. The early years were difficult beyond our imagination. Survival depended upon their success at accomplishing enormous amounts of physically demanding work, dealing with the monotony and isolation of frontier life, and facing courageously events of fear and terror. In these early years, the Paybodys and their neighbors lived with a dread of Indian attack and fear of natural disasters over which they had little control. Their commonly-held spiritual vision served to anchor, inspire and to bond them together.

Natural Disasters

Several natural disasters occurred in New England soon after the Paybody's arrival. Greeting Francis was a devastating hurricane whose fury descended upon the area on the 15th day of August, 1635. Having sailed from England on April 2, 1635, he would have landed just a few weeks earlier.

According to Bradford in *"Of Plymouth Plantation"*:

It began in the morning a little before day and grew, not by degrees, but came with great violence from the beginning to the great amazement of many; it blew down sundry houses, and uncovered divers (diverse) other; divers vessels were lost at sea in it, and many more were in extreme danger. It caused the sea to swell in some places to the southward of Plymouth, as it rose to twenty feet right up and down, and made many of the Indians to climb into trees for safety. It threw down all the corn to the ground ...It blew down many hundred thousand of trees, turning up the stronger by the roots and breaking the high pine trees—very strange and fearful to behold...The greatest force of it at Plymouth...The marks of it will remain for many years in those parts where it was sorest.

Just three years later, in 1638, another natural phenomenon occurred.
A great earth quake in New England this year, on the first day of June. The quake shook with such violence, that in some places, the people could not stand, without difficulty, in the streets and most of the movable articles in their houses were thrown down.

Earthquakes rarely occur in New England.

The previous winter had made history as well. Author Robert Usher, in *The Pilgrims and their History*, reported that the winter of 1637-38 was exceptionally cold. Plymouth harbor was frozen solid enough that for five weeks oxen and carts could cross it safely. Everyone called it fortunate that the *Mayflower* Pilgrims had not encountered such extreme cold during their first winter. (The 1620-21 winter had been a typical winter) The Paybodys, however, faced this extreme cold their first year. We wonder how they fared as they tried to establish roots in a wilderness environment while enduring these hardships.

Not only forces of nature but animal predators threatened the Paybody settlers. In 1641 families banded together to fight the menace of wolves attacking their livestock. Thacher writes,
It was ordered that every house holder within the town shall pay a half penny for every person in his family, except poor people who have no cattle, for every wolf that shall be killed within the liberties of the town. The killer shall bring the skin to Mr. Jenney, and there receive coin for his pay, Mr. Jenney to have the skin for his pains.

But Indians* posed the most ominous threat of all. As the Paybodys began life in the New World, hostilities came to a head. To understand the conflict it helps to understand the early pioneers' attitudes toward these native tribes. So, we will depart from the family chronicle briefly to describe the Indians who shared their New World.

---

*The author often uses the word "Indian" when referring to the Native Americans, in keeping with the terminology used in those times.

The Native Americans in New England

For the first few years the English immigrants and the Native Americans co-existed in an uneasy alliance. The Indians, curious about these newcomers, experienced no excessive threat from their presence. They enjoyed trading with each other and being mutually helpful. They shared a balance of power. However, the two groups faced inevitable collision. Shiploads of new settlers kept arriving. As the English continued to grow in numbers, their needs for land kept expanding, and the Indian tribes felt increasingly hemmed in.

Neither group understood the other and both had vastly different attitudes toward the ownership of land. The colonists thought of the natives as savages who neglected to establish "civilized" settlements. Thus the Christian newcomers felt entitled to the land. Quoted in the *Historical Atlas of Massachusetts,* John Winthrop wrote:

> they in close noe habytation, nor any tame cattle to improve Land by, and soe have noe other but a Naturall Right to those countries.

This contrasts the Indian view. According to writer Eugene Stratton, "The land was something to roam in, hunt in, fish in, build a temporary home in." Land "belonged" to the one making use of it. The mere signing of a piece of paper was meaningless to the Indians and in their minds did not transfer exclusive rights to an uncultivated piece of land.

Though the English settlers believed they naturally deserved the land, they were scrupulous about paying the Indians for all the acreage acquired. These Plymouth leaders honored their code of ethics in refusing to take the land from the Indians. For example, in 1649, Massasoit sold to Captain Myles Standish all of the township of Bridgewater, a tract of land about seven miles square, used by the Duxbury settlers. Thacher records: "The price paid to the Indian leader was seven coats of a yard and a half each, nine hatchets, eight hoes, twenty knives, four moose skins, and ten and a half yards of cotton cloth."

However, the natives may not have fully understood the English method of purchasing land. Indian scholar Douglas Leach explains,

> ...frequently the colonists bought large tracts of land from the Indians, and then left the land unused for many years before dividing it up into

individual lots. Since the Indians would still make use of this land, they must have thought the white men rather foolish at times. But, ultimately the settlers came to take over exclusive rights to "their" land and the Indians, perhaps a bit astonished (and angry!), now had to retreat to a constantly diminishing piece of territory.

The Indian served many functions for the English settlers of the 1600's. He met many of their needs: a customer for their alcohol, guns and glass beads; an ally in war against their enemies; a helper who taught them to fish, hunt and cultivate new crops; and a guide in exploring the wilderness. Immigrants could trade with him for furs to repay their debt to England. Missionaries could preach to him to save his soul. He was also a convenient embodiment of evil and depravity which provided the newcomers a reassurance of their own moral goodness. Cotton Mather, as reported by Bandelier in *Delight Makers,* reminded his faithful, that the Red Man was a creature of the Devil himself — so, in exploiting the Indian, the Puritans could be confident they were fulfilling their obligations to God.

The following is a summary of James Thacher's 1832 description of the Indian natives encountered by the early colonists. This account appeared in his book, *History of the Town of Plymouth from its First Settlement in 1620 to the Present Time with a concise History of the Aborigines of New England and their Wars with the English.* (It is important to note that Thacher wrote this nearly two centuries later, so it provides a view of the "aborigines", as he calls them, that may not reflect 17th century attitudes.

Aborigines or Indian Natives of New England

Although generally the men were naked except for a slight covering at the waist, occasionally they dressed in the skin of a deer or wolf. Women were commonly clothed in beaver skin. They believed that the idea of cultivating the earth was degrading to men. "Squaws and hedge hogs were made to scratch the ground." Men were designed for war and hunting and holding council. Their women were held in complete slavery being made to do all out-doors drudgery. The women did the planting and weeding and carrying burdens while the men indulged in idleness. They called the white people "much fool to spoil their women by keeping them from out-door labor and making them into lazy women."

The preparation of the natives from infancy was entirely directed to fit their bodies for enduring the greatest of hardships and to form their minds to suffer and to inflict the most appalling of evils. Infants from birth were tied down to a board for months at a time. Young men, in preparation for powwows, had to undergo the most horrible of tortures. The chief occupation for men was hunting and war. When their hunting season was over, they generally loitered in their wigwams in entire indolence, eating and drinking with unbounded excess as long as their stores lasted. After alcohol was introduced to them they would drink without restraint and in this drunkenness they would be exposed to the weather and would often perish.

When preparing for warfare, to give themselves a fierce appearance, they painted their faces and plucked all the hair on each side of their head leaving a narrow tuft of hair extending the entire length of their head and tied up at the crown. The war dance and ceremony of smoking and passing the pipe was a sacred brotherly bond.

Their style was to ambush and attack, whether it was one tribe fighting another or in making war on the pioneer settlements. Taking their enemy by sudden surprise, they suddenly descended upon the unsuspecting prey screaming blood curdling savage yells. The indiscriminate butchery was marked by savage cruelty without the least regard to humanity or mercy. The inhabitants were either murdered or scalped or carried into the wilderness and put into the Indian wigwams as servants. Or they were tormented for amusement by their captors. Stories of savage cruelty are beyond belief. The prisoner was condemned to suffer the most cruel torment by being roasted alive, while the savages danced around the fire with awful yells; or the prisoner's body was tortured by tearing or biting off the flesh, tearing out the finger nails and protracting life as long as possible so that the tor-

ment may be increased and lengthened. When the Indians were the victims, they suffered the most exquisite torture with a fortitude also beyond human nature.

Stories of ambush, attack and torture did not characterize the peaceful early years of colonist-Indian coexistence. But the Paybodys settled just when tensions were beginning to erupt.

Greeting the Paybodys soon after their arrival was a terrifying turn of events—the Pequot War (1637). A group of 75 settlers from Massachusetts and Connecticut colonies joined forces with Indian allies from the Narraganset and Mohegan tribes. Plymouth forces were also raised for this but never sent. In the early morning hours these joint forces viciously assaulted the Pequots who were still sleeping in their wigwams. They stormed in and slaughtered them, not sparing a woman or child. Then the village was set afire and the entire tribe was vanquished. The colonists showed no mercy as they burned alive more than 600 natives. William Bradford wrote about the burning of the village: "It was a fearful sight to see them...frying in the fire...and horrible was the stink and scent thereof."

Pilgrim Justice

A year later, John Paybody became involved in an event of an opposite nature. In 1638 four young men who were servants at Plymouth deserted their masters and hid in the woods. They met an Indian and killed him to steal his wampum (beads made from quahog shells and used as money). One murderer escaped, but the other three went to trial. Confessing their guilt, they were executed by hanging. John Paybody served on the jury which convicted them on June 4, 1639. Although some might have considered hanging three Englishmen for one Indian excessive, it illustrates that, especially in these early years, the Pilgrims attempted to uphold standards of justice for the Indian nations as well as themselves.

Nevertheless, tensions escalated. Householders received an order to provide themselves with firearms and ammunition. Each town had to submit a list of all adult males able to bear arms. William Paybody's name appears among 76 men from Duxbury listed in 1643. To alert each other of the need for help, settlers agreed in 1644 to sound an alarm, or build a great fire on Gallow's Hill in Plymouth or Captain's Hill in Duxbury. The colonists lived in a state of preparedness. Sporadic incidents continued to happen. Without warning, Indian attackers descended upon homesteads and killed men and women as they worked in the fields.

King Philip's War

Hostilities finally came to a head during the vicious King Philip's War in 1675. Philip (or Metacomet), was the son of Massasoit, the Wampanoag chief who had been a great friend of the Plymouth colonists. Philip, who rose to assume the leadership of all the area tribes, was determined to regain the land for the natives.

He assembled a force of 4,000 warriors to accomplish his goal of driving the English out and returning the land to the native peoples. Both sides raided villages and massacred hundreds of victims. The English troops finally trapped Philip where he had fortified himself in the middle of an immense swamp in South Kingston, Rhode Island. Within the enclosure 500 wigwams served as the winter quarters for at least 3,000 natives. Thacher described the Narraganset Great Swamp fight of December, 8, 1675:

> The Indians were driven from their posts at all points and from wigwam to wigwam in great confusion. Then an immense slaughter took place; neither men, women nor children were spared; all were hewn down and the ground was encumbered with heaps of the slain. In the midst of this awful sight, fire was communicated to their wigwams. When the howlings and yells of the savages were mingled with the roar of musketry, the raging of consuming fire, and the screams of women and children altogether forming a scene inconceivably appalling to humanity. The battle continued for three hours. Carnage and death were the order of the day.

Warfare continued even after this horrible battle for another few months. In August, 1676, Philip finally succumbed in another swamp fight near Mount Hope, Rhode Island. Now it was the colonists who behaved in a primitive, savage manner. They initiated the barbaric practice of 17th century

England of beheading and quartering the enemy. The colonists performed this act on the body of the unfortunate Philip.

> His head was brought to Plymouth on Thanksgiving day in great triumph. Then it was exposed to public view for more than twenty years. One of his hands was preserved in rum and afterwards exhibited through the country.

Both sides fought the King Philip War at enormous cost. The Indians killed nearly 1,000 colonists and completely destroyed 12 towns. Three thousand Indians perished, causing the virtual extinction of Philip's tribe.

When peace finally came, the abandoned towns were reoccupied and a new expansion began. Over the years, the colonists multiplied in numbers and strength. But calm only lasted a few years. Beginning in 1689 another long series of Indian hostilities, known as the French and Indian War, began and lasted nearly three-quarters of a century.

One hundred years later, in 1789, a number of Indian Sachems (chiefs) assembled at New York on a mission to President Washington. General Knox, as Secretary of War, invited them to dine at his table. A little before dinner two or three of the chiefs went out onto the balcony from which they had a view of the city, the harbor, Long Island, and the adjacent country. On returning into the room they appeared dejected. General Knox, noticing this, said to one chief, "Brother, what has happened to you? You look sorry! Is there any thing here to make you unhappy?"

Historian James Thacher reports the Chief's answer:

I will tell you, brother, I have been looking at your beautiful city, the great water, and rivers, your mighty fine country producing enough for all your wants. I see how happy you all are. But then I could not help thinking that this fine country, and this great water was once ours. Our ancestors once lived here, they enjoyed it as their own possessions in peace; it was the gift of the Great Spirit to them and their children. At length the white people came here in a great canoe. They asked only to let them tie it to a tree, lest the waters should carry it away; we consented. They then said some of their people were sick, and they asked permission to land them, and put them under the shade of the trees. The ice then came and they could not get away. They then begged a piece of land to build wigwams for the winter; we granted it to them. They then asked for some corn to keep them from starving; we kindly furnished it to them, they promising to go away when the ice was gone. When this happened, and the great water was clear, we told them they must now go away with their big canoe; but they pointed to their big guns round their wigwams, and said they would stay there, and we could not make them go away. Afterwards more white people came. They brought spirituous and intoxicating liquors with them, of which the Indians became very fond. They persuaded us to sell them some land.

Day of Mourning. Wampanoags look across the bay at the Mayflower. The proposed wording for a new plaque on Cole's Hill expresses the tribal sentiment: "Since 1970, Native Americans have gathered at noon on Cole's Hill in Plymouth to commemorate a National Day of Mourning on the U.S. Thanksgiving holiday. Many Native Americans do not celebrate the arrival of the Pilgrims and other European settlers. To them, Thanksgiving Day is a reminder of the genocide of millions of their people, the theft of their lands, and the relentless assault on their culture. Participants in a National Day of Mourning honor Native ancestors and the struggles of Native people to survive today. It is a day of remembrance and spiritual connection as well as a protest of the racism and oppression which Native Americans continue to experience."

Finally, they drove us back from time to time, into the wilderness, far from the water and the fish and the oysters. They destroyed the game, our people have wasted away, and now we live miserable and wretched, while you are enjoying our fine and beautiful country. This it is that makes me sorry brother! and I cannot help it.

The native people of the forest, the first possessors of our country, became a vanquished people.

The Peabodys built and established homesteads, spread over fertile lands and flourished. The Indians, decimated or driven off, retreated from their ancestral lands. Years passed and Peabody generations came and went. Their name shifted in spelling from Paybody and Pabodie to Peabody.

The following summary of the lives of a few descendants of Francis Paybody spans about two hundred years before Almeda Peabody was born in 1844 and the story of her life begins.

Saga of the Next Six Generations (1700-1844)

John Paybody (1)*, is considered the originator of the Peabody family in America. He arrived in the New World about the same time as his son, Francis (2). Francis had eight sons and six daughters. From these fourteen children a myriad of branches in the Peabody family tree originated. In fact, if we assume each descendent had six children by 1998, twelve generations later, there would be two billion descendants of John Paybody! But, let's trace the one particular branch that proceeds forward in time to Almeda, and ultimately to my immediate family.

Isaac (3), the fourth-born son of Francis inherited the family mansion and mill, the orchard and farm land at Topsfield. Historian Selim Hobart Peabody explained Francis' generosity by quoting from his will, "I have given y more to my son Isaac in consideration (of) y providence of God disinabling him by y loss of one of his leggs." Francis' will also made elaborate and detailed provisions for the continued

care of his wife, Mary, after his death. Reserved for her was the South End of the family house, along with her choice of two "milch" cows, two or three swine, use of oxen as needed and a horse to ride on when she had the occasion. Isaac was to pay his mother 20 "bushells" of Indian Corne yearly, five "bushells" of wheat, four of rye and six of malt and to provide her a pasture for her "cowes" and fodder for them in the winter. "In the case that she should marry again then all y privildges above said shall cease." (See the Family Foundations section for for the complete text of Francis' Last Will and Testament.)

Isaac (3) married Sarah Estes and together they had 12 children. He lived in Topsfield all his life and died in 1727 at the age of 79 years. In his will he signed his name Isaac Peabody, the first to use the present-day spelling of the name in America. He left the family mansion to his second-born son, Isaac (4) who did not marry. After his death the house passed out of the family.

Isaac's oldest son was Coronet Francis (4), born in 1694. He lived in Middleton, Massachusetts, and he and his wife had 13 children. In 1711 when

---

*The number in parentheses refers to the generation number. See the Family Tree in the Family Foundations section.

Francis was only 17 years old he sailed under the command of Ensign William Hilton and they gave chase to a fishing sloop stolen by a French man and three Indians. The sloop was ultimately captured after a difficult pursuit in a very rough sea. The Indians were put to death, scalped and thrown into the ocean. The French man was taken prisoner. The New England Historical and Genealogical Register printed the letter written by Francis as he describes the incident.

> York November 8th 1711. Wee who are your Escellencies moast humble Servants gives Our Duty to your Escellency and do hereby Assert that on the Eight day of Nouembr wee Embarqut on Board a Small Sloop with Ensigne Wm Hilton & made Saile into the Oacion in Chase of a Sloop taken out of York Harour ye night before when wee came about Three Leauges without York Harbour Wee see a Saile in the Offing which Wee Expected to be the Said Sloop taken out of York Wee gave her Chase shee try'd uss upon a Wind Wee gain'd upon her apace shee went away a point or Two of the sheet Wee gain'd upon her Still wich much Encouraged uss Wee Chast her upon that Course about two hours Wee began then to Raise the man that Stood at Helm very plain then shee bares away before the Wind it Seem'd to uss as though Shee gain'd Ground on uss. The next thing Wee put up our Blankits to Starbord to make more Sail Wee came up with her apace Wee fires upon her Ten or Twelve Guns shee bringing too Wee boarded her Ensigne Wm Hilton Leaps On Board the Prize with Two other men he orders the Enemie to Jump into the Sloop he came Out of the Night coming on and the Sea Runing so Extraordinarie Bigg Wee made the Best of our way for the Harbour and Secured these Rebells till Ensigne Wm Hilton came in. As Soon as he Arriv'd in the Harbour Capn Wm Heath & Capn Abraham Preble sent Jobe Young a man belonging to York to Said Hilton to know what should be done with ye Rebels He Immediately Went on shore with ye messenger Capn Heath & Capn Pregle Invites him up in a Chamber at Esqr Doonniels what past between them We do not Know but quickly said Hilton returns & goes to the place were said Rebels were & they were put to Death & thrown into the Sea what Ever your Excellency may have otherways this is the truth.
>
> —Frances Peabody

Coronet Francis (4) named his eighth child Isaac (5). Born in 1727, Isaac grew up to become a private in Captain N. Adams' company during the French War in Nova Scotia in 1755. Isaac Peabody also served as a soldier from Wilton, New Hampshire, in the American Revolution.

The youngest of Isaac's nine children, Moses (6), was born in Middleton (1765). He moved first to Keene, New Hampshire, then to Weston and then to

Mt. Holly, Vermont. Moses also had a large family of 13 children.

Historian Alden B. Rollins, in his comprehensive two volume work, *Vermont Warnings Out*, lists Moses Peabody's name as having been "Warned Out" of two Vermont towns. First, on September 29, 1803, Moses and Elizabeth Peabody and their seven children were Warned Out of Weston. And then again on December 1, 1810, Moses and his family were Warned Out of Mt. Holly, a small town a few miles to the north.

Warning Out was a common practice in early New England in which local authorities ordered unwanted newcomers to leave town. If they did not leave willingly, officials escorted them to the town borders or returned them to their town of origin. In the early years Warnings Out were issued to a wide assortment of individuals—people who were dangerous or of an undesirable personal character, poor, transient, of the "wrong" religion, or anyone who looked like trouble.

Gradually, economic considerations came to predominate as the rationale for ejecting newcomers. In these later years the practice came to be used almost entirely for removing new arrivals who were poor. A town had 12 months to ask a new arrival to leave town. If after that, because of sickness or poverty, any person needed relief, town poor laws required their needs be provided for.

Most New England states abandoned Warning Out by the middle 1790's. But Vermont alone revived it in 1801. Local towns then had the power to exercise this law at their own discretion. Enormous variation existed between communities. Some towns Warned only the poor or the transient. Others routinely Warned almost all newcomers in order to avoid future responsibility for their welfare. Selectmen in these towns believed that if they failed to Warn Out people who later became welfare cases, they would be proven remiss in their duties. So, they thought, why take a chance? Give everyone a Warning. The unstated corollary in these later years was that anyone Warned Out could stay there without much fear of being removed. Selectmen were indifferent to whether the Warned Out person actually left town or not. They had accomplished their duty of protecting the town from new arrivals who might be added to the relief rolls later on. As it came to be practiced, Warning Out was not a sentence of banishment but a disclaimer of responsibility. In 1817 Vermont repealed the Warning Out law, and it never was used again.

When Moses and his wife and seven children (at that time) received their Warnings Out in 1803 and 1810 it was probably because they were poor. Town officials wanted to avoid ever having to assume financial responsibility for them if they should be in need of help. This was their Welcome Wagon!

We have seen how the previous generations migrated northward from Massachusetts, to New Hampshire and to Vermont, each following the receding frontier.

The next generation brought the Peabodys to New York State. Moses' eighth child, Benjamin Bigelow (7), was born in Mt. Holly, Vermont, but married his wife, Maria Wright, in Ohio, New York. They moved to East Pitcairn from Herkimer County, New York.

This brings our 200-year journey to my great-grandfather, Edwin, and his historian sister, Almeda Peabody. She was the seventh of Benjamin and Maria Peabody's eight children. Almeda, with her brothers and sisters, grew up in the wilderness country of northern New York, the land of the big trees. Though they would eventually follow the lure of gold to far-off Colorado, they began life knowing only the forest primeval . . .

Almeda Peabody,
Northern New York

The gloom of the dense, ancient, silent forest is awe-inspiring.
—Isabella Bird

This is the forest primeval.
The murmuring pines and the hemlocks,
Bearded with moss, and in garments green,
indistinct in the twilight,
Stand like Druids of eld, with voices sad
and prophetic,
Stand like harpers hoar, with beards that
rest on their bosoms.
Loud from its rocky caverns, the deep-voiced
neighboring ocean
Speaks, and in accents disconsolate answers
the wail of the forest.
This is the forest primeval...
—*from* Evangeline,
Henry Wadsworth Longfellow

The Big Woods

Before the colonists arrived, this "forest primeval" covered all of northeast America, a dense, dark barrier. An ancient forest, it had stood undisturbed since the end of the Ice Age, 20,000 years ago. It spread as an endless wilderness of trees, except for a few square miles along the river banks where the Indians lived. They had girdled and killed trees with their stone axes, or had burned off a few acres to make a little space to grow their corn and pumpkin.

A virgin forest. These trees had lived and grown their natural life spans and died and lived again for 200 centuries—undisturbed, except for an occasional hurricane or fire. The trees in these New England forests sometimes grew to immense proportions. *The Yankee Pioneers* tells of Samuel Williams, in his 1809 history of Vermont, describing pines commonly growing up to six feet in diameter and up to 247 feet in height.

Grass could not grow in the deep forests where sunlight never reached. The only part of New England where wild grass grew to any extent was along the seacoast where the sunlight bathed the shore. Deer and moose survived in the inland forests but only by eating twigs and gnawing off the tree bark. Cattle and oxen depended on their owners to clear the land so grass could grow.

Rivers, rather than land routes, became the wilderness highways. Rivers also provided bottom land on either side favorable for planting and developing farms. The uplands, on the other hand, only offered the settlers an abundance of rock with poor soil. Thus, early settlements rose along the rivers.

Gradually, settlers made inroads. Villages sprang up and lower New England was settled.

Vast and forbidding mountains created another formidable barrier to westward expansion. Maps reveal that the northeast is made up of several mountain ranges, all running north and south. The White Mountains of New Hampshire, the Green Mountains of Vermont, the Berkshires of Massachusetts, the Adirondacks of New York, and the Appalachians and the Alleghenies of New York and Pennsylvania form a barrier. These mountainous systems blocked expansion, not so much because of their height, but because of their collective width of parallel ranges that lay directly across the path of westward movement into the midwest.

Instead of moving westward, the thrust of migration now turned to the north. Nearly all the settlers in Maine, New Hampshire and Vermont had left homes in states to the south—Massachusetts, Connecticut and Rhode Island. After the end of the French and Indian War in 1763, an ever increasing flood of people pushed northward.

Why did they choose the hilly rock-strewn North rather than the rich, flat, rock-free meadow lands west of the Alleghenies? The West was less attractive because of the mountains. But even more important, the fertile farmlands beyond the mountains were deep in mud! The

same rich soil that made the land desirable also made it impassable. Mud. Author Franklin Hough describes it:

The route to (the Genesee country and Ohio) was through miry swamps, and along streams and valleys, which when overspread with the decaying foliage of a luxuriant vegetation, were

Logging in St. Lawrence County, New York.

infested with deadly miasms, and offered to the adventurous emigrant but little inducement for the exercise of industry, when his little earnings were liable to be demanded by the expenses of sickness. His frame on alternate days, chilled, parched, and drenched, with fever and ague.

Accordingly we find, that during the years between 1802 and 1807, the tide of emigration from that prolific hive, New England, poured into the valleys of the Black and St. Lawrence rivers, which settled with a rapidity, especially in the former, which has been seldom equaled...Winter was usually selected for moving, as the streams and swamps were then bridged by ice, and routes became passable which at other times would be wholly impractical.

The Peabody family over the generations also migrated northward. Francis (2) and his son, Isaac (3), and grandson, Coronet Francis (4), all lived in the Massachusetts area just north of Boston. Then this branch of the family moved along with the receding frontier. Isaac (5) and his family settled in New Hampshire, his son, Moses (6) moved to Vermont and his son, Benjamin Bigelow (7), ultimately settled in northern New York.

In the midst of the great forests of northern New York, in the little settlement of East Pitcairn near the St. Lawrence River, Almeda began her life on January 22, 1844. Her childhood in this wilderness area, her mother's untimely death, her struggles to survive while working for pennies on neighboring farms, and finally her adventuresome journey to the Colorado gold camps all come alive in Almeda's memoirs. She met and fell in love with a young man, was married, worked as a cook in a mining camp and raised her family in the high mountains of Colorado.

I have printed her journal with a minimal amount of editing. Except for rearranging the paragraphs so the story reads in a chronological order and breaking up run-on sentences, little has been changed from Almeda's original biography.

Let us hear her account...

Almeda's Story

Some time in the earlier years, two brothers came from England and after wandering around finally settled in the Green Mountain Country of Vermont—settled down and became what was called "Green Mountain Boys." Their names was Peabody.

These thrifty Green Mountain Boys were productive and raised large families, one having eleven living children, being my grandfather. His children—James, Moses, Joseph, Blake, Harvey, Lorenzo, Sally, Betsy, Cynthia, Nancy—were my uncles and aunts— and Benjamin was my father. Many lived from seventy-five to ninety and past in years.

This family then drifted up to central New York. Four of the boys and two girls finally settled in Northern New York in St. Lawrence County. Most of them raised large families.

My father, Benjamin Peabody met my mother, Maria Wright in Herkimer County, New York. My mother's father was killed in the Army [American Revolution]. And then when my Mother was eight years old her mother died, leaving her a lone orphan. Her grandmother took her and cared for her, they two being alone made their living by knitting and sewing.

My father met her when she was eighteen years old, a beautiful delicate girl, while he, like most of the Peabodys, was a large tall man—six feet two inches. All were poor. Three months

Erecting a log cabin.

before my birth, in 1844, (I was their seventh child) they moved up to Northern New York and settled in East Pitcairn, St. Lawrence County, in what was then known as the big woods.

My father chopped down big hardwood trees to build a cabin. And then when they got moved in their little cabin, after using the fallen trees to build it, he chopped down more trees to get room to build a log house, which had two rooms, one upstairs and one downstairs, and a good cellar. That log house being the only home that I ever knew until after I was twenty-five years old, when I came to Colorado. Our whole family grew up in that log house. My Mother died there and is buried there in a little cemetery in East Pitcairn, St. Lawrence County, alone.

These were early times, and hard. There were no wealthy people near, every one living as we did, in log houses. The winters were quite severe, and men banked up their houses in early fall by shoveling the ground up around the base to keep the cold out, and to keep their cellars from freezing. We lived mostly on buckwheat, corn and potatoes, of which we had an abundance as soon as ground could be cleared to raise enough on. There was a great deal of wild fruit, and there were great numbers of maple trees, so we had plenty of maple sugar. We knew no other.

Nearly every one had a few sheep, and made their own woolen cloth and stockings. The women carding the wool into rolls and then spinning and weaving into cloth, redoubling the yarn and twisting and then knitting stockings and mittens. No one could buy these things ready made. Then all girls learned very young to knit, and did knit their own stockings. When I was eight years of age I had the proud pleasure of boasting that I had knit a pair of gloves for my Father and one for my brother Daniel. I never wore but one pair of stockings that I did not knit until I came to Colorado, past twenty-five years of age. My Mother's old spinning wheel was still there in the old house when I left there, and I with my sisters had learned to spin on it. I heard my Father say after I was a grown girl that none of his eleven children had ever worn a pair of shoes until after they were seven years old. We had no coddling and grew up hale and hearty. We, one and all, had to amuse ourselves with no playthings purchased for us, and was no doubt happier for it. In winter we had a hand sled to slide down hill on, and to haul our loads of wood and other heavy things on. While green things were growing in summer we had all kinds of vegetables to eat, and melons, both watermelons and muskmelons. Green corn was either boiled or roasted before the coals of fire; beech nuts and butternuts we had in great quantities by gathering them and laying them up to dry. And what one doesn't see now, we peeled pumpkins and hung them up under the rafters to dry. In winter these great rings of dried pumpkin were cooked and used for sauce or pies. In those days there were no apples in Northern New York, so our everything and anything that children love to eat we gathered and dried for winter use. Everyone raised their own pork and deer were very thick there. So we had plenty of meat, but not much butter. But in summer we had butter.

If the hay and other feed gave out, the men went into the woods and cut down the young limbs from trees, and drove the cattle (which no one had many of) into the woods to eat or browse on it.

Sometime about the twentieth of March men began their sugar making. Men made their spikes or spouts by cutting the required length of wood, shaving a trough in it and boring a hole for the sap. Then they drove it into the tree about two feet from the ground and put large buckets underneath for the sap to run into. When the buckets were filled they drove around with a sled on which was a large tub and gathered up the sap. Those were busy days, for men had to boil the sap, keeping a fire night and day. When it was about as thick as syrup it was taken up and after standing overnight to settle, then boiled into sugar, or as we said, "sugared off".

Log cabin at East Pitcairn.

Money was a scarce article in those days. Quite a good many men hunted deer for about three of the coldest months in winter. They used the fore-quarters for meat, and the hindquarter, or saddles as they were called, were sold to venison buyers. They came from cities of Boston, Philadelphia and New York, and purchased all they could get and shipped it to those cities. That hunter's life was a hard one too, but it must have been fascinating too, as well as some money in it. Some days a man would not see a track, and other days might get one or two, or even three once in a great while.

My father (with my mother) had eight children—five boys and three girls. Their names were:

Benjamin Peabody,
borne January 1, 1830; died April, 1906
Daniel Peabody,
borne April 27, 1832; died April, 1900
Lelon Peabody,
borne February 4, 1834; died April, 1898
James Peabody,
borne April 14, 1836; died August 4, 1917
Alvira Ann,
borne March 15, 1839; died August 4, 1917
Salome,
borne April 7, 1842; died September, 1913
Almeda,
borne January 22, 1844. died---
Edwin Judson Peabody,
borne May 9, 1848, died 1918 [the author's great grandfather]

I was borne in East Pitcairn, St. Lawrence County, N.Y. and so was Brother Edwin. All the older ones were borne in Herkimer County, New York. Brother Lelon was the youngest of all my father's children [when he died], he being only sixty-four years, but he did not die a natural death.

When I was eleven years old my Mother died October 4, 1855. She lies buried in a little cemetery in East Pitcairn, N.Y. all alone, so far as her family is concerned. My youngest brother Edwin J. was seven years old. My father married again the next spring, and had three more children, one of which died in infancy. The other two I have lost track of. I do not know whether they are living or not. When my Father remarried that summer we children all left home except the two younger brothers. James remained with Father until he was twenty-one. When Edwin was ten years old he went away to live at our brother Daniel's on a farm fifteen miles from home.

Almeda's feelings about her stepmother or what life was like after her father's remarriage are noticeably absent. Taking a closer look at the known facts may shed light on the emotional reality of those years.

A year and a half after their mother died, Almeda's father remarried (May 13, 1855). He was 53. His new wife, Sarah Holden, from Yorkshire, England, was only 23 years old—younger than some of her step-children! By the summer all the children moved out except James and Edwin. We also know that a baby, Anna Elizabeth was born to their father and his new wife on May, 5, 1857, but she died less than a year later (March, 1858.) The very next month (April 24, 1858) another little girl was born who was also given the name of Anna Elizabeth. And that was the year Edwin, age ten, left home to live on brother Daniel's farm!

Under the best of circumstances life on the frontier was hard with survival requiring a strong family unit. Their mother's death was a tragic loss for the family The new stepmother was blamed for the family's disintegration. Almeda's daughter, Beatrice Lulu, later wrote: "She had a hard struggle to live and grow after her mother died. Her father, after a few months had remarried, hoping to be able to keep the family together until all could go out on their own. The stepmother was very difficult, however. So Almeda had to go out to work, child as she was."

From Sarah's point of view, to enter the grieving family as the stepmother to nine children, some older than she, must have been daunting. Raised in England, Sarah may have found frontier life primitive, unfamiliar and a trying ordeal. When her first baby died and another born to replace her—one can imagine her emotional turmoil. Overwhelmed with the needs of her stepchildren, grief stricken over the loss of her first baby, and preoccupied and anxious about her new infant—she hardly had the emotional reserves to nurture ten year old Edwin. So off to brother Daniel's farm he went.

Gouverneur Wesleyan Seminary.

Almeda seemed to be a person who kept her unhappy feelings to herself. Her indomitable spirit probably grew strong by not feeling sorry for herself or lingering in self pity. Positive thinking was essential for survival.

Hard Work and Poverty

I wandered around a year or two, and then went to work by the week. The year I was fifteen I received 75 cents a week for 28 weeks, which had to clothe me. Of course I had to go scantily clad, with no shoes most of the time. I was very small for my age, but the next year I received one dollar and glad to earn it. If I was absent or sick one day, that day was lost time. It was a great farming country. People hired girls, and men too, for about eight months of the year. We were in demand so we never need hunt a job or place to work. We were sought. I have had men drive thirty miles to hire me to work for them. No girl need ask for work if she was old enough and would work.

When I was sixteen years old I was very sick with typhoid fever. I was then working for a family named Hildreth. There was a Homeopath Doctor called who came 2 1/2 miles, charging one dollar each trip. He came three times and cured me. I worked at that place 34 weeks for one dollar each week. They were very good people to work for. They had a dairy farm and made cheese part of the time. One morning when we went to the vat to strain the milk there was a big spotted adder sailing around in the last night's milk. The lining of the vat was smooth tin and he could not climb out. We did not make cheese that day. I also worked at my brother Daniel's, where they also made cheese, and I think I could make cheese yet. I don't mean cottage - I learned to make that from my husband's brother, Karl, as it takes a German to know how to make good "Schmearcase" or cottage cheese.

The hardest place I ever got into (although I had other hard ones), was

Back from deer hunting.

named Almira Hazelton. She had two sons and two daughters. I received $1.25 a week there. I was then eighteen years old. I stayed there 27 weeks, arising at 4:30 in the morning, milked nine cows (each of their boys the same). I could retire at 9:00 most of the time, but never allowed to sit down except Saturday p.m. and then only to do the family mending. I was only allowed to sweep my bedroom on Sunday. If I was gone a few hours I lost my days time, even not allowing me the Fourth of July. If I sewed a little while for myself I lost my time. Most of my mending I did on Sunday. If she purchased anything for me, and could over-charge a dime, she did so. I was not allowed to enter the pantry where she kept her provisions. Of course I was not in love with her, but being a very timid girl I did not dare say anything, no matter how badly I was treated. But now after 59 years I can truly say I am satisfied and am glad I did not do her any harm, and she and her family have gone to their resting places. After that I had life a little easier and I learned to do most required of me and do it well and make friends.

Then I had an opportunity to attend school at the Seminary (Gouverneur Wesleyan) or Academy. It was supported by the Methodist Episcopal Church, and was under the Regents of the State of N.Y. I think the M.E. Church sort of adopted me, as it got me a free tuition and soon I received an education enabling me to teach school. I studied hard and did my very best, very thankful for the support that was given

me. The teachers were very kind to me and who shall say that I do wrong to love that church that did so much for me. It was the church of my Father's and Mother's choice, and is the church of the poor people, and the poor who belong to it are looked after and helped. We welcome all to our church who do not belong to other churches and come asking admission, wanting to live Christian lives, God being their Judge.

Gouverneur Wesleyan Seminary kept close watch over its students educationally, morally and spiritually. Students were required to keep study hours, beginning at seven o'clock at night, after which none were allowed on the streets or in other rooms unless excused by a teacher or some member of the faculty. All were required to be at chapel at night and morning for sound and prayer service. Very soon after the beginning of each school term there was a social given in Chapel so that students would get acquainted with each other and we all enjoyed it very greatly. It is now 52 years since I left that dear old Seminary. Most of the students and teachers have done their work and gone to rest. My brothers and sisters have all gone, I alone remaining, I might say, of all that throng.

Almeda continues in the next chapter to describe leaving New York and traveling to the mining camps of Colorado.

"An endless wilderness of trees" awaited settlers in the forest primeval of upstate New York. Here, workers float logs on St. Lawrence, New York waterway

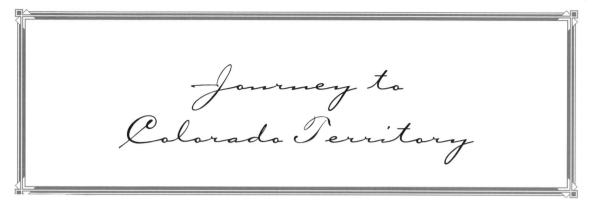

Journey to Colorado Territory

The story of how the earliest Paybodys ventured into the unknown and established life in wilderness New England holds many parallels to the Peabodys and other pioneers who migrated westward in the 1800's. Although separated by 200 years, remarkable similarities appear between the hardships the pioneers of each era encountered—the primitive living conditions, the endurance of women despite privation, the harshness of the environment, the menace of wild animals and the fear of Indians.

Many Parallels

The newcomers' attitudes and behavior towards the Native Americans—both the English settlers in the 1600's and the pioneers of the American West—were sadly similar. The Peabodys experienced consequences of this intolerance firsthand as Almeda's journal will reveal.

A powerful thread runs through the generations—the magnetism of the West. There seems to be a pull, beginning with the earliest colonists from England, to look westward, towards the horizon, whether it was crossing the ocean, or crossing the plains and mountains. The lure of the unknown was compelling. The same indomitable spirit carried them forward.

Brief History of the Gold Rush

Only ten years after the craze of the 1849 California gold rush, another discovery rocked the nation. In late 1858 prospectors found flakes of gold in the sands along Cherry Creek, near the present site of downtown Denver. Wondrous tales of huge fortunes just waiting to be scooped up electrified the people back home. "Pikes Peak or Bust" became the Colorado gold rush slogan, not because Pikes Peak held the precious metal, but because Pikes Peak, visible for miles around, stood as a landmark to guide newcomers. Pikes Peak represented the entire Colorado Front Range.

To the average young person "back East," travel to Colorado seemed more attractive than the three or four month's trek over the mountains to California. Many a farm boy started off on horseback or wagon, by stagecoach or even on foot, with dreams of riches.

The surface (or placer) gold at Cherry Creek soon played out, but prospectors swarmed deeper into the mountains. Miners agreed that the Continental Divide, the granite spine running down the country's mid-section, was the richest source of gold. In 1859 prospectors struck gold on Clear Creek near the site of Idaho Springs. Then, a rich gold-bearing quartz deposit was discovered at Gregory Gulch, which led to Central City's birth.

The rush was on. Some 50,000 people flooded to the gold fields during the summer of 1859. Miners soon made big strikes at Hamilton, Tarryall, Fairplay and Breckenridge. Small camps of rough shacks and tents sprang up around these gold strikes and the population mushroomed overnight. The effect of each new strike resembled fireworks on the Fourth of July. Each discovery created a new burst, bigger and more spectacular than the one before. Easterners gasped in wonder. They thronged to the West hoping to become rich. Most failed to gain their fortune.

The First Peabody to Join the Stampede

One of New York farm boys who got swept up in the excitement of '59 was Almeda's older brother, Lelon Peabody, the first Peabody to go West. Almeda describes the journey:

When Mother died my brother, Lelon, left New York in 1856 and stayed in Iowa for three years. Then in 1859, when gold was discovered in Colorado,

he joined an emigrant train and traveled across the plains with ox teams, 40 men with their families together. There was no railroad further than Omaha. It took six weeks to make the journey to Denver, that city consisting of three houses.

He then left the others and all scattered, roaming around the foothills and into the mountains. There were small colonies there. At one place two miles east of where Golden now stands there was at one time five hundred people living. The name of the place was Arapahoe City, but not one mark is left now to show where the little city stood.

Lelon Peabody penetrated mountains as isolated and remote as the upstate New York forest had once been.

Picture the tranquil wilderness which greeted the first white settlers. Here and there meandered an animal trail or a simple Indian path; vast herds of buffalo roamed the open spaces of Colorado's South and Middle Parks; pristine creeks and rivers made a home for the beaver; abundant flowers and wildlife flourished. Visualize the jagged peaks of the Ten Mile range protecting the gentle valley below. Feel the warmth of sunlight filtering through golden aspen trees and the coolness of the night-time air with stars dazzling overhead. In the distance hear the call of a lone coyote.

Then came the white invasion. News of the discovery of gold on Denver's Cherry Creek infused the economically depressed nation with hope. A mass scramble began. Hordes of men, and an

"It is Jan. 20, 1868, and the David Bruce Powers wagon train has just arrived from Leavenworth, Kansas, and is circled in the 1500 block of Market Street."

occasional woman, swarmed up every valley and gulch, prospecting every creek bed. Like invading ants, the prospectors fanned out pushing deeper and deeper into the mountains, higher and higher toward the Continental Divide.

Discovery of Breckenridge Gold

During the summer of 1859 Ruben Spalding's party of 14 men and one woman scaled what is now called Hoosier Pass and viewed a vast unspoiled wilderness. These were the first prospectors to cross the Continental Divide. Breckenridge became the first mining camp on the western slope. This crossing brought about the end of an era for this lush, tranquil valley—and the beginning of the next.

Spalding and his party descended from the high mountain pass into the secluded homeland of the Ute Indians. Following the rushing river into the valley below, they made camp about one-fourth mile downstream from the present site of Breckenridge. Here in mid-afternoon on the tenth of August, 1859, Ruben Spalding panned the first gold. The yield in the first few pans was so promising that all the members of the party immediately staked off 100-foot claims along the Blue River. The men soon set to work building sluice boxes ("Long Toms") and diverting the channel of the river in order to placer mine the gold that laced the drained river bed.

News of the strike in Breckenridge quickly traveled back over the range. By October, 1859, there were nearly 100 prospectors on the Blue, living in lean-tos and tents. However, only a few of these men had enough provisions to risk facing the hardship of the mountain winter.

With winter coming on, the handful of prospectors remaining in the camp felt isolated and vulnerable on the western side of the divide. They knew they had intruded into the hunting grounds of the Utes whose wary presence could be felt in the distance. To protect themselves from becoming "big game" hunted by the Indians, the miners erected a green log fortification that autumn.

The fort was located less than a mile north of today's Breckenridge on the west bank of the Blue River. The prospectors named it Fort Mary B (also called Fort Maribeh or Fort Mabery) in honor of the lone white woman who crossed the range with the Spalding party. The fort consisted of sod-roofed block houses, joined together and all facing inward around an empty square.

Among the block houses was a store run by Mr. Iddings whose merchandise consisted of a variety of miners' goods and clothing. The prospecting party constructed the fort with only two entrances making it easy to defend. Reports indicate that for three weeks during the winter several hundred Utes camped near the Blue River diggings. The Utes far outnumbered the 25 miners who wintered at the fort. Fortunately, defense proved unnecessary. The fort was occupied during the winter of 1859 and 1860 and deserted by 1861. (Now it lies buried under massive rock piles disgorged by the gold dredges.)

The little band of settlers hunkered down for a long, rugged winter. Snow fell to a depth of six to 12 feet that year (depending upon who reported it). Although settlers hunted the abundant game and caught plenty of fish, they missed the luxuries of home—coffee, tobacco, whiskey, flour, bacon and soap.

Among other activities, the miners occupied themselves making a pair of "snow shoes" for each of the men. These skis, as we would call them today, were made of boards from spruce trees. They were ten to 13 feet long and four inches wide and weighed a hefty 15 pounds. Having designed for themselves a means to travel about, the prospectors did not have to wait until the spring thaw to begin further exploration. The glittering gold that lay buried out of reach beneath deep snow cover was tantalizing. Author Mark Feister reports Spalding's writings in *Blasted, Beloved, Breckenridge:*

Gold panning.

In January or February, 1860, (I can't remember which), we all mounted our snow shoes, taking blankets, tools and provisions and went down Blue River about six miles where we built a cabin of small pine logs and claimed a town site, calling it Eldorado West. It was from this cabin Mr. Balce Weaver went prospecting and discovered Gold Run diggings beneath snow eight feet deep.

News about Gold Run quickly made its way back over the divide to the mining camps in South Park. Even though it was still the middle of winter, 50 men from Tarryall lashed on their snowshoes and trudged over the range to stake out claims at Gold Run. They promptly began shoveling off the snow or building bonfires to try to thaw the frozen ground. But the snow proved too much for them, forcing the prospectors to wait until spring.

The present-day skeleton of the Jessie Mill is a landmark in Gold Run Gulch. In 1885 the ten stamp Jessie Mill was constructed to crush the mine's gold ore on-site. In 1894 owners replaced the original mill with a larger one, and in 1898 it was remodeled with up-to-date equipment added.

Twenty-plus years before the Jessie Mill was built Lelon Peabody located his 1863 claim across the road from what would become the Jessie mill site. (Today you can visit the Jessie Mill by driving north from Breckenridge 3.5 miles on Highway 9, turning right onto Tiger Road, and after .9 miles turning right onto Gold Run Gulch Road. Then proceed another .6 miles up the valley on a little dirt road until you arrive at the skeletal ruins of the Jessie Mill.)

Throughout the long winter news of the gold strikes on the Blue River and Gold Run Gulch smoldered and sizzled in the dreams and imaginations of the folks back East. Finally in May, 1860, the big explosion came. It was as if a bomb had gone off. Once the snow had melted enough to travel over the high mountain passes, miners began pouring in at the rate of one or two hundred a day. Pack trains with much needed provisions and tools arrived daily.

Opposite: Two miners, Edwin Peabody on the right.

A typical outfit and provisions for a party of four miners might include these items listed in the book *Bayou Salado:*

. . . a wagon with three yoke of oxen, a tent, tools—including picks, shovels and gold pans—a wooden bucket, a Dutch oven and kettles, tin plates and cups, flour, bacon, dried beef, lard, beans, dried fruit, coffee, pickles, three gallons of brandy, soap, gun powder, lead, shot, gun caps, ten yards of drilling for a sluice, candles, rope, a five-gallon water keg and so on ad infinitum—all for a little over $600 or $158.58 per man.

Miners developed a real taste for oysters, an unusual item in the mountains of Colorado. Canned oysters were a luxury, but became an essential part of their diet. The empty cans then were used as containers for the gold flakes and nuggets.

Rich discoveries were made everywhere—up French, Georgia, Illinois, Humbug, American, Galena, and Brown's Gulches as well as Salado and Nigger Hill. (Years later this name was changed to Barney Ford Hill after the first African American who prospected the Breckenridge area.) Tents and white-topped wagons dotted the hills wherever prospectors panned for gold. Mining camps sprang up in every gulch and gully.

Sometime during this early rush era, Lelon Peabody arrived at the Blue River Diggings, a scene of frenzied growth.

Mark Feister tells about a Breckenridge resident who wrote on June 10, 1860:

> One month ago you could scarcely see a human being away from the fort; now I can scarcely look in any direction without seeing herds of stock and scores of wagons, tents, cabins and bower houses. For twelve miles on the river, and from the mouth to source of every gulch the skirts of timber are lined with the canvas of wagons and tents. Breckenridge is improving rapidly...Many new buildings of substantial character are going up, and what was a few weeks ago a forest, with the exception of eight houses, is now a clearing with streets extending each way and built along with stores, dwellings, shops and saloons.

Population soared. Breckenridge boomed. In just one year, 8,000 people thronged the area. Reports document only two women among these thousands of male settlers. One lived in Breckenridge and the other in Gold Run. It is hard to imagine such a raucous scene. Thousands of men, living far from the influences of civilized society, with gold to burn in their trousers—what a wild and primitive horde!

Not everyone mined. As many people worked at separating the prospector from his gold as there were miners laboring to get it. What a sordid and motley assortment—saloon keepers, gamblers, dance hall ladies, madams, thieves and claim jumpers. In the midst of the tents where they camped, saloons and dance halls and hotels opened up enticing the men into wild drinking and spending sprees. Miners worked hard on their mining claims all week only to lose it on the weekend as they drank, gambled and generally "whooped it up."

One of those in the 1859 stampede to Breckenridge was Lelon Peabody.

Lelon Peabody, Gold Run Gulch

As Almeda wrote in her journal, Lelon had joined an emigrant train in 1859 and traveled by ox teams across the plains. Once in Colorado, the men and their families in the wagon train scattered, everyone hoping to strike it rich. Lelon prospected the streams and gullies in and around Breckenridge for the next four years.

In 1863, a few years after the initial rush, Lelon Peabody purchased a claim from the famous naturalist, Edwin

Carter in Gold Run Gulch. This district of Breckenridge was by then a hotbed of gold mining success. He selected a choice site just beyond Balce Weaver's original 1860 discovery claim. Twenty-five years later the famous Jessie Mill would be constructed at this rich site. Lelon Peabody's original claim lies across the road from the present ruins of the Jessie mine and stamp mill.

In the early years miners staked out scores of claims up and down this gulch. Some men became more successful than others. Lelon Peabody numbered among the fortunate. An entry in the July 17, 1868, *Rocky Mountain News* singled out four miners: "In Gold Run John Shock, Peabody, Mumford, Eberlin & C. are hard at work and are getting good pay."

Almeda's Journey West

The work grew so demanding that Lelon Peabody needed help. Almeda's story highlights how her brothers, and then she and her sister, traveled west during the Colorado gold rush.

My two brothers, Benjamin and Edwin, came to Colorado in 1868. Then my brother Lelon wrote and asked me to come to Gold Run and cook for the miners in his camp. Being young and liking a little adventure, I decided to go. So in the spring of 1869 my sister, Alvira, and I also left our home in Northern New York. Alvira was a widow, her husband being recently killed in the War of the Rebellion.

On the way we stopped at Coopersville, Michigan to visit my father and brothers who had moved there from St. Lawrence County, New York.

During the trip she met a fine young man:

It was there at my Brother James' house I met Henry Wagner, about the last of April, 1869. My sister and I and Henry Wagner and one of his Army chums left Coopersville and crossed to Chicago on a boat, arriving in Chicago at 7:00 am. We purchased tickets there which cost us each $75.75 to Denver.

Almeda provides no details about their getting to know each other or their courtship. A young unmarried woman traveling unchaperoned with a young man was unconventional in those days. Our imagination must fill in the blanks about how this young couple fell in love and decided to undertake the journey together. Two weeks after arriving at Gold Run, their Colorado mining camp destination, Almeda and Henry were married. Although Almeda does not share her personal feelings nor the details of their romance, she does provide a picture of the man who became her husband:

My knowledge of the Wagner family is very limited. Henry was borne around 1843 in Prussia, one of the German states. He was left motherless at the age of ten months and fifteen days. Soon after this his father married a second wife. When he was only thirteen years old he came to America. He had come across the ocean on a sailing vessel using six weeks on the trip. Living

Stagecoaches

with his grandfather in Milwaukee he only spoke German. At sixteen years of age he left the Germans and went to live with Americans, where he soon learned to speak and read the American language. He being a good worker always had employment.

The War of the Rebellion broke out before he was eighteen years old. He tried to enlist but could not on account of his youth and because he was not quite tall enough (5' 4"). But the time soon passed and he entered the Army where he served as a wagoner, driving a six mule team, until the close of the war. He served in any

other capacity whenever ordered; sometimes as a forager, or reconnoitering, or in any place where ordered. He could always be depended upon to do his duty. He was in the Army over three years. He was one of Sherman's "Bummers" on the March to the Sea at the close. He received an honorable discharge and returned to Milwaukee from which place he enlisted. At that time a soldier received thirteen dollars a month. Henry saved his wages, as he did not smoke or chew or drink, so had over three hundred dollars, which he loaned to a soldier chum to start a meat market with.

He then started business for himself, that of furnishing oak barrel staves and ship timbers. He went to Michigan, into heavily timbered woods and purchased oak and other hardwood trees. He cut and got them hauled to the lake and shipped them by shiploads across to Chicago and Milwaukee. While he was in Michigan he became acquainted with his future wife's family and boarded with them.

Rough Wagon and Stagecoach Journey

Almeda journeyed by train west from Chicago to Cheyenne. From here she traveled the remainder of her trip to Colorado by stagecoach and wagon. The Transcontinental Railroad was nearing completion when Almeda made her journey. Although in April of 1869 the eastern and western portions had not yet been connected, the railroad did go through Cheyenne by that time. Workers laid the final tie and drove the golden spike on May 10, 1869. The Union Pacific had started from the east at Omaha and the Central Pacific started from Sacramento in the west. Many years of arduous work allowed the two railways to finally meet at Promontory, Utah.

Almeda did not provide details about the portion of her trip between Chicago and Cheyenne. However, when Professor Brewer made his trip to Colorado just three months later (July, 1869), he followed the same route as Almeda. His vivid description of the journey across the plains helps us to imagine the scenes Almeda viewed.

As he left Omaha to cross the Platte Valley, Professor Brewer described the desolation he viewed from the window of his train:

...the Platte Valley, the truly great plains of the West...stretching away on both sides limitless almost as the sea, mile after mile, league beyond league...Every fifteen or thirty miles there is a station - the water tank and wind wheel loom up above the waste for miles ahead.

...The country becomes almost treeless, except for a line of cottonwoods that fringe a distant river...this is the picture for hundred miles after hundred miles - dreary and monotonous. Two hundred soldiers are posted at many stations to protect the road from Indians...Animal life seems sparse - a few birds, but the impression is one of desolation.

As he neared Cheyenne:

The country has grown drier and drier as we go west, first fertile and later not...low table-like hills are around us, treeless and barren. About twenty miles before reaching here (Cheyenne), I had my first view of the Rocky Mountains - great masses piled up against the sky along the horizon. Their snows glittering in the morning sun, a sight I had longed for years was before me.

Professor Brewer describes the inhospitable town of Cheyenne:

It (Cheyenne) is a cheerless place...not a tree in sight. The winds sweep over it and raise a dust, the sun blazes fiercely

Ute encampment near Denver, 1874.

on it - the glare is painful - the houses look comfortless. Money, not homes, have tempted settlers there. At the south and southwest, the Rocky Mountains, bold, rocky, forbidding, covered with snow are the only things to relieve the weary eyes.

Now we leave Professor Brewer because Almeda picks up her account, depicting her journey from Cheyenne to Denver.

When my Sister (Alvira) and I, together with Henry Wagner and one of his Army chums arrived in Cheyenne, we were compelled to finish our journey by stage. There were many people traveling through then, but the two soldier boys, through strategy, succeeded in getting a seat for the four of us on the same stage. There were three seats so nine of us rode inside and six on the out, besides trunks and other baggage strapped on. It was a hard ride for we were packed in like the proverbial sardines. There were four horses on all the time. When we were nearing a station which was every ten miles, it being one hundred miles to Denver, the driver gave a shrill whistle and four fresh horses were standing ready. As our tired horses were unhitched, the fresh ones were instantly hitched up and away we whirled, riding all night. At the last station there were six white horses taken, so we rode into Denver in style; stopping at the Car House, where we remained overnight.

Almeda does not elaborate on her impressions of Denver. However, Professor Brewer makes some interesting comments:

Denver—a quiet little village of perhaps four or five thousand inhabitants, lying out on the plain some dozen or sixteen miles from the base of the great chain—rather dull just now for a mining town...No miners about, or at least conspicuously, and no trees about either.

It started here a dozen years ago as a convenient place to enter the mountains...supplies being brought in on 'trains' or wagons, and the place where trains start out for various surrounding regions. Denver appears to be in the stage...(where) the old mining excitement has ceased...business is dull, the town quiet...I see scarcely a new house going up, plenty of places 'To Let'; yet it will perhaps start again and have a healthy growth, although I see no reason to predict an especially brilliant future.

By day, great trains come in under the guidance of dirty, sunburned men, swarthy Mexicans, bringing freight from or loading for distant points. Men throng the streets, woman are few, all are not beautiful, and alas, quite a percentage are reputed frail.

As I look out my window, I see the campfires of an Indian encampment just over the Platte, perhaps a mile from here...and about thirty or forty lodges gleaming in the sun...These Indians are the most picturesque objects of the region. Many are in town every day, seeing the sights and trading - decked out in all their glory with brilliant paint and profuse ornamentation, their faces painted with vermilion, trapped out with lots of finery, intelligent and fine looking, yet wicked looking enough. This morning I saw lots of warriors in town, nicely mounted. They are the Utes - the only tribe here that dares come near the cities.

Almeda Enters the Colorado Rocky Mountains

Almeda made preparations in Denver for the final portion of her journey over the mountains to Breckenridge.

Henry and his chum, a soldier too, hunted another team to carry us to Hamilton. Henry went with us, but his chum remained in Denver, as he was a maker of fine shoes. Hamilton was to be our last stopping place before crossing the Range.

We stayed our first night at Slatt's Ranch, where we had snow on our bed, and our breakfast consisted of very salty salt side, potatoes, bread and coffee. I could not eat.

Slatt's Ranch (or Slaughts, Slaghts or Granite Vale) was one of the earliest stations for stagecoaches to South Park. Located east of Kenosha Pass, it provided meals and overnight accommodations and a change of horses and water. Azel Slaght and his wife, Alice, homesteaded this land in 1860 after having journeyed from Wayne County, northern New York. Over the years the Slaghts gradually established a thriving

Wagon Train.

ranch which grew into a small town, a post office and a stopover for the Denver to Leadville stage coaches. Jane Gelsinger in the *Park County Republican* and *Fairplay Flume* tells about an 1868 article in the *Rocky Mountain News* which describes Slaghts:

> Slaght's Ranch, on the Platte, Denver and Buckskin road is a pretty place, the comfortable home of the weary and hungry traveler...Mr. S. cultivates some 200 acres, cuts all the hay he wants near home...He is now building a sawmill with which to cut his own lumber. Mrs. S. treated us to aquadente in a milk pan, which we considered the full measure of hospitality, and since which we have entertained the most chivalrous and affectionate respect for her.

An 1870 article states, "At Slaght's the coaches meet and stop over night and he (Slaght) is always busy; he runs the saw mill besides, has a fine mountain farm, and is evidently getting rich." By 1874 Slaght's had a population of 25. The hotel was constructed of logs until 1874 when it became a frame building. By 1886 Slaght's was a popular summer resort along the railroad. However, with the establishment of Shawnee, the town of Slaght's gradually deteriorated and today there is no indication that it ever existed. Today it is mostly hay fields.

The earliest route from Denver to the pastoral upland valley of South Park followed an old Indian trail over Kenosha Pass. From South Park several passes provided access to Breckenridge—Georgia, Hoosier and Boreas, the most frequently used route.

Almeda's story continues:

Some rode on. Just before reaching South Park, our driver, "Bob", stopped at his mother's house, as she kept an eating place. He got us a real good breakfast, inviting only Henry and Sister and myself to eat with him. It was a free lunch and a good one. After which we drove on across the park to Hamilton, where the Lelon Peabody ranch now stands, arriving early in the p.m. There were then two hotels there, one of which was kept by a German and his wife named Leillienthal where we remained.

A Memorable Night in Hamilton

A few years before Almeda came through, the town of Hamilton served as the center of activity for the entire South Park region. Actually two towns, fierce rivals, shared this location. Across the creek from Hamilton and downstream about a half-mile lay a cluster of tents and cabins named Tarryall. When gold was first discovered in Tarryall the sudden deluge of prospectors caused the original settlers to become jealous and run off the newcomers, gobbling up the promising claims. As a result, Tarryall earned a horrible reputation as greedy and unfriendly and was nicknamed "Grab-All." Disgruntled late arrivals went off to start the town of Fairplay, a name chosen in mockery of "Grab-All" and to announce a welcoming atmosphere where all comers could be treated fairly. Others established the town of Hamilton which in time surpassed Tarryall as the center of activity for the South Park region.

In 1860 when gold was first discovered, 3,000 settlers lived in Hamilton. They built about 40 houses this first year; the rest of the miners camped in tents around the town. The one main street was rutted and crowded with oxen. Simmons reports that by July of 1860, the names of 20,000 miners were recorded in the book at the Hamilton post office which served the entire district in the north end of the park

However, by 1869, when Almeda passed through, the town was desolate. A visitor to the area wrote about finding "about fifty empty cabins, two log hotels and about twenty people living in the grimy, dirty-looking village...with manure heaps in front of the houses and a few sorry looking horses and mules scattered about the pastures." Like so many frontier boom towns, Hamilton's meteoric rise to fame was followed by a pathetic fall. It collapsed like a punctured balloon.

Almeda continues her story:

(At Hamilton) I wrote a letter to my Brother Lelon, which the mail carrier, S. Davenport, carried eighteen miles on snow shoes to Gold Run. My brother returning with him the next day. We had not seen him for fourteen or fifteen years. We left the hotel after supper and rode in a wagon as far as the horses could haul it through the snow. Then we waded further for a while and camped east of the Range where we waited for the snow to freeze so we could walk over the crust. There were twenty-two people there at camp that night. Some made beds on the snow by cutting down limbs of trees and putting blankets on them and other bedding over. But there was a big camp fire and my Sister and I and some others sat up all night.

Wagon en route to high altitude mining camp.

Almeda's daughter later wrote, "If I remember correctly my mother told me that night was when my father 'popped the question' and probably in capital letters."

Next morning early we walked over the crusty snow until we reached a place where Lelon Peabody had horses to carry us to Breckenridge. But we were not used to horseback riding and so our ponies had to be led.

We arrived at Breckenridge at nine o'clock and had breakfast there.

When 25-year-old Almeda Peabody rode her pony into the little mining town of Breckenridge that 1869 May morning, a new phase of life for the Peabody family began. Her long journey was nearly complete.

Weeks earlier Almeda and her older sister, Alvira, had said good-bye to their home in far northern New York. They had journeyed across the country chugging by railroad, and bumping along by stagecoach, laboring through rough country by wagon, climbing above timberline to cross a mountain pass on foot and finally navigating steep hills and water crossings by horseback. Without knowing what to expect they had set off following the footsteps of their older brother, Lelon, who had joined the hordes migrating to Colorado in the 1859 gold rush. Two other Peabody brothers, Benjamin and Edwin, had also felt the magnetic pull of gold and had settled there.

One wonders: what magnetism did the West hold for these unmarried, young women traveling alone? Were they looking for adventure, or a place to meet single, eligible men, or to be with other family members who had emigrated West—or was there simply nothing holding them in New York? Whatever their motivation, it certainly wasn't the glamour of 1860's Breckenridge.

Breckenridge, A Shabby Log Town

Almeda spent her breakfast stop in this primitive, log mining camp. The Breckenridge that greeted Almeda was scruffy and dilapidated.

Like other Colorado mining towns, Breckenridge had risen to stellar heights in the 1859 placer mining rush and then crashed. In the first boom, from 1859 to 1863, the mining camp flourished. Placer mining using sluices and Long Toms had extracted the gold flakes and nuggets from the stream beds. But then the streambeds became washed thin and the placers were abandoned. For the next 15 years the town was almost deserted.

When the second wave of Peabody siblings came to Colorado (Edwin and Benjamin in '68 and Almeda and Alvira a year later), Breckenridge was a crude little town whose population had plum-

meted. The first frenzied rush was over, and the next hadn't begun. Bayard Taylor, editor of the *Rocky Mountain News,* visited the town in 1866 and described it as "a long street of log-houses; signs of "Boarding," "Miner's Home," and "Saloon"; canvas-covered wagons in the shade and a motley group of rough individuals."

The Princeton Scientific Expedition, a party passing through the settlement in 1877, expressed disgust with what they saw:

> To get out of the reach of the noise was impossible and you might think there was a den of wild animals being fed, or something worse...the most fiendish place we ever wish to see. We were forced to spend the morning and afternoon in the company of men whose language was vile and whose actions were tinged with a shade of crime that shocked and hurt our sensibilities.

A humorous story describes how two men settled a dispute one day. Most men in Breckenridge carried a pistol. Gunfights were common. Life was cheap. Men of the early West often found an honorable death more attractive than living with shame. Nevertheless, Judge Silverthorne was consulted one day to settle an argument of two men who had come to blows over a woman. He decided that the men should fight a duel in the streets of Breckenridge. At the appointed hour they were to stand back to back and at a signal start walking. After fifteen

Breckenridge in the early 1860's.

paces they would whirl around and fire their pistols until one of the two died. The whole town turned out for the big event and watched with great anticipation. The two men stood back to back and began walking, but instead of turning around and shooting they each kept on walking, faster and faster, and hightailed it out of town.

The rough condition of the log village Almeda encountered at journey's end failed to daunt her enthusiasm. Although she was weary after her long, arduous journey and felt anxious riding a skittish horse which had never before carried a woman with long skirts, Almeda was still excited to begin her new life. Gold Run, her final destination, lay just over the next hill...

over Gibson Hill, one side of which was, as we thought, almost perpendicular. What a climb for a Tenderfoot! We had to cross Gold Run ditch, which was wide. We crossed it on horseback over a bridge made of poles lengthwise. My pony's feet went down between the poles which frightened him so the man who led him grabbed my arm and pulled me across. The pony never allowed a skirt to approach him again.

Arrived at last on May 17th at our destination: Lelon Peabody's great log house where we were to cook for our brother's men who worked his mines.

Two weeks after arriving in Gold Run Almeda married Henry Wagner.

The first wagon to cross the range that year was on May 31st. It brought us our trunks which we needed badly. My Brother Lelon was Justice of the Peace and so officiated at our wedding on June 3, 1869. He being the only person in thirty miles that could perform that ceremony. I am sure it is safe to say that it was his last. He was pleased to do so as he was very fond of my husband. He paid him better wages than other men for he could trust him to do

anything that needed to be done and never soldiered on his job.

My Sister and I cooked for my Brother's men until in July another woman got sick so she went to take care of her. So I cooked for the twenty five men alone, cooking 175 pounds of beef and a barrel of flour each week, besides much other foods, until the mines closed. My brother Lelon took $12,000 from his mines that summer. He paid $1,000 for his next winter's provisions.

In today's dollars, Lelon's summer gold yield would equal $96,000.

Mr. Wagner and I lived with my Brother until the fall of 1871. He worked by the month in winter and by the day in summer; I for my board in winter and $50 per month in summer. Our daughter, Marie, was borne in his log house August 12, 1870. She was the first white child borne in Gold Run. Lelon went to the Pit and told the miners that there was a four-pound nugget up to the house.

It was necessary to keep pretty close together on account of Indians. The Sioux, Arapahoes, and Cheyennes being troublesome and all fighting against the Ute tribe who were as friendly with the Whites as Indians are expected to be. But the Whites were something of a protection to the Utes, so the Utes were a protection to the Whites.

Let's take a closer look at the Indians Almeda encountered in her new life in the Colorado Rockies.

Burros haul boards for early-Breckenridge building boom.

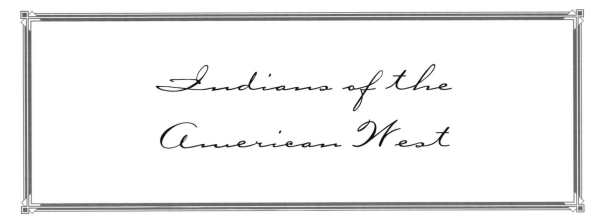

Indians of the American West

When Almeda began married life near Breckenridge in 1869 the West was still embroiled in sporadic but often savage conflicts between the settlers and the Indians. Rumors of Indians on the rampage colored the pioneer experience.

Only a decade earlier, before the deluge of white people, the Utes had lived for centuries in peaceful harmony with the land. These natives of the Colorado mountains were nomadic hunters. Their hunting grounds abounded with wildlife. Streams teemed with trout. Nature was prolific in providing for the survival needs of the native people. Although these mountain dwelling Utes constantly warred with the Plains Indians, the various tribes had achieved a balance of power. An equilibrium existed between the land, the wildlife and the Indian people. The white people's invasion into this idyllic setting shattered permanently this delicate balance that had been in place for thousands of years.

When the early trappers and traders began to drift into Colorado the Indians at first showed no fear. Just as in the 1600's, when the first white colonists settled in New England, the western Indians viewed these strangers with curiosity and saw an opportunity for trading. Only when settlers began moving in and building permanent homes did the Indians become alarmed.

As the white people continued their influx into the hunting grounds of the Indians, tension began to mount. Several major events encouraged this rapid settlement of the West. The great financial panic of 1857 had wiped out the fortunes of thousands in the East and left many in a state of poverty. With the discovery of gold in 1859, many gained new hope and the promise of great wealth. The Homestead Act of 1862 implicitly took the land away from the Indians and provided hard working settlers a way to own their own land. The completion of the Transcontinental Railroad in 1869 provided the means to reach the vast western lands.

Opposite: Pioneer women dreaded the Indians. Colorow, a Ute subchief, frightened Almeda Peabody Wagner, according to her diary.

As the trickle of white settlers turned into a flood, the Indians, realizing the intent of the white government, began to panic—and then to retaliate. The nomadic tribes of the western plains were the most fierce. Daring and warlike, they refused to step aside as they saw their ancestral lands encroached upon and the buffalo slaughtered.

The Indians had lived for centuries as a Stone Age culture. They had no metal of any kind. The buffalo was their mainstay of survival, providing more than just meat to eat. The Indians found a use for every part of the buffalo, leaving no waste. After consuming what they could of the fresh meat, they pounded the surplus flat and covered it with berries and dried it, making pemmican to eat at a later date when food supplies ran short. The Utes made buffalo hides into blankets, robes, mattresses, teepees, papoose cradles, snowshoes and drums, ropes and lariats. Horn provided ladles, cups, toys and impressive adornments for headdresses. Bow strings and thread were made from sinews. And bones were used for many things—jewelry, paint brushes, war clubs, shovels and hoes. Pouches and medicine bags were made from the buffalo bladder. Squaws used the stomach lining to carry water. Rocks, after being heated in a fire, were dropped in to cook soup and stews. Even the scrotum became a rattle.

The near eradication of the buffalo ranks as one of the most tragic events in American history. White hunters slaughtered the buffalo recklessly. They butchered herds for meat for railroad construction crews and sold hides for two or three dollars to commercial tanneries. Marksmen killed buffalo for popular sport, just for the fun of it, leaving the carcasses to rot.

An estimated 30 million head of buffalo roamed the plains in the early 1800's, and in 1850 at least 20 million still remained. Twenty years later the great American buffalo herd was virtually extinct! The settlers and their government treated the buffalo as they treated the Native Americans.

As the buffalo slaughter continued the plains tribes became increasingly frightened and enraged. Desperate to hold onto their lands, in 1863-64 they began raiding outlying ranches and small wagon trains. As conditions worsened, overland trails were closed from time to time. Author Anne Ellis wrote about her terror of the Indians as she journeyed westward across the plains in 1879:

A dreadful fear of Indians was born and grown in me...driving our wagon across northeastern Colorado we feared the Cheyenne and Arapahoe Indians. Everyone kept watch every moment, many times being frightened by a mirage, or they would see a line of objects running toward them as Indians would— these usually turned out to be the ever-shifting tumble weeds driven by every passing wind.

The 1864 Battle at Sand Creek sparked full-scale warfare. The following

Shooting buffalo on the line of the Kansas, Pacific Railroad, from Leslie's Illustrated News, June 3, 1871.

account by historian Eugene Sprague describes the horror of this tragedy.

The Sand Creek Massacre

At sunrise on a clear, cold November 29, 1864, Colonel Chivington and his Third Colorado Cavalry of nine hundred mounted men topped a ridge and saw on a bend of Sand Creek the many teepees of Black Kettle's village with Old Glory flying above them. The soldiers had ridden all night from Fort Lyon, nibbling on maggoty hardtack. They were miserably cold, unkempt, resentful, and near exhaustion, but sustained by Chivington's promise that they would be heroes like Gilpin's Lambs because they were about to wipe out this vile nest of murdering savages and end Colorado's Indian troubles forever. A few Indians sighted the troops and made for their nearby herd of some six hundred horses. Chivington ordered the soldiers forward, shooting. Artillery men on a bluff manned their four twelve-pound howitzers. As the teepees began to shrivel and collapse under cannon fire, men, women, and children, disheveled and bewildered, poured out, some with guns and bows and arrows, some with hands raised in surrender. The Indians ran toward the creek bank for protection, but the space between the village and the bank was soon covered with bodies, dead and dying. Throughout the morning the one-sided carnage continued as the soldiers cleared Sand Creek for two or three miles of its defenders and completed the destruction of the village. According to the testimony of witnesses later before two congressional committees, a madness seemed to possess some of the soldiers as they took to scalping fallen bodies, male and female, cutting off fingers, breasts, genitals for souvenirs, raping dead squaws in relays, using toddling children for target practice. By 4 p.m. the horror had ended - the village a flat litter, the flag purloined, the area gruesome with blood and torn corpses. Black Kettle was among those who escaped northward. There were no other survivors. Chivington allowed no prisoners to be taken. He forbade burial. The Third Colorado Cavalry simply rode away, leaving the dead to the coyotes and vultures. The Third Colorado lost eight men killed, some of them in their own crossfire, and forty wounded. A "credible" estimate put the Indian dead at 'something under two hundred.' Two-thirds of the bodies counted later were women and children.

Instead of terrifying the Indians this massacre aroused them to fury. Ten years of almost continuous warfare followed. Ranches and farms were plundered and burned. Emigrant trains and stagecoaches were captured.

Pioneer families lived in a constant state of dread.

Warring Indians made it difficult to build the Transcontinental Railroad then extending west from Omaha. As the Civil War ended, troops became available for duty on the frontier. Attempts at treaties proved ineffective. (It was often the whites who reneged.) Indian wars continued to disrupt the frontier.

Gradually the tide began to turn, however. In 1868 Chief Roman Nose was decisively defeated. Chief Black Kettle's village in Nebraska was destroyed in the winter, 1868. In the summer, 1869, Tall Bull suffered defeat at Summit Springs. However, the northern Cheyenne continued on the warpath, joining the Sioux in the Custer Massacre in November, 1868. They held out until their surrender in 1878. In the heat of these critical times (April, 1869). Almeda and her sister ventured forth across the plains.

Mountain-dwelling Utes

In contrast to the Plains Indians who were notorious for warfare against the whites, the mountain-dwelling Utes were less hostile. In the early days the Utes and white settlers banded together in mutual protection from the tribes of the plains. However, from time to time there were tales of the Utes plundering occasional prospecting parties and taking their scalps. The most serious outbreaks occurred after Almeda and her siblings had been in Colorado for ten years.

In 1879 the increasing resentment of the Utes finally culminated in the

Here, 200,000 buffalo hides await shipment (1874). In twenty years time the American buffalo was virtually extinct.

Meeker Massacre in northern Colorado. Nathan Meeker had the lofty goal of lifting the "savages" out of their misery. Insensitive to the differences in culture, he failed to understand that the Utes preferred their way of living, free and in harmony with the environment, over the white man's way of conquering and sometimes destroying the land. With missionary zeal, he urged them to push the plow, build barbed wire fences and become farmers. Meeker proposed to "cut every Indian down to the starvation point if he will not work."

In one misguided effort Meeker plowed up the meadow the Utes used as a race track and fenced off their land. Outraged, the Utes retaliated by slaughtering the white men and carrying off women into captivity. Chief Colorow led one of the war parties that attacked Meeker in the Battle of Milk Creek. Legend says that the Indians took Meeker's stiff body and ran it along the ground as one would a plow to mock their farming lessons.

Word of the uprising leapt from one settlement to another. The pioneers were dreadfully frightened. The Meeker Massacre caused a big scare for the Blue River miners. Reports circulated that Utes on the warpath were headed to South Park and over the mountains to Breckenridge. Governor Pitkin advised the terror stricken settlers: "Indians off the reservation, seeking to destroy your settlements by fire, are game to be hunted and destroyed like wild beasts."

Fear played a large role in the settlers' response to the Indians. The rumors and stories of distant Indian attacks frightened them. The Peabodys shared that concern. Yet, few families, including the Peabodys, personally experienced Indian violence. Almeda wrote:

Lelon's house was built of the largest logs he could get as a part of the protection from Indians, which often came there in crowds and demanded to be fed. Sometimes there was what was called an Indian Scare, as they occasionally drove off stock and murdered the Whites. Especially the tribe Sioux, Arapahoes and Cheyennes did this. The Utes were always at war with those tribes and so did not often do much damage among the Whites. But there was one old ugly Chief that we feared, if caught anywhere alone. That was "Old Colorow". I remember him for he would come and gaze at me through the windows (which were not made of glass, but instead oiled paper were the panes). Or he'd come in and sit in my way. Once he asked my brother to open the door and let him in. They never stopped for an invitation but threw the door wide open and entered, at the same time hallowed, "How!"

Pioneer Women's Dread

Tales of Indians on the rampage were a part of the pioneer experience. Women were especially vulnerable. Out of necessity they were frequently alone with their younger children when the men and older sons went out hunting or mining. They lived in a state of apprehension until their husband returned. Any sudden noise or mysterious shadow alarmed them. No Indian, friendly or not, ever seemed trustworthy.

Almeda feared Chief Colorow and other female pioneers described similar reactions. *Pioneer Women* author Joanna Stratton wrote:

She was always startled when an Indian face would suddenly and noiselessly appear at the window or door. Although she soon learned that they meant no harm, but were only curious to see the room, she never could conquer the sudden fear that gripped her heart.

Panic shadowed the August, 1870 birth of Almeda's daughter, Marie, the first white child born in Gold Run. As a new mother recovering from childbirth with a frail four-pound newborn daughter, Almeda experienced this sudden fear:

During our first year in Summit County the Indians were somewhat troublesome. When my first child was only a few days old there was an Indian scare. It was reported that they were on a raid, and people living anywhere near came to my Brother's bringing what they could of their valuables. They remained a few days, keeping sentinels and watching for the Indians. We had the best and largest house, built of large logs. The scare proved false which was a great relief to

Ute Indian family.

me as I was unable to be out of bed. I think that was the last time the Indians troubled us, though they still came on peaceful terms.

When most of the men had gone across the range one day I looked up at the window and saw a big Indian looking at me. I was startled and quickly went to the doors and locked them. Another day Old Colorow, the big chief, came with beads, arrows and ponies which he wanted to give my brother in exchange for me. But my brother told him I was a bad white squaw, and wouldn't do it.

The newcomers' fear of the Indians was matched only by their ignorance of Ute customs and ways. For instance, common courtesy among the native tribes demanded sharing food as a token of hospitality. So when an Indian approached the settler's wagon or cabin, he expected such tokens as a way of greeting. However, the white pioneers often wrote of Indians who came up to their wagons "begging" and they found the habit "disgusting." Indians made their visits a surprise, Joanna Stratton reports:

> The Indians would often go begging from house to house for food. They were apt to stalk uninvited into the family kitchen and demand tastes of the freshly baked bread or the roasting meats. The frontier housewife, frightened by their unrelenting demands, would hastily offer them plates of food just in order to get rid of them. Many a dinner was sacrificed to appease hungry visitors.

Contrary to the prevailing myths, the native Americans were by nature a curious, sociable and often friendly people. Thus, they sometimes became persistent visitors at the cabin door.

Unaccustomed to the formal etiquette of white society, they felt free to wander into any dwelling, whether it was a fellow tribesman's teepee or a white person's cabin. Without bothering to knock they marched in and made themselves at home. "I was told they were harmless but I did not like the way they had of stalking into the house unbidden or of looking in at the window," one Kansas woman remembered.

The settler's sedentary ways intrigued the Indians. To them the pioneer cabin was a place of great curiosity with its unusual furnishing, strange and delicious aromas, and array of household items—like the spinning wheel, the clock with its rhythmical chiming, the assortment of cooking utensils and dishes, the quilts, pillows upon the beds. The Indians gazed upon these newcomers with an insatiable curiosity.

Almeda did not understand Indian customs and habits any more than they could comprehend hers. Other pioneer women shared Almeda's fear of Chief Colorow. Anne Ellis, in *The Life of an Ordinary Woman,* wrote about this notorious Ute:

> For years Chief Colorow used to frighten me—he was an Indian outlaw and a very bad hombre. I thought he had special designs on me because of my long yellow hair, and many times in my dreams I have felt him lift it from my head and seen it dangling from his belt.

Accounts differ in how Colorow is viewed by history. Summit County, Colorado historian Mary Ellen Gilliland in her book, *Summit,* describes "Chief" Colorow as a "scallywag", a "fat, blustery coward." Although he led a group of Ute renegades, he was no hero. A story tells how he led a band of Utes to fight the Sioux. Upon reaching Sioux country, Colorow declared, "Ponies heap tired, no can go" and he turned around and "hightailed" it back to Ute country. Early tales say that he once shot a man in the Gore Range of the Blue River for refusing to cook his dinner.

There is no disputing the anxiety the settlers felt towards Colorow. Out of fear, Wolfe Londoner one day reluctantly agreed to feed Colorow. His wife was horrified, historian Mary Ellen Gilliland writes. Although they were nearly without provisions she managed to come up with a soup to serve the guest. Colorow arrived with an entourage of three or four of his squaws. "I gave the old devil the head of the table. They got the soup, but we did not get any soup that day. He would take a spoonful of soup and then spit. He would spit alongside the table. It was the most villainous thing I ever encountered, but durst not say a word."

On the other hand, *Who's Who in Native American History,* Carl Williams, paints a more impressive warrior-like picture of him:

Chief Colorow (Colorado, "the red"; Toop'weets, "rock"). Ute-Apache. (ca.1810-1888), Leader in the Ute War of 1879.

Colorow's mother, an Jicarilla Apache, was captured by the Comanches. Colorow in turn captured by the Mouache Utes and adopted into this tribe. He established his reputation as a warrior while young and became known for the strategy of attacking enemies from high ground.

After the 1868 treaty signed by Ouray in Washington, D.C., Colorow and his band lived on a small temporary reservation outside Denver, Colorado. In 1875, after the reservation had been closed, he and his followers settled on the reservation at White River along with Northern Ute bands. Traditional hunters, the Utes had difficulty in adapting to reservation life and farming. In 1878, the Indian agent Nathan Meeker deposed Colorow, whom he considered too militant, and appointed his rival Sanovik as chief of his band, further adding to ill-feeling.

The next year, after a confrontation with the medicine man Canalla, Meeker called in troops under Major Thomas T. Thornburgh. Colorow led one of the war parties that attacked them in the Battle of Milk Creek in September 1879.

Through Ouray's efforts, the war chiefs Colorow and Nicagat were pardoned for their roles in the uprising because they had been engaged in what was deemed a fair fight.

In 1881, Colorow and about 50 of his warriors again threatened to revolt rather than move from White River to the Uintah Reservation in Utah. Colonel Ranalds Mackenzie ordered four companies of cavalry to meet the Utes in battle formation; the Utes backed down without violence and were soon relocated.

Colorow eventually left Uintah to settle on the Southern Ute Reservation in the vicinity of Ignacio, Colorado. During a hunting trip off the reservation, he and some of his men were again involved in a confrontation with whites. Sheriff Jim Kendall requested help, and the Colorado National Guard and cowboy volunteers chased the Utes back toward the reservation. In the one skirmish of the so-called Ute War of 1887, two whites were killed and two wounded, and about seven Utes were killed. It is thought that Colorow received a wound in the fight and never recovered; he died the following year.

Ute Exodus

Phyllis Dorset, in her book *The New Eldorado,* described the sad day of the Ute exodus as a warm lazy Sunday in September, 1881:

> Slowly and sullenly they filed along the Uncompahgre, down the Gunnison to the Colorado, and then westward on that sprawled-out river toward their new lands and home. Fourteen hundred fifty-eight homeless Indians including squaws, bucks, braves, and children, driving ahead of them over 10,000 sheep and goats, riding, leading, or herding 8,000 small ponies, made their way down the historic river, indifferently drinking in the beauties of the late summer sun playing on the mountains. Chief Colorow... was the last to leave the valley - a dull, prosaic dash of copper at the end of a long Indian sentence.

The prevailing attitude of the time affected, and in turn was affected by the tensions between these two cultures. Just as the colonists of the 1600's had viewed the native Americans as "Aborigines", the white settlers perceived the western Indians as savages. Both the white pioneers living on the frontier in New England and the settlers of the American West 200 years later believed the Indian to be sub-human. It is a sad irony that after fighting the Civil War to restore human rights to African Americans, or Negroes as they were then called, society failed to consider Native Americans as deserving these same human rights.

The condescending descriptions and scathing denouncements written about the native people embarrass readers today. For example, the October, 1878 the Boulder *Colorado Bulletin* declared, "There is no use of making much ado about the Indian question. The only solution of the problem is extermination."

Isabella Bird, in *A Lady's Life in the Rocky Mountains,* stated:

> The Americans will never solve the Indian problem till the Indian is extinct... The only difference between the savage and the civilized Indian is that the latter carries firearms and gets drunk on whiskey. 'To get rid of the Injuns' is the phrase used everywhere.

Ned Farrell published a small book, *Colorado, the Rocky Mountain Gem, as it is in 1868.* He writes about the need to defeat the Indians:

> The [plan] of Mark Twain is full as sensible as any- he says, 'the time has come when blood curdling cruelty has become necessary. Inflict soap and a spelling book on every Indian that ravages the plains, and let him die.'...The Indians, ever hostile, have been gainers by their depredations...Our Eastern friends, misled by rum inspired poetry...and dime novels, written by men who never saw one of the thieving rascals, cry out against the injustice of driving the "noble red man" from his land and do not hesi-

tate to condemn the pioneers as aggressive...They should bear in mind that the frontier settlers are the children of eastern mothers and what mother would condemn her son for defending his hearthstone from the attack of the savage?...The people of the plains and mountains have sprung from good blood; they with their ancestors have redeemed from the hand of the savage the Atlantic States and the Mississippi valley and will not stop till they have accomplished the same thing in the Rocky Mountains. Let those remember that the East as well as the West was Indian property, from which the occupants were driven back to give way to a higher civilization. The Indian has rights and the frontiersmen have no wish to disregard them, but they have no right to a foot of our soil for the use of barbarism. They were the original occupants, it is true. The claim of civilization is paramount to theirs. Might makes right the world over, and the die is set. (The Indian) must give way - his days are few and soon the red man will be known only in history... my private advice to Mr. Indian is in the vernacular of the plains, to "git up and git!" or behave himself.

For 10,000 years the Utes roamed all over the high mountain country of Colorado. Within 22 short years after the gold-seeking prospectors' arrival, the Utes were driven out.

A series of treaties gave the Ute ancestral homelands to the U.S. government. Except for those living on a small reservation in the southwestern part of Colorado, the Utes have departed forever from the state. Like the vast buffalo herds that once roamed South Park and the Blue River Valley, the Utes have vanished.

How Can You Sell the Sky?

Responding to a 1852 U.S. Government offer to buy his tribal lands, Chief Seattle eloquently expressed the Native Americans' vision of nature. This reply, addressed to "The Great Chief in Washington" (President Franklin Pierce), was jotted down by an English speaking witness in 1855. Over the years various writers have exercised dramatic license with the Chief's words. In effect the speech we have here is a piece of folklore in the making. Joseph Campbell gives this version in *The Power of Myth*:

The President in Washington sends word that he wishes to buy our land. But how can you buy or sell the sky? The land? The idea is strange to us. If we do not own the freshness of the air and the sparkle of the water, how can you buy them?

Every part of this earth is sacred to my people. Every shining pine needle, every sandy shore, every mist in the dark woods, every meadow, every humming insect. All are holy in the memory and experience of my people.

We know the sap which courses through our veins. We are part of the earth and it is part of us. The perfumed flowers are our sisters. The bear, the deer, the great eagle, these are our brothers. The rocky crests, the juices in the meadow, the body heat of the pony, and man, all belong to the same family.

The shining water that moves in the streams and rivers is not just water, but the blood of our ancestors. If we sell you our land, you must remember that it is sacred. Each ghostly reflection in the clear waters of the lakes tells of events and memories in the life of my people. The water's murmur is the voice of my father's father. The rivers are our brothers. They quench our thirst. They carry our canoes and feed our children. So you must give the rivers the kindness you would give any brother.

If we sell you our land, remember that the air is precious to us, that the air shares its spirit with all the life it supports. The wind that gave our grandfather his first breath also receives his last sigh. The wind also gives our children the spirit of life. So if we sell you our land, you must keep it apart and sacred, as a place where man can go to taste the wind that is sweetened by the meadow flowers.

Will you teach your children what we have taught our children? That the earth is our mother? What befalls the earth befalls all the sons of the earth.

This we know: the earth does not belong to man, man belongs to the earth. All things are connected like the blood that unites us all. Man did not weave the web of life, he is merely a strand in it. Whatever he does to the web, he does to himself.

One thing we know: our God is also your God. The earth is precious to him, and to harm the earth is to heap contempt on its creator.

Your destiny is a mystery to us. What will happen when the buffalo are all slaughtered? The wild horses tamed? What will happen when the secret corners of the forest are heavy with the scent of many men, and the view of the ripe hills is blotted by talking wires? Where will the thicket be? Gone! Where will the eagle be? Gone! And what is it to say good-bye to the swift pony and the hunt? The end of living and the beginning of survival.

When the last Red Man has vanished with his wilderness, and his memory is only the shadow of a cloud moving across the prairie, will these shores and forests still be here? Will there be any of the spirit of my people left?

We love this earth as a newborn loves his mother's heartbeat. So if we sell you our land, love it as we have loved it. Care for it as we have cared for it. Hold in your mind the memory of the land as it is when you receive it. Preserve the land for all children, and love it as God loves us all.

As we are part of the land, you too are part of the land. This earth is precious to us. It is also precious to you. One thing we know: there is only one God. No man, be he Red Man or White Man, can be apart. We ARE brothers after all.

Pioneer Women and the West

Women dream many dreams and see many visions while bending over the washtub.
—Anne Ellis

Stories of the West enthrall us. We savor pictures of the magnificent landscape, heroic figures engaged in combat, tales of brave people struggling against extremes of weather and terrain. The frontier myth creates images of adventure, challenge and courage. History books tell us of wars fought, speeches delivered, and territories acquired.

Yet if we really think about it, these heroes of the legendary West are almost all men—explorers, mountain men, trappers, cowboys, miners, soldiers, desperadoes, vigilantes, Indian chiefs and braves. Women are nearly invisible in this picture. The male bias underlying the western story leads us to believe that women were incidental. If they existed at all, they remained in the background.

When women do appear they are one-dimensional stereotypes—the refined lady and husband's helpmate at one extreme and the prostitute at the other. The refined lady, who may be a schoolteacher or missionary, is depicted as a woman with civilized tastes, too genteel for the rough and primitive West, sorely out of place in its harsh environment. The helpmate, is a strong, stoical woman who adapts to the West but becomes an oppressed drudge, completely lacking in individuality. This view lends a bleak picture of women as reluctant pioneers, dragged West by their men and silently hating it all the way.

These images of the lady and the helpmate reflect Victorian attitudes toward women that prevailed in the 19th century. To be a "true" woman she must embody the four cardinal virtues of piety, purity, domesticity and submissiveness (to male authority). These qualities were cultivated to better meet the needs of husbands, fathers and children. Popular magazines and newspapers of the day carried countless articles and advice columns stressing women's domestic responsibilities and their role as helpmate to their husbands.

Victorian values polarized images of women and divided them into the good women and the bad women, the saint and the whore—sunbonneted, workworn helpmates or prostitutes.

The loose woman of the streets, in contrast to the refined lady in her parlor, epitomized moral degradation.

While grains of truth exist in these stereotypes, the true picture is richer and more complex. For example, a "reluctant pioneer" flavor does show up often in the diaries of women immigrating on the Overland Trail. And it is certainly true that men usually made the decision to move West. But women didn't just meekly submit to their husband's will. Women found the decision a complicated one. Women felt torn about making the journey. Loyalty to their family struggled against sorrow over leaving behind a network of friends and emotional supports.

Feminist writers stress the importance of erasing the negative stereotype of women. However, we make a similar mistake in viewing men's behavior in a biased, one- dimensional way. The ordinary man who moved to the West probably experienced his own range of feelings about uprooting his family, leaving the comfort and predictability of home. Men have the same needs as women for love and connection. These feelings were rarely written about as they did not fit the image of the "real" man in the macho West. Understanding these social pressures for men to hide their vulnerable sides makes my grandfather's tenderly expressed love letter to my grandmother (page 149) all the more remarkable.

If any passion drove women, it was the belief that survival depended on keeping their families together. So, rather than staying behind and fearing abandonment, pioneer women gathered up their children and a few meager belongings and traveled the arduous road together. This goal of maintaining family unity made the difficult journey bearable. Success in getting married, producing healthy children and creating a family was the ultimate test of womanhood. In facing this challenge women proudly resigned themselves to the hard, monotonous work, the isolation and primitive living conditions.

In the diary of Amelia Buss, written her first year on a lonely homestead near Ft. Collins (in 1866-67), we have an example of one woman's suffering and resilience:

> George went to the mountains yesterday morning to be gon all week... After he had gon gave vent to my feelings in a flood of tears. It may seem foolish to those that have neighbors and friends around them. I get along very well through the day but the long evenings and nights are horrible.

A year later she has come to accept her new life.

> Now I have settled down with the belief that here I shall end my days, and the sooner I make it home the better... this little book may seem full of trifling trouble to you, but at the same time they were great to me, more than I knew how to bear... now farewell little book you shall not carry more complaint to my friends at home.

Covered wagons going West

No Simple Answers

At first glance this woman seems to fit the stereotype of the reluctant pioneer. Looking closer, however, the picture becomes more complex. Amelia's life was in transition and so were her feelings about it. Many women who may have initially felt reluctance or resignation later came to accept, and even enjoy, their new life.

Key factors affected a woman's enthusiasm or reluctance to journey west. Both her age and her stage in her life cycle were significant. Lillian Schlissel, in *Diaries of the Westward Journey,* found that young women on the Overland Trail were more likely to approach the journey with enthusiasm than older women.

"There are mighty few bravos and huzzahs for the new territory in the accounts of the older overland women," Schlissel wrote. When these older family women recorded in their diaries the decision to leave home, they usually wrote with anguish, a feeling conspicuously absent from men's journals.

The fact that these older women with families had no voice did not make for eagerness of spirit. Wives understood that the decision to pack up, leave home and transplant their family across the continent was their husband's. Social norms prescribed that men headed their households. Women could voice no dispute. This pattern of paternal deference emerges in the next chapter when Almeda's husband, Henry Wagner, decided the family would leave Colorado and get a farm in Missouri. Then he changed his mind and decided to stay in Colorado. Almeda had no say in the matter. The culture supported the attitude that women were to be subordinate to men—as were the Indians and the buffalo.

In Stratton's book *Pioneer Women,* Mrs. W. B. Caton writes of her husband's decision to relocate to Kansas:

My memory goes back fifty years to a humble home with the library table strewn with literature extolling the wonderful advantages of the new haven for immigrants—Kansas. To me it spelled destruction, desperadoes and cyclones... I could not agree with my husband that any good would come out of such a country, but the characteristic disposition of the male prevailed, and October 1, 1879, saw us—a wagon, three horses and our humble household necessities—bound for the 'Promised Land'.

To say I wept bitterly would but faintly express the ocean of tears I shed on leaving my beloved home and state to take up residence in the 'wild and wooly West.' However, my fears vanished as we traveled toward our Mecca.

The pioneer experience varied widely for men and women. Embarking upon the frontier adventure dovetailed with the developmental needs of a young man. Journeying into the wilderness with challenges to confront gave men a unique opportunity to test their bravery, to become autonomous, self reliant and independent.

However, the opposite was true for women. While men found the journey an opportunity for their free spirit to discover itself, women viewed the journey as a dislocation. Since most women were married, giving birth and raising children, they needed to create a home where they could nurture and care for their families. Constantly on the move, living with chronic fear, their physical energies taxed by the extraordinary demands of frontier life, and being dehumanized as a cultural norm made them weary in spirit.

Strong Ties

Uprooted from their homes and communities, they broke ties with other family members and friends. Communication was difficult, rupturing women's sense of connectedness and continuity. For most women, the demands of life on the frontier directly opposed their emotional needs.

Young, single, or newly-wed women adjusted better, according to Schlissel:

Youth carried its own resilience of spirit and of body. Youth adapted to the patterns of work and dress demanded by life on the frontier. The fact that one might not look 'the lady' seemed to matter less to those whose years had ingrained these prescriptions only lightly. The landscape appeared far more magnificent when one was not searching for a lost child or carrying a babe in arms as she walked.

Almeda Peabody's story fits this pattern. In her memoirs she regards the trip west and her early days in a Colorado mining camp as the adventure of her life. Meeting a young man along the way, who by the end of the trip had proposed to her, must have been not only romantic, but also have given her a sense of security. The prospects of beginning a new life in a new land was full of positive anticipation. We feel the enthusiasm in her words.

Earlier we questioned why Almeda and Alvira embarked upon such a journey. Like other pioneer women these two Peabody sisters were drawn west by family ties. Most of their immediate family had disappeared from East Pitcairn by 1879. Their mother was dead. Their father had remarried and moved to Michigan along with their stepmother and two other brothers. Their brothers, Lelon, Benjamin and Edwin, had already settled in the Breckenridge, Colorado area. Alvira's young husband had recently been killed in the "War of the Rebellion." Nothing held them in New York. It seemed natural for these two unmarried women to pack up and join their brothers out west.

Schlissel's research reveals that the overwhelming majority of women who journeyed west were married. Out of 103 women who made the overland crossing only nine women between the ages of 16 and 30 were unmarried.

Even these nine single women traveled with their families. As pointed out earlier, Victorian values viewed Almeda and Alvira traveling unchaperoned in the company of two single men, Henry and his Civil War "chum", as highly improper.

Almeda does not comment on how others perceived their trip or her own feelings about leaving East Pitcairn. Nor does she share any details or feelings about her whirlwind courtship with Henry. Almeda does not discuss private or uncomfortable aspects of her life. Personal subjects like menstruation, sex, pregnancy and childbirth are avoided altogether. These intimate details of life were often not recorded in diaries of pioneer women. Throughout her journal, Almeda formally refers to her husband as Mr. Wagner—it must have seemed too personal to call him Henry.

We yearn to know more of pioneer women's private feelings. What was life really like? What were their hopes and dreams, their sorrows? How did it turn out in the end? The more we can know of their inner reality, the more of a bond we feel—for this is the stuff that makes up our own lives. Though much has changed from the pioneer days, women's inner experience is timeless—the joy of falling in love, anguish over the death of a child, worry over not providing for one's family, fear of abandonment and dreams for a better future.

We are grateful to the pioneer women for what they did put down on paper. Their diaries and memoirs shed light on the dailiness of life. Details of

Four generations of Peabody women, left to right: Edna York Gateley, Linnie Peabody York, Mary Elizabeth Gateley, and Almeda Smith Peabody.

work and family relationships dominate their words. Women's stories offer a more peaceful version than men's. The male frontier myth plays up courage, honor, physical bravery and individualism. Novels, movies, art work and histories portray the drama of how the West was conquered as a violent saga. Women are not concerned with individualism, but with human connection. Their writings express either sorrow over the loss of loved ones left behind, the appreciation for one another's support on the journey or the utter isolation when that connection was lacking. We will later read my grandmother's

poignant letter about the absence of nurture in her young childhood. This lack of loving connection scarred her deeply and had its ripple effect upon generations to come.

Regardless of their many differences, one idea joined women to men: that the move West would bring them and their children a better life. This made the strenuous journey and the hardships of the first few years bearable. The women, as well as the men, had seen the limitations of staying in their old home. Hope for a new life gave husband and wife a unified vision.

Almeda, Mining Cook to Ranch Wife

In the early 1870's Breckenridge continued to see its placer mining rush diminish. The Indian problem, in contrast, only escalated. These two factors probably helped form Almeda and Henry Wagner's decision to leave the Breckenridge area.

Leaving Summit County

We lived in Summit County two and a half years. Then I went back to New York state in the fall of 1871. I stopped in Michigan on my way, to see my Father, and Brothers, Daniel and James. I passed through Chicago a few days before the great Chicago fire. The weather was very hot and dry everywhere, and as I went on down to home and to St. Lawrence County, 800 miles, I was not out of sight of fire. Many buildings, fences, haystacks, and trees, everything inflammable, seemed on fire; often the heat almost burning our faces through the (railroad) car windows.

I arrived at my Sister Saloma Thompson's in October and remained there until January 8th among friends and relations. When I went East Mr.

Wagner was intending to go to Missouri and get a farm, but he changed his mind and sent for me to come back to Colorado.

I arrived in Georgetown January 13, 1872. Mr. Wagner worked there in the stamp mills until the next spring, and I had taken boarders and worked by the month. Both of us saving as best we knew how, so that we had in all $2500. In April, 1873, we moved to the Valley on a ranch and bought a team of horses, harness and wagon. We homesteaded, pre-empted and purchased land of the railroad company and other ways until we owned 1200 acres. This was mostly stock or grazing land. Mr. Wagner being exceptionally good at handling cattle and horses. We lived at that place for twenty seven years. It was and is now called the Wagner Ranch.

Our oldest daughter had been borne in the mining camp of Gold Run. Our eldest son was borne in Georgetown. And our three youngest children were borne on our ranch.

Early Days on the Wagner-Peabody Ranch

When we first went on the ranch the house was only a shell. But we kept building on until we had a comfortable house of seven rooms, besides a large store-room and milk house, with a chamber for men to sleep in. But all these things took much time and money and hard work. For to begin with we had no cellar, no well, just a little spring down in the meadow - no fence or sheds. Many cold mornings Mr. Wagner drove up to Coal Creek Canon over impassable roads to get slabs and poles and posts to build with. Until at last we had sheds and corrals, miles of fences. Our son Lelon dug a cistern, so then we had plenty of soft water on the porch, as well as hard. Also we had hydrants in the cow yard, one in the barn, one in the house lot, and one in the slaughterhouse.

One winter after a dry summer there were severe storms and we were obliged to haul hay and grain from Golden. We lost heavily of our stock that spring after paying $700 for feed. Then we both got down with pneumonia - I in bed at the ranch and Mr. Wagner in Golden, unable to come home. Our oldest girl, Maria, or Rie as we called her, only ten years of age, together with her two brothers, John (8) and Lelon (6), doing their best to care for the stock and get their own meals. The snow was two or three feet deep in places. Those two boys, so young, worked like men, and Rie had no idle moments for weeks.

During the winter I taught the children at home. They had never been in school as we lived three miles from a school house. But they studied well, so that when they began to attend school they were well able to stand with any class of their ages. Now when I think how hard those dear little ones worked, making no complaints, it brings the tears, even yet.

But taken all together, I believe that our happiest days were those spent on that big ranch. And it was not always hard or bad after we got well started. We had plenty to supply all our needs or wants. We had teams and wagons and buggies and saddle horses, to go and come as we chose. Those big fields and mountains seemed all our own. Mr. Wagner was an extra good man with stock and he and his sons could guess the weight very close of our stock. He was also good at breaking horses to the saddle or harness, and he took good care that his stock did not suffer from hunger.

The years flew by. All the children except the youngest grew up in the old home and married and left us to make homes of their own. Beatrice Lulu, our youngest, was our stay and helper during our last six years on the ranch. Mr. Wagner's eyesight was failing, so she and I were needed with him constantly to be eyes for him while driving or riding or doing any kind of work.

Our oldest son was named for his Grandfather John Adam Wagner. He was seriously injured while riding a horse. He died at the age of 36 from the effects of this after eighteen years of great suffering. He left three orphaned children. His wife was killed by a gunshot wound nearly three years before, he being shot at the same time though not fatally. After her death our daughter Rie kept house for him until her own marriage. After John's death the sisters of his wife took their three children and finished raising them.

In 1909 we sold the ranch for $14,500 and moved into Golden. We had the pleasure of raising our children in the country, among the hills and valleys and in the fresh mountain air, with plenty of room, no other building in sight but our own. All but one married while we lived there. And here let me say I have thanked my Maker for the privilege of raising our children in that country home, and of having a husband that did not play cards or use tobacco; had temperate habits, was kind to his family, and had many good friends who shed tears of sorrow at his death on May 20, 1906.

The end

These pages are dedicated to my children, by their mother

—Almeda Peabody Wagner
May, 1921

[Note: These memoirs I have copied from notes in Mother's own handwriting, written as the dates will show, when she was 77 years of age. At the time she was making her home with her youngest daughter, Lulu, at 2801 Second Avenue, Los Angeles, California. The original pages, written at my request are my most treasured possession, I hope to retain as long as I live, in memory of that which all men recognize as nature's most noble creation - Mother.

—Lelon Wagner
P.S. Mother died at Los Angeles, December 31, 1921]

Woman brings lunch to placer miners. Sluice boxes (or "Long Toms")
were used to separate the heavier gold ore from the soil. Later, lode
mining was discovered and later still dredging was used.

Lelon Peabody,
A Progressive Pioneer

Lelon Peabody, who drew Almeda to the Breckenridge area, also departed Gold Run Gulch. While she moved to lower altitude at Golden, Colorado, he shifted his mining activity to nearby Hamilton, back across Boreas Pass.

Shortly after Almeda and Henry married (and after Lelon's much younger brother, Edwin found himself a wife), Lelon decided that he was not getting any younger. So, in 1871, at the ripe age of 37 he married 13-year-old Mabel Rudeler from Beaver, Pennsylvania. Nearly triple her age he truly robbed the cradle! In 1876 when Mabel had attained the "mature" age of 18 their first child was born at Gold Run.

It is unclear when Lelon left the Gold Run area to move back over the divide to Hamilton. In 1878 a daughter, Minnie, was born in Breckenridge, but mining reports indicate that during the 1879 summer he employed 15 men, netting $7,000 at his placer in Hamilton. Between 1882 and 1888, three more children were born (one of whom died).

A long-time employee of Lelon's, Jimmie Jones, shares his memories about this pioneer miner whom he admired greatly. It was published in the August 27, 1953 edition of *The Denver Post:*

Leland Peabody started his placer work on the Middle Fork of the Tarryall, which rises on the east slope of Silverheels Mountain, as soon as he could get his ditches set. He struck gravel so rich that a stampede began. Miners poured in there and that built up the old town of Hamilton, which was located about two miles up the creek and north of Como. Of course, there wasn't any Como then.

Hamilton was some town while she lasted. In 1860 a Government report showed 5000 people there. It was a stage station on the line that ran over Mosquito Pass; Leadville was built over there later. The old toll road that ran out of Boreas Pass also left out of Hamilton.

When all the rest of the people pulled out of Hamilton, Leland Peabody stayed. He took up a little ranch on the creek and kept right on placering. When I knew him he was known as Old Man Peabody.

He was a man of medium height and build. He always wore a full crop of whiskers, pretty well sprinkled with grey by that time. He had a young woman and a fine family—five children. The finest people in the world. That old man was one of the men who opened up that country. There never was a nicer man lived than old Leal Peabody.

I went out there to work for him when I was 12 years old. He'd been in there 33 years then. He had one ditch which was never decreed. If it had been, it'd been the oldest ditch in that part of the country.

He'd start working in May as soon as the ice was gone out of the creek and the ground thawed out a little. The 80 Chinamen and 20 white men that he worked had holed up there on the place or in Como. They were always glad to see the Spring break-up so they could get to work again.

For water pressure Old Man Peabody had dammed off the whole creek. Of course he had an over flow to keep from tearing his dam out. He kept gradually working up the creek, for he had claims on both sides for about two miles.

He built his sluice boxes out of planks. They were four feet wide and four feet deep and sat on the ground. In the bottom were riffle blocks about six inches in diameter, enough to go across the box in a row. They were fastened in there by boards on each side nailed to the box. These blocks were 6 inches high and were made right there on the job by two old brothers. Maybe he'd have 50 feet of them or 100 feet. It all depended on what he had com-

ing through there; he sampled the gravel first.

White men loaded the wheelbarrows and the Chinamen dumped them in the sluice box. They went down to bedrock, cleaning it very careful.

Along about 11 o'clock in the morning Old Man Peabody'd pull that headgate and let the full force of water go through and wash out everything except the gold. He had men along the sides with long-handled forks to throw out the big rocks.

He made two cleanups each season, which ran about five months up there. When he got ready to cleanup, he'd shut off all the water. He'd pull the riffles (blocks), gather up all the gold, black sand and everything that went in between the cracks.

He'd take that down to the house and pan it all down. I've watched him many a time. You should have seen him handle a gold pan, he was as artist with it. He'd have buckets full of gold. He'd ship that on the narrow gauge (Denver, South Park and Pacific) down to the Mint in Denver.

That old bird took out millions there but he put it all back in the ground up there in that country. He had several lode mines that he always thought were going to pan out big— but they never did. His placer mining, though, was a great success.

He was the best placer miner on the Middle Fork of the Tarryall but he wasn't the only one working. Right above him was the Fortune Placer, run by old John Fortune, that had a

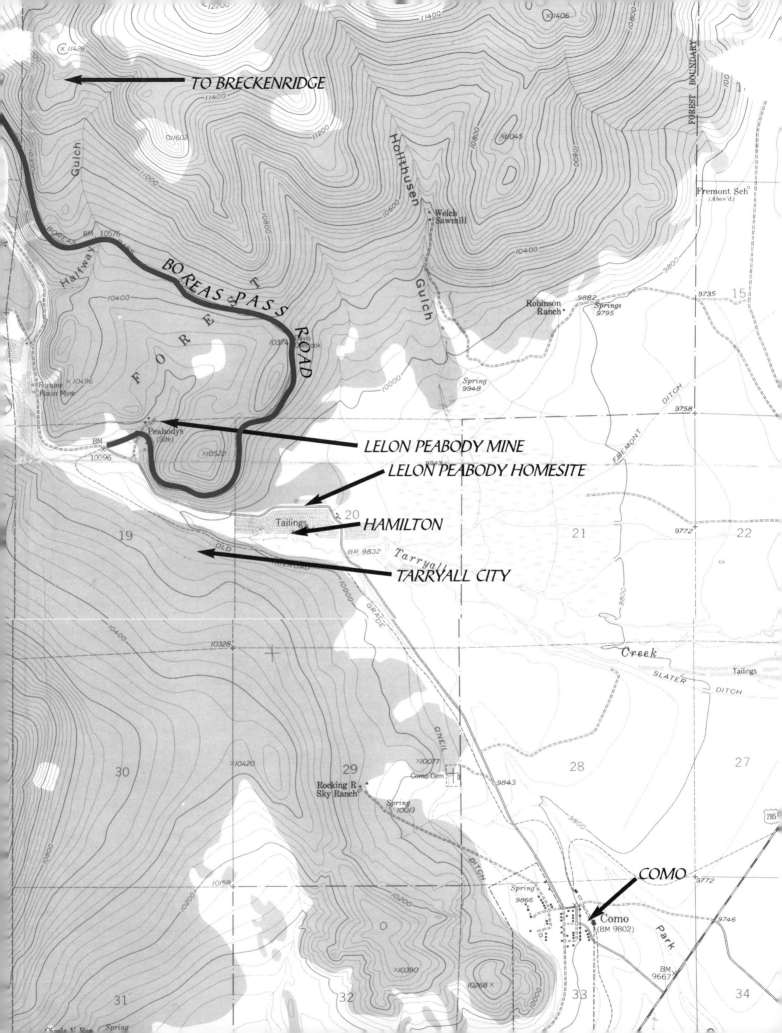

TO BRECKENRIDGE

LELON PEABODY MINE

LELON PEABODY HOMESITE

HAMILTON

TARRYALL CITY

COMO

hydraulic outfit. It went on up the creek to the Montague Placer, which went on up on the sides of Silverheels Mountain.

This was the mountain named in honor of a lovely dance hall girl who stepped from the Denver stage one day in Buckskin Joe, hurrah placer mining camp. 'Tis said that the miners fought to dance with her, this girl who wore silver slippers. She repaid their devotion, for when the smallpox struck she nursed the sick, held many a man's hand at the last. Some say she took the disease herself, the pock marks erasing her beauty. Be that as it may, these Old West adventurers who knew character gave her an imperishable monument.

Old Man Peabody shut down operations about the first of October. By that time the creek would commence freezing over. All his men and the others would make a rush for Como. What a celebration! They'd boom the devil out of things. There were six saloons in Como then.

Old Leal kept on placering right there in that same place until he had to quit. He was still taking out gold there at the last, for I worked off and on for him for years.

Years afterwards a dredge outfit come in there and bought up Old Leal's claims, which another man had bought after his death. This dredge man was sure he'd clean up big, for he said the old man hadn't known how to save the gold. I told him he'd find out different but he only laughed at me.

He went ahead and moved that big dredge in there and started up the creek. About two weeks later he came to me and wanted to know more about Old Leal's operations. He finally had to admit that they hadn't recovered a thing. The gravel was clean all the way down to bedrock. He believed then what I told him—that Old Leal Peabody was one of the best placer miners that ever hit the West.

Chinese in Colorado

For many years Lelon employed a large number of Chinese in his mines. He was progressive for his time. Many people looked down on the Chinese and wanted as little to do with them as possible. Like the Native American Indians, the Chinese in this country were at first treated as a curiosity, a picturesque novelty. Later they joined the community of women and Indians who suffered treatment as sub-human and endured discrimination.

The first Chinese were attracted to California by opportunities in the gold fields, and then they spread to Colorado and other western states as well. Since most of the Chinese were at first engaged in mining, it was in the mines that the first opposition to the "Celestials" showed itself. As their numbers increased so did the bitter protests against them. *The Colorado Magazine,* describes the growing anti-Chinese sentiment:

"The Chinese must go" became the chant echoing in the halls of Congress as the people of the East, thoroughly inmbued with the principle of free immigration, bitterly contested the eager western Congressmen in their fight to save America from the ruin that might follow in the wake of the "pig-tailed Celestials..." The major reason for their unpopularity in mining towns was fear of the competition the Chinese coolies would give White labor.

In the Chinatown section of Denver public outrage focused on the vice and filth of "Hop Alley." A nest of opium dens, gambling joints and houses of prostitution pushed anti-Chinese sentiment to a fever pitch, sometimes culminating in open violence.

The great majority of Chinese, however, were hardworking men who gravitated to the occupations of mining. Others were merchants of fine silk, restaurant owners and launderers. They came to America without their families intent on making a fortune and returning to their own country.

Lelon Peabody located his placer mine a short distance upstream from Hamilton where the road forked off to Boreas Pass. Today one can still locate the neatly laid out rock terraces that mark the location of the shacks built by the Chinese whom Lelon employed in his mines. These remains are scattered in the woods on the outside of the big hairpin turn.

Boreas Pass

The rough trail Lelon first traversed in 1859 from Hamilton to Breckenridge was just an Indian path over the Continental Divide. Within a year pioneers had hacked out by hand a crude wagon road. For 22 miles this trail wound its way up and over the high altitude range, sometimes clinging precariously to the mountainside.

On Boreas the snow arrived early in the winter and lasted late into the spring. Because there was deep snow on the path, spring-season travelers traversed the snow-covered pass before the sun softened it. As Almeda mentioned in her diary, they left in the early morning while it was still dark and rode their horses over the frozen and crusted snow. Travel continued in this mode for many years.

In 1881, two years after Lelon moved to Hamilton, the Denver, South Park & Pacific Railroad workers graded and laid track. At 11,488 feet, Boreas Pass was the highest narrow gauge railroad route in the United States. The rails snaked their way up from Como in South Park, crossed the high divide and then wound their way down into the Blue River valley. Difficult for railroad crews to build and challenging to keep in operation during raging winter storms, the pass was notorious for its ferocious timberline blizzards. Howling winds, drifting snow and bone-chilling cold made the going treacherous.

In its early history, Boreas Pass had several names. First known as Hamilton, or alternately Tarryall Pass, it took its identity from the early mining camps which it served. Later, switching its loyalty to the mining settlement on the western side of the summit, it was renamed Breckinridge Pass (using the original spelling of the town name). In the course of trying to operate a railroad in the face of the vicious winter storms, it seemed appropriate to rename the pass once more. This time it was named Boreas in honor of the ancient deity of the north wind.

To service the railroad and provide shelter for the crew, a small town, also named Boreas, grew up on the top of the pass. Only a few remnants of this settlement remain visible today.

Stories are told of harrowing experiences in the history of Boreas. Snowbound residents wrote letters describing their terror being marooned in blizzards and temperatures that plummeted to 60 degrees below zero. During the Winter of 1898-99 the people of Boreas were snowed in for 90 days. No trains were able to reach the station from either side. When supplies dwindled below the danger point two men made a desperate effort to reach Como. Shortly after noon they headed out on snowshoes into the stark, white wasteland. They never got there. Their frozen bodies were found along the trail during a search which was attempted the next day. Food was finally brought in from Grant by using horse-drawn sleighs after a trail had been broken through the drifts.

Ice and snow covering the track caused Boreas Pass trains to jump the rails. In addition, the steep, winding grade proved too precipitous for some trains descending from the summit. Horror stories of runaway trains were

far too common. Brakes on the locomotive would give out as the train careened down the steep curving railroad grade. Sometimes the crew and

The steep, windy grade with ice-covered track made travel treacherous. Derailments were not uncommon on Boreas.

passengers would jump to safety from the runaway. But the brakeman, pulling desperately on the brakes, often died in the crash.

The stories of Boreas are not all disaster tales, however. One colorful and bizarre incident involved a P.T. Barnum circus train attempting to chug up

Locomotive descending Boreas Pass.

Boreas on its way from Denver to Leadville. Robert Brown, in *Ghost Towns of the Colorado Rockies,* indicates it faced a challenge:

> Shortly after it had played at Denver, the circus train crossed Kenosha Pass and huffed its way across South Park to Como. In the course of trying to reach Leadville, it became stalled about three miles below the town of Boreas. Seemingly no amount of steam was capable of carrying the ponderous cargo of wild animals over the crest. Since the line, at this point, consisted of only a single track, all other traffic from both sides was effectively blocked as the sun went down and darkness began to descend. To add chaos to confusion, the lions grew hungry and started roaring. In desperation the elephant keeper offered to remove his huge

animals from their car, allowing them to push against the rear of the train. Frantically, the engineer is said to have replied, "Anything to get to Leadville." Carefully the pachyderms were arrayed behind the last coach. Impatient little knots of people gathered to watch hopefully as the strange hookup was arranged. Almost simultaneously, the brakeman released his iron shoes while the caretaker uttered an impressive string of Arabic oaths. Up front, the shrill whistle split the darkening sky. From the rear of the train, a powerful snort was heard as the strange procession actually began to move. When the top was reached, a few Boreas residents are said to have taken a hasty pledge of alcoholic abstinence, but Leadville got its circus anyway.

The Peabodys lived close to all the action. A station for the Denver, South Park & Pacific narrow gauge railroad stood nearby Lelon's placer claim. There the railway tracks made a wide hairpin turn to start the climb from the valley up and over the pass. Windy Point, a railroad landmark, lay just above the station.

Old Man Peabody, as he was affectionately called, was well liked and respected by those who knew him. Almeda's memoir recorded his passing near Hamilton, Colorado,

where he died at the age of 63 years and 8 months. His wife and two daughters (and son) are living there yet.

His obituary, in the *Fairplay Flume* written at his death in 1898 said: Mr. Peabody being a man of exceptional character - open hearted, honest and trustworthy to a remarkable degree, he enjoyed the respect of all with whom he came in contact. He came to Colorado in 1859 and has since followed the avocation of a placer miner and was more successful than the average man. He was 63 years of age and leaves a wife and five children to mourn his loss in the community from which he will be sorely missed.

Almeda indicated that Lelon did not die a natural death, but how he died remains a mystery.

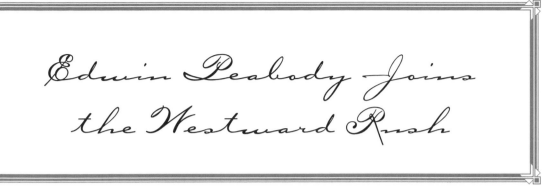

*Edwin Peabody Joins
the Westward Rush*

Lelon Peabody introduced his siblings to the lure of gold and the magnetism of adventure in Colorado. Now we turn our attention to his brother, one of the youngest Peabody siblings, and pick up the story of Edwin Peabody, my great grandfather.

Readers will remember that Edwin, born in 1848, grew up with Almeda in the northern New York wilderness on the family's East Pitcairn farm. He was seven when his mother died. His father soon remarried, and at the age of ten, when the new baby arrived, he was sent miles away to his brother Daniel's farm. At some point Edwin moved with his father (and perhaps his stepmother) and brothers, Daniel and James, to Ravenna, Michigan.

When he was a young man of 20, Edwin and his oldest brother Benjamin, 38, set off to seek their fortunes in Colorado. Edwin, like his two sisters a year later, joined Lelon at Gold Run. Here he worked for a year in Lelon's mines. In the fall of 1869, a few months after sister Almeda arrived and was married, Edwin left Gold Run Gulch. Six months later he, too, married his sweetheart.

My brother, Edwin, returned to Michigan that fall and married Almeda Smith (March 27, 1870). But after a few years he came back to Colorado.

Edwin probably met Almeda Deborah Smith earlier when he first lived in Michigan. When they were married, Almeda was not yet 16 and Edwin was only 20. Her father had served as a Union soldier, and after having been taken prisoner, died in the Andersonville prison. The young couple lived for three years in Ravenna, Michigan, and their first two children were born there, Cecelia Rosetta on February 20, 1871 and Marshall on October 10, 1872.

Many Moves for a Young Family

Apparently, Edwin had tasted enough excitement during his year spent in the mining camp at Gold Run that he yearned to return. Colorado was in his blood. So in 1873 Edwin and his young bride journeyed back to the Breckenridge area. The couple made

Peabody family, 1892. Linnie and Cecelia in back row; Edwin, Almeda and Cliff in front.

The Extension and Jumbo Mines lay just beyond Preston on Gibson Hill.

the last part of the difficult trip over Boreas Pass on horseback, each one carrying a baby in their arms. Can you imagine the hopes and fears and great anticipation that this young couple must have felt as they finally reached the summit of the steep mountain pass and looked down into the Blue River valley below?

Edwin brought his little family over Boreas Pass and they settled in the town of Preston, not far east of the original Peabody placer. Here they lived and worked in the mines of Gold Run Gulch. Another child, Linnie May, was born four years later on May 10, 1877. At some point Edwin and his family returned briefly to Michigan. But they found Colorado compelling. So, once again they loaded up their belongings and made the strenuous trip back to

Colorado. This time they resided in Golden near where his sister, Almeda, and husband, Henry, were by then homesteading their ranch.

On Christmas Day, 1884, a joyous event occurred. While much of the world celebrated the birth of Jesus, another special baby was born, my grandfather, Elmer Clifton Peabody. His arrival had a special significance to the Peabody family. For years, Marshall had been a sickly child. No medical treatment available could heal him. Just a few months after Cliff (as he was often called) was born, Marshall died. Cliff was beloved by all—the youngest child, the only surviving boy, and the only son of this branch of the Peabody family to carry the name. Cliff's sisters were a good deal older than he and probably enjoyed having a little brother to spoil.

Teams and wagons depart from Breckenridge-area ore mill.

(Linnie was seven and Cecelia was thirteen when he was born.) Cliff's presence may also have eased the family's sorrow over the loss of Marshall.

After a few years the family moved again from Golden to Como in South Park. This time they chose to live where brother Lelon had now settled. Edwin apparently had trouble finding a place to call home. Perhaps this difficulty resulted from the losses he experienced in early life. So every two or three years he pulled up stakes and moved on. Over the course of about 20 years Edwin and the family relocated at least seven times. He always moved to be nearer to one or another of his older siblings. The person he really sought in all these moves couldn't be found—his mother!

His older sister recorded the end of Edwin's sojourns in her memoir:

After living in Golden and in these mines in the mountains he finally settled in Breckenridge.

So, in 1891, Edwin and Almeda made their last move to Breckenridge where they lived the rest of their lives. The couple discovered a prosperous town quite different from the log and shanty gold camp they'd left years earlier.

Lode Mining Transformed Breckenridge

The discovery of lode mining in 1879 set off a second population boom and greatly changed Breckenridge. Miners discovered how to mine the gold-bearing veins, or lodes, which ran deep beneath the surface. These lodes were the source of the gold which eroded and washed down into the stream beds.

Originally placer mining was used to mine the stream beds. This was first done in the form of panning for gold which was quickly replaced by sluicing.

Both relied on the simple process of gravity to separate the gold from the gravel. A sluice box (or Long Tom) might be as long as 100 feet and one and a half feet wide. Sand and gravel were shoveled into it and water, diverted from a stream, poured through causing the heavier gold particles to settle to the bottom. Here the gold was caught by battens nailed to the bottom of the sluice.

Placer mining was then superseded by hard rock, or lode, mining which used vertical shafts and horizontal tunnels to mine the gold ore from deep within the earth. (A few decades later another form of placer mining, dredging, would become the most lucrative method.)

Like busy gophers, the prospectors burrowed their way deep into the hillsides rising high above Breckenridge. Today if one looks up at the high mountain slopes above timberline, often a narrow little trail can be seen, clinging to a near vertical slope and winding its way up to some remote abandoned mine. There, perched precariously, sometimes on the narrowest of ledges, one might see the remnants of an old mine with its tailings dump of discarded rock—silent reminders of a bygone era. With a little imagination one can visualize stalwart little burros bearing heavy loads of supplies as they plod up the trail. Or, we may try to imagine the owner of this isolated mine. Were his hopes of success realized? Or did he give up in disillusionment after having expended an extraordinary amount of effort?

Anne Ellis, in *The Life of an Ordinary Woman*, talks about the difficult job of a hard rock miner. There was always, she points out, that terrible fear of accidents which ever hangs over a miner's wife. Miners should have good wages, as, aside from risking their lives every time they go underground, there is the feeling of being buried; at least this is my first feeling whenever I have gone down a mine; then the dampness, the sound of dripping water, the smell of burned powder and bad air, the feel of darkness, the dirt sifting and slithering around rotten timbers, rats slipping around corners, the fear of a companion's carelessness, or of an open trapdoor not noticed in the darkness...A drunken engineer might miss their signal and hoist a cage or bucket full of men in the shive wheel—I have known them to. If a mine is working

Burros going to high mountain lode mine.

Ore car and track emerge from Breckenridge mine tunnel.

Arrival of supplies by wagon train to Victorian Breckenridge.

three shifts, it is hard to get used to the different hours for sleeping and eating. The 11 p.m. to 7 a.m. graveyard shift, is hated by all miners and their wives.

Population Soars

Despite the well known dangers in a miner's life, the new lode discoveries brought hordes of prospectors. In 1880 the Breckenridge population which had shriveled now skyrocketed. Within a couple of years the population soared from 500 to 2,000 to 8,000. Excitement over the new discoveries ran high and newcomers again stampeded to Breckenridge.

In Breckenridge hammers and saws banged out new two- and three-story frame buildings next to the log cabins built in the 1860's rush. In addition to the necessary provision stores, restaurants, blacksmith shops, boarding houses and sawmills, the town had three dance halls and 18 saloons. "There was a saloon or gambling house at every other door," remarked one visitor.

Western architectural style of this era featured false-fronted buildings. Breckenridge architecture became known as well for its impressive Victorian flair. The traditional method of hiding a one-story building behind a facade was carried out much more elaborately. In Breckenridge, designers added ornate cornices and built the two-story false-front to make the building appear much higher. To deceive the passerby, one building even displayed two false windows.

The arrival of the railroad also helped transform Breckenridge. The massive peaks making up the spine of our continent served as a barrier isolating Breckenridge from the rest of the world. This little mining camp on the Colorado western slope had since its inception felt cut off from the civilized world. But in 1882, when the first train snaked its way over Boreas Pass, Breckenridge was given a much needed transportation breakthrough.

The Denver, South Park & Pacific line boosted the economy of the already flourishing town. Breckenridge entered an era of prosperity and culture. Now, gold-bearing ore could be more profitably hauled out. And luxuries for civilized life were hauled in. Newcomers, who became stable citizens intent on building a civilized community, swelled the town. A newspaper

Edwin James Peabody

was published. Beautiful Victorian homes with wall-papered parlors were built. Churches, schools, hospitals, a fire and police department all sprang up to meet the needs of town families. Breckenridge was no longer a transient mining town. Culture and social graces had arrived.

Elmer Clifton Peabody, A Mischievous Youth

My grandfather, Elmer Clifton Peabody grew up in this affluent Breckenridge. Cliff came to Breckenridge in 1891 when he was six years old. Years later Cliff would entertain us around the dining room table with his tales of "the good old days." I was entranced by the stories of this fun-loving, often mischievous young boy. I think he was quite a prankster in his younger days. Cliff entertained readers of the *Summit County Journal* with his colorful articles entitled "Reminiscences of the Good Old Days."

Breckenridge was a great place for a boy to have fun, that is if he would try to make his own fun with the others. There were no school activities, no youth center, no P.T.A. Just a little swimming. Fletcher's Lake was the favorite place, until the town took it over and made it into the present reservoir. After that Rocky Point Lake or some lily pond was used. A little skating in the fall, skiing and bob-sledding in the winter.

One cabin of especial interest to the young fellows was located on the edge of the placer on Yuba Dam Flats, a bit southeast of the old Two Mile Bridge. Here a crowd of us young boys would gather with our picnic lunches and play batching. In those days you could buy a dozen donuts for 10c, a lemon pie for 20c. A pound of Arbuckle's or Four X or Lion brand coffee could be bought for 20c a pound, a can of milk for 10c or less, sugar could be had from the home sack. So it wasn't very expensive for half dozen boys to go there and have coffee, pie and donuts.

In those days a boy had to prove himself, before he could "belong" and if he was unable to show himself worthy, he was out of the activities such as they were.

Cliff recalls a boulder rolling escapade involving Tom Abbott's cabin. Tom was a no-good character in town. According to Cliff:

Over a period of years all the cabins near town were burned, one by one, by Tom Abbott. When one burned he found another, moved in and it would then go up in flames.

(But here Tom gets his comeuppance by the youngsters in town.)

On one of our trips to this cabin, the crowd decided to roll a big boulder down the hill, in the direction of Tom Abbott's cabin. We never dreamed of the good results we would get. Just before the boulder reached the cabin it struck a log or another large boulder, bounced into the air. Then it landed on the roof of the cabin and then fell inside. Little did we suspect that "Old Tom" was inside. When he came running out, it was every boy for himself. We scattered in the timber in every direction. I personally never made town, before that day or after it, in so short a time. That was the last time I ever went there. I don't remember if the older boys continued to use the cabin for their rendezvous any more or not.

I remember Pags (which is what I called my grandfather), reminiscing about other rowdy incidents in his boyhood. He told these stories with great delight, but also a tinge of embarrassment—as if he shouldn't be telling his granddaughters that he took pleasure in such pranks.

One Halloween night, looking for some fun, he and his friends roamed around and found someone's outhouse which they proceeded to tip over. They discovered afterwards that someone was in it! That always left me wondering—what happened next?

Rolling boulders down hillsides and knocking over outhouses seems to have been quite the entertainment—at least for Cliff and his buddies. It certainly was mischievous, if not bordering on malicious. Fortunately, as is true for most of today's youths, luck was on his side. No one was hurt and he emerged from his devilish days unscathed.

When Cliff was 14, Breckenridge experienced the historic Winter of the Big Snow. Snow started falling on November 27, 1898, and by morning five feet blanketed the area. This was just the beginning. Snow continued falling steadily until February 20th, inundating Summit County. Breckenridge was buried up to its rooflines. People either had to crawl in and out of their second story windows or they dug steps in the snow creating a staircase down to their doorways. The railroad was paralyzed. For 79 days Breckenridge was snowbound. Cut off from the rest of the world, supplies dwindled and nearly ran out. In 1952, years later, Elmer Clifton Peabody recorded his memories of the Big Snow for his granddaughters

The Winter of the Big Snow

Dedication: *To Cynthia Charlotte Peabody and Sally Ann Peabody, daughters of Elmer Clifton Peabody Jr, son of Elmer Clifton Peabody, your grandfather. You knew him as Pags and love him and called him by that name, Pags.*

Winter of the Big Snow, 1898-99. Streets of Breckeridge.

Your grandfather was born in Golden, Colorado. His family moved to Como, Colorado because your great grandfather had a brother living in Como, and both men were interested in mining, placer and hydraulic mining.

Your grandfather came to Breckenridge, Colorado in the year 1891 at the age of six. This would make him 14 years of age at the beginning of the really BIG SNOW.

In this year of 1952 so much has been re-told and some written about the Big Snow of 1898 in Summit County, some of it factual, some half remembered facts. So your Pags has decided to give you a picture of the storm, the railroad, the town and the people as viewed through the eyes of a wide-awake 14-year-old boy.

So Here It Is

The railroad, that came to Breckenridge from Denver and then on to Leadville, Colorado was part of the Union Pacific System. Later it became a part of the Burlington, and this branch was known as the Colorado and Southern.

In 1898 this branch was declining in its activities. Freight hauling and passenger travel was getting less and less as the ore was getting harder and harder to find. No new spectacular uses for the available minerals had been found. At one time there was a sleeper or as it is now called, a Pullman, running daily between Denver and Leadville. There was one train called an "accommodation freight." This freight carried mail and passengers from Denver to Leadville and mail from Denver each afternoon. This was plus the mail from the accommodation freight. The railroad station, or depot, was across the river and about one block south from the house in which your Daddy was born. A "Y" extended toward Shock Hill where the switching, changing and turning of the railroad cars was done. This station was large enough and nice enough for the train dispatcher and his family to use for living quarters. Ore was hauled to this station in very heavy tired wagons, by horses that were not very large, but they were strong and always kept nice and fat. The ore was unloaded by the men using shovels. Nothing had been mechanized in those years. Wages were very low. There were no unions, no strikes, no foreigners. The few foreigners, Swedes, Germans, and so on, all were taking steps toward citizenship.

Anything anyone would write or talk about the winter of 1898 and '99 would have to be from their personal recollections unless they kept records, or obtained records from newspapers or personal diaries. Anything I write has to be as I remember it and the things with which I came in contact.

Snow Blockade for 78 Days

The setting for me is Breckenridge alone. I saw nothing further than a few miles outside the town. Jess Oakley was quoted in the Summit County Journal of Feb. 10,

Winter of the Big Snow, 1898-99. The only way to travel was on skis.

1939, "The railroads started blocking in December, and the snow grew steadily worse; more and more trouble was had getting through. On the 5th of February, 1899, the last train left Breckenridge for Como, with seven engines, one passenger car and a rotary plow." The blockade lasted until April 24th, 1899. That means for 78 days no train could get in or out of Breckenridge. After the real storm started, the snow fell day after day, all day long and with no sunshine.

As days and days passed with no let up in the storm the townspeople began to think about how to get mail in and out, especially first class mail, since the possibility of a train coming in was so doubtful. Jess Oakley volunteered to make the trip to Como on skis and bring back the most important letter mail. A collection was made to pay his expenses. The principal contributor was George Engle. With a few quarters from here and there, the sum total was probably about twelve dollars. At this time that seemed ample compensation for the trip, and time required to make it. If you were capable, physically, to make it you could buy three squares (meals) and a nights lodging for one dollar, and oh yes, two drinks of whiskey for twenty five cents.

The Feb. 10, 1939 article in The Journal quotes, "On February 8, Jess carried 45 pounds of 1st class mail to Como. When he arrived at Boreas, he looked for the station to get some coffee before going on into Como. When he found the story and one-half station house, the smoke stack was about 6 inches under the snow. He looked for the entrance and found a dug out in steps. Mr. Oakley estimates the snow there was about 20 feet deep."

I do not know how many trips Oakley made alone. One trip he was accompanied by Horace Post, returning with about forty pounds of mail each. If anyone thinks forty pounds isn't much let them try to carry that much on skis (they were called snow shoes at that time and webs were webs.)

Kaiser Cow Butchered, Peabody Cow Escaped

During this time groceries, meats and other food supplies were being consumed and supplies dwindling. One item was Mellin's Baby Food and Horlick's malted milk. Again Oakley had to make a trip over the pass called Boreas for food for his own son Clyde. Meat in the markets finally ran out as did butter and eggs, and so did the vegetables, except what the individual householder may have had on hand.

There were amusing incidents, and one for me that contained quite a little humor. The meat situation was getting quite acute. When Mrs. Christ Kaiser went to her barn to milk her cow one evening, she found that her cow had been butchered right there in the barn. Ed Theobald and George Moon were then operating the Christ Kaiser Market. That building still stands. Mr. Kaiser was in the cattle business with Billy Sanborn at Jefferson. When the two butchers of the cow explained the matter to Mrs. Kaiser, they told her it was done in the name of necessity. She was paid for the loss of her cow.

My mother had a cow also. After the Kaiser's cow was sacrificed, she daily expected they would demand her cow for the same reason. I believe the difficulty of getting the Peabody cow out of the barn saved her. The fact that supplies were dribbling in might have been a factor toward saving her life also.

It was quite a problem to care for that cow. That was one of the small chores delegated to me. All water and feed had to be carried into the barn as it was impossible to get the cow out of the barn. The snow was nine feet deep in the cow yard. I don't remember how many weeks

Winter of the Big Snow, 1898-99. Two photos taken at same location at the top of Boreas Pass show depth of snow in spring and then in summer, 1899.

she stood in the barn. By the end of March the snow storms had become intermittent and I was able to clear a space in front of the door. Then I shoveled a circle trail, wide enough so the cow could follow this trail and walk around the circle and come right back to the barn. She could then at least stand outside during the warmth of the day when it did get warm. This barn was in the alley close to the Catholic Church.

Inventive Minds at Work

The problem with getting places confronted everyone. Since "necessity is the mother of invention" someone was going to try to improve the skis, skis being the best and easiest way to move about. Previous to the opening of the road several parties made the trip back and forth to Como on skis or webs. They only person using webs, that I recall, was one Felix Martin, a French Canadian. When I saw him go up Ridge Street on a pair of webs, I got a thin board and fashioned some shoes. My tools were a saw and hammer; that was all I had to work with. I went out after dark to try them out so no one could see me struggling with them. I still have them and believe they could be used by putting on some foot straps. The one difficulty I found with them was the snow gathered on top of them and did not fall through, as it does with webs.

Where the Court House now stands was a row of houses that extended as far as the tree which still stands near the corner of the Treasurer's office. George Engle owned a building at the corner of Ridge and Lincoln. This was used by a contractor named Mitchell. Since there was little carpenter work to do his men had plenty of time to work on their ideas which ran to Snow Bikes. This was what was wanted the most. The first attempt was an idea of Walter Henderson. His idea was a pair of skis with a frame built on them with a pair of pedals, a sprocket wheel made of wood with nails driven at regular intervals with the heads sawed off. The belt was of leather about one and one half inches wide, with holes punched and spaced to engage the nails in the sprocket. The belt went back to a wooden shaft on which was another wooden sprocket with nails driven in for sprocket teeth that were supposed to engage the holes in this leather belt. On this shaft was placed four or six wooden paddles that were to push this sled as they rested on the snow a little below the bottom of the sled runners.

To steer this bike was a third and shorter shoe placed between the runners and a little ahead. This operated by a pair of handles, like bike handles. The power was derived by leg power the same as a regular bike. Gas and small engines were not much in use in those days fifty three years ago.

The day this snow bike was taken out for its trial run was a Sunday, just after noon. It was moved out of the shop and given a start at Ridge Street on Lincoln Avenue, and was headed for Main Street. Henderson was unable to steer it in a straight line. By the time he got to Main Street, the power plant was exhausted. So with the help of five or six men it was pulled back up the hill and put back in the shop for future use as kindling wood. At the same time two other Mitchell men began building a sled. However they used the frame of an old tandem bike, mounted on runners, using the regular sprockets and chains to the rear wheel hub. On the rim of this wheel were placed triangular pieces of metal with the point outside which was supposed to dig in the snow and thereby drive the sled forward. This sled looked much better than the Henderson sled, but one trial was no more of a success. Two men could not furnish enough power to drive it on a level road, in soft snow it would not move at all. That venture ended any ideas of making skiing easier.

The demand for skis was great that year as that was the only outdoor sport to be had, as well as the only means of travel. Bob-sledding wasn't good as snow fell so regularly the hills could not be kept open for sliding.

The only skis anyone saw those days were made locally. They were made with just a strap across the instep and a bridge or block placed under the arch of the foot. Skis were never fastened to the feet as that was considered too dangerous. One might get a leg broken on a fall. But many a ski took off alone down the hill, sometimes to be lost or broken.

The best skis were made by Eli Fletcher. The kind of wood used was native spruce or pine, ash, oak or Texas pine. Texas pine, quarter sawed, were the fastest skis made and needed no waxing. The more they were used the better and faster they became. The usual length of the ski at that time was twelve feet.

Dancing the Winter Away

There being no radio, no train coming in each day with mail, no road or pass open for teams to get to the world outside, you have to try to imagine some of the things the people had to worry them. One was entertainment. What was there to do? It has been said that Breckenridge never had such a sociable time as that winter. Certainly never since has any time equaled that winter. As an example, four dances were held most of the time. One on Saturday afternoon was given by Professor Clisbee for the juniors at the GAR Hall. This was really a school for beginners and cost fifty cents a lesson, boys and girls paying alike. On Saturday nights one was given by the Professor for the general public. On the same nights a dance was held in the Old Firemen's Hall. This was given by the Club. As I look back these dances were perhaps more grown up and formal. Professor Clisbee scraped the fiddle while his daughter, Edna, was the violinist, with Mrs. Robert Williams at the piano. She was the Mamie Hilliard whom you call Aunt Mamie. These dances, as I said, were held at the Firemen's Hall. On Wednesday nights Professor Clisbee had a dancing class in the dining room of the old Occidental Hotel where he lived. That building is gone.

After a few Saturday afternoon lessons a few of us decided we were good enough for the Saturday night dances. In order to be sure we had partners, or at least a partner for part of the dances, Marion Fletcher and I would see that one or the other of us took Vera Stephenson to the dance. Then we paid for the lady as well as for ourselves. So we would check our finances and decide who would take her to the dance. We decided that weighty matter on Friday at school Sometimes we had to pool our money, sometimes borrow, but we always were sure that we had someone for some of the dances. You see we were just "punks" then and most of the older and better dancers didn't like to dance with us. More than once I have seen a lady wearing a red face while dancing with us. But it didn't mean a thing to me then. Of course we stepped on their feet, but I think women's feet were larger then than now. Or at least as I remember them more stuck out in front and not so much up in the air in their high heeled shoes.

The Wednesday dancing class given by Professor Clisbee was attended by the older ladies who had never learned to dance and wished some instruction before attending the public dances. The Professor would round up a few of the punks (I was one) for these dances to dance with the ladies. This was one time we did not pay. The ladies had to. I don't know if we helped teach them anything or not, but we were something to lean on while they were moving about. When twelve o'clock came on Saturday night the music stopped and there was no more dancing. The big dances were always given on Friday night and dancing lasted as late as 4 A.M. At the end of the dances everyone went home, walked home. This is just a side light about the entertainment of the children during the blockade. Speaking of social parties, there was in school every age group having parties almost every night, at some house or home. The home of Eli Fletcher was one of the favorite places for the group to which I belonged, however that was not the only place we met. Refreshments were not often served.

We just had a good time, usually dancing. Not many of the class of '99 are left. Probably the "Four Hundred" or Elite society spent their evenings playing cards. Five hundred was the game of that time.

Struggling Out for Food

Naturally there was much talk and speculation as to what the railroad was doing about opening the road, and also, what about the wagon road? People gathered in groups to discuss the situation. I attended every meeting held anywhere that pertained to anything concerning the town railroad. I was everywhere. One of the first parties to make the trip by skis was Eli and Will Fletcher. They fashioned a sled from ski shoes with a tongue and rope for pulling. They brought back some pork and beef. On the way down from Boreas the sled became unmanageable and tipped over. I don't think they ever tried a second trip. After the road was opened to Como, George Moon and another man went to the Park, probably to the Sanborn and Kaiser place near Jefferson. They went on horses expecting to drive some beef cattle to Breckenridge to butcher. On the day of their expected arrival, I went about a mile beyond Rocky Point Lake to see if they were coming so I could report to Ed Theobald, another butcher. But they didn't arrive in Breckenridge until the following day. Probably held at the Kaiser barns and corrals and slaugh-

An 1890's Breckenridge parlour.

tered there as it would have been next to impossible to have brought them in on the hoof. Another party that went out was the "Finding" party. There were several in that party who went out to Denver. I don't recall if both the Finding girls, Agnes, now Mrs. Miner, or her sister Tonnie [went]. I have seen pictures of this party taken at Boreas. I have no Book of Memories or clippings, to turn to in this narrative, just the things and incidents that came into the line of my vision and a 15-year-old boy isn't supposed to see and remember much. I bet though there are some who wish they couldn't remember as much as they do. At one time or at about the lowest ebb of the food situation, Bob Foote (no one ever called him Robert), owner of the Denver Hotel, came to my mother who owned the Colorado Hotel, and asked her for some butter. He was completely out of butter, and his daughter, Ella, wouldn't eat without butter. My mother told him he could have butter for Ella but none for his boarders. I take it from that that the supplies were not so very low for my mother.

A grand character, Bob Foote; many a prospector was grubstaked for months at a time by him and many a man lived on Bob when he knew he would never get a cent for boarding. In the span of a man's life you do not meet many grand men like Bob Foote.

Mass Meeting Called

Things finally reached the stage where something had to be done as food for the stock as well as the food for the human population was getting near zero. On a Sunday afternoon a mass meeting was called and it was decided the time had come when the wagon road over Boreas to Como must be opened. On Monday morning about seven o'clock the Fire Bell was tapped. More than a hundred men with several teams of horses gathered at the Firemen's Hall. The men began the opening of the road to Como. All the teams and men returned to Breckenridge the first night. They made Como the second or third day. By teams going to Como one day and returning the following day the road was kept open. Finally it was built up to the height of the surrounding snow; thereafter there was no trouble keeping the road open. Meats, groceries and animal food began to flow in to Breck-

enridge, three days a week, but not in such quantities as to fill the empty store shelves. But the crisis was over and the necessities were available as well as some of the luxuries. After the opening of the road a short time contract was given to one Shaw to bring in mail by team and sled. I saw the first sled load of mail and other supplies arrive at the post office. My great interest was to see if Shaw brought in any bananas. "Yes I have no bananas." Later Carl Ecklund and I bought part of the first stock of bananas that came in and proceeded to eat a dozen each. We had heard that no one could eat a dozen. We could have eaten more but wanted our supplies to last two or three days. I remember Shaw very well but do not remember his partner. I knew where they started their "Steam Laundry," on Washington Avenue. It was short lived.

Whiskey First!

I don't know the condition of the road between Dillon and Breckenridge but it probably had to be broken open after the Boreas Pass Road opened. More than once I have heard it said the first load of supplies that came into Dillon by sled that winter was a load of barrel whiskey. Their thirst must have been greater than their hunger.

So far as I know, only one life was lost on Boreas Pass by those skiing to Como, Loren Waldo. Others died elsewhere, but have no place in this story. Loren Waldo worked as a clerk in John Hartman's grocery store. Receiving word that his wife was ill, he, with several others left Breckenridge for Como together. On reaching Boreas, Waldo decided not to stick with the other members of the party but to go on by himself. He did this against the advice of the agent. It was about 5:30 P.M. when Mr. Waldo left Boreas for Como during a blizzard and 18 degrees below zero. He never reached Como. So goes the story that was told at the time.

The family of Waldo offered a reward of two hundred dollars to any person or persons finding the body. There was little chance of finding him during the winter since the snow and wind had erased all marks of his travel and covered him with snow. Joe Marz, Sam Wells, Jess Oakley and I spent a day searching, after the snow had partly melted. This was probably at the end of May or early June. How many others had been searching I do not know. The body was not found until a week or two after our search. It was found by a Louis Craig just a short distance from the snow sheds. Waldo probably became exhausted. Realizing he could go no further he had apparently tried to write a letter or note, as a pencil and note book were at his side.

The above are the highlights of the wagon road opening. As I said before, the speculation was long and some of it vociferous as to what the railroad was doing. I don't know much about what went on until the time arrived that the railroad's rotary snowplow had passed Rocky Point and reached Illinois Gulch. Many of the townspeople and school children went up to meet and see it. The snow at that time and place was deeper than the height of the rotary. When the rotary reached the point of Nigger Hill above the ball park, one engine became useless. Just what was broken I do not know. The only repair was to disconnect and remove the connecting rod. I watched the engineer do that work. It was on a Sunday morning.

First Train Arrives

That Sunday afternoon a mass meeting was held at which time a spokesman for the railroad asked for assistance from the citizens. Some heated arguments resulted. Many were against giving the railroad any assistance. Some were for helping and getting the road opened into town. Finally, the Superintendent, or whatever he was for the railroad, asked all those in favor of helping the road to line up on one side of the hall. After they did this he said he would give each one two dollars a day to help. It didn't take long for the ranks to swell. I attended that meeting but my parents would not let me stay out of school that Monday to earn that two dollars. Several of the boys did. The shovelers did not shovel the full width of the track. They cleared one rail which relieved the rotary as only one cylinder was working as I previously stated. One connecting rod was removed. About three o'clock that Monday afternoon the whistles of the locomotives began blowing as they entered town. Stewart dismissed school. It was like an ant hill disturbed—two hundred school children and most of the citizens going to the depot to see the first train arrive after the blockade. The blockage was ended, but there still remained feet and feet of snow on the hillsides. Only that deep, narrow cut the rotary had made which could again become filled with snow, if snow should fall, and the wind blow. From the records, it did again, causing a delay in train service.

Time passed. So did the school term end and the out-of-doors called to the dancing youths of the blockade, through the love of a swimming pool and fishing stream.

Oh, magic town of Breckenridge. One of the best and cleanest mining towns that ever existed until prohibition came to change it. The population of Breckenridge at that time was about nine hundred. On Saturday when the men from the hills came in it might make a thousand. At least that was claimed for it. There were two meat markets, six grocery stores, three dry goods stores, one or two bakeries, two barber shops, five saloons, several hotels, two livery stables, two hardware stores and other business establishments.

Let me give you a little sketch of the social-public activities. One has to remember, there was little money paid in the little towns, isolated as Breckenridge was. The old water system and lights consumed all the money collected for maintenance. So anything carried on in the town was done by donations. The largest donors were always the saloon keepers all a fine class of men. Dancing was the most popular form of entertainment. Any person appearing at one of these dances under the influence of liquor was escorted from the hall and told not to come back. There was always a floor committee to take care of such matters, and two would usually take an arm of the frolicsome guest and go toward the door, usually laughing. So far as most of the persons present knew, the men were just going to the smoking room for a friendly smoke. There were none more insistent on keeping the dances free from drinking than the saloon men themselves. When Theodore Knorr, Ed Weaver, Arlington Fincher, Bob Williams, Charlie Marz and some others on the floor committee escorted a man to the door as an undesirable, they told him to leave and don't come back. They did not need to threaten what they would do later. Those boys were organized, and like the fellow who was asked to disturb the hornets nest said, "No, they are organized."

Undesirables Screened

The big dance of the season was the Masquerade given by the Red Men's Lodge. To make sure that no undesirables got in under mask, then later boast that they crashed the dance, every one, ladies and men, were required to step in a booth and unmask before the town Marshall as he knew all the undesirables. Strangers were not required to give their names or furnish a character reference as all local questionables were known. This dance was usually given on the last Friday in March each year.

The society dance of the years was given by the Odd Fellows around the end of April. There at that dance the ladies were always given a bouquet of cut flowers at the door. The lodge members all wore some of the lodge regalia for the Grand March.

The ladies and men also were beautifully dressed, the men in tuxedos, Prince Alberts, sack coat, seldom a cut-a-way, or claw hammer. Vests were always worn, often a white one. Every man owned a black suit for evening wear. It was a necessity. No man would think of appearing at a dance or party dressed otherwise. Yes, even in Breckenridge, those were the days of beautifully dressed men and women.

No Fuel Shortage

I want to say something about the fuel, why nothing so far as I have read has ever been said about short-

Almeda Smith Peabody, the author's great grandmother, ran the Colorado House with her daughter, Cecelia.

"Fatty's restaurant," formerly the Colorado House.

Almeda Smith Peabody in front of the Colorado House which she operated.

ting and others hauling the poles and logs to town. In town there were three or four small mills cutting it into various stove lengths. Many a Saturday I would help T.B. Thompson deliver wood around town. His sled box would hold one-half cord of wood. I would get five cents a load for helping load and then unload each load. Some days we could deliver as many as ten loads if we worked until it became dark, which was around five o'clock. I had then for my work, earned fifty cents, enough to go to the Saturday night dance.

Breckenridge had no day service or electricity. There was a small light plant at the west end of Lincoln Avenue. This was the Breckenridge Light Plant, not owned by the town but privately owned. This plant had two DC generators driven by one small steam engine. During the day the plant remained idle. But when it got dark enough and the lamps were to be lit, they would start up the generator and run through the night or to such a time that it was not needed. This plant used wood for fuel almost exclusively, cut in cords of four foot lengths. T.B. Thompson had several men and teams hauling wood from the woods daily. He paid his men every night and furnished board to his men. At the supper table he placed one dollar and fifty cents at each man's plate. What would our boys think of working for a dollar and fifty cents now? The men had to supply their own lodging, however.

ages. There wasn't any shortage that really amounted to much. There was very little coal burned in Breckenridge at that time and what was used was generally put in the house bins early in the fall. Wood was the principal fuel and furnished quite a number of person's employment, some cut-

There was no telephone service in Breckenridge at that time. It did not come into Breckenridge until two or three years later. However, I believe the Western Union lines remained in service through the winter. The rate was twenty five cents for the first ten words to Denver and corresponding distances, but who had twenty five cents?

The Mountain Pride Mine on Baldy was about the only mine to run through the winter that employed any force of men at all. The Mountain Pride and wood chopping and hauling were about the only sources of revenue that winter.

This, my story of the winter of 1898 and '99, has not been written for publication. It is for the members of my family who will hear about that winter as long as any remain who passed through it. Any one of a dozen persons could write, perhaps, a more interesting story because of their experiences and memory of it that makes it live again in their minds. My one regret, a boy's regret, is that I was not allowed to ski to Como. I was a better skier than some of the men who made the trip.

Affectionately,
—Your Pags

Victorian Breckenridge

By the 1890's Breckenridge had reached its peak of affluence. Business flourished. Cliff's mother, Almeda, with her oldest daughter Cecelia's help, went into business. For many years she oper-
ated the Colorado House. (The building, at 106 South Ridge Street, is now the home of Fatty's restaurant.) Like other boarding houses in Breckenridge, the Colorado House offered the miner and traveler a delicious home cooked meal—a welcome relief from the beans, hard tack, salt pork, oats and coffee on which the prospector subsisted. Guests who stopped at the Colorado House relished a favorite delicacy: Blue Point oysters shipped all the way from the Atlantic.

Almeda gave freely and generously to the hundreds of wayfarers and neighbors she knew and met. She was a much-loved pioneer of Breckenridge. Edwin also was a respected member of the community. In his later years he served as the police magistrate for the town and justice of the peace for Summit County.

The successful mining operations in the area provided the source of Breckenridge's prosperity. With this new wealth, a class consciousness and racial discrimination developed that attempted to separate out those who were "undesirable" from the rest of society. Breckenridge entered the Victorian age.

Turn-of-the-century Breckenridge had no tolerance for "undesirables," whether at the Masquerade Ball or working in the mines. Cliff, in his "Reminiscences of the Good Old Days," describes citizen committees, or vigilantes, who took matters into their own hands to keep law and order as they saw it.

Breckenridge always protected its own interest. When undesirables came in they were quickly moved out. In 1898 a large number of workmen were brought in by the Pence-Miller people to work on their ditch and placer. Wages were $2.50 a day for ten hours. The men brought in were to work for less. The citizens objected and kept the men in the willows, west of the depot, for a day or two. After much oratory, threats of the militia, etc. the men were loaded into one or two boxcars, the doors sealed and the car was sent to Denver. There was no violence, no one was hurt, except for a street fight or two between townspeople.

Another example occurred a few years later.

Early in the 1900's a firm was cutting paper wood around Lincoln Park and Brown's Gulch. This company attempted to bring in some laborers, 20 or 30 as I remember it. After the passenger train on which they were riding had left Como, someone telegraphed someone in Breckenridge about the matter. It was easy in those days to gather a hundred men. Just a few taps on the fire bell and, presto, there you had them. On this occasion, T. B. Thompson quickly organized a party, gathered up a few shot guns, some clubs and other things, then went over and met the passenger train. As the men got off the train, they were lined up, marched through town, and escorted to Illinois Park, almost to Rocky Point Lake. They were told to keep on that road and go back to Denver. The town Marshall was at the reservoir and the sheriff was asleep in his office. There were no more importations.

Breckenridge citizens lacked tolerance for cultural diversity. Residents looked down on the Chinese. The "Celestials," as they were called, were considered acceptable to operate laundries, but not good enough to work in the mines. The editor of the Summit County Journal wrote about the Chinese in 1884:

We are not favorably impressed with the idea of flooding our town with a class of labor which is calculated to drive out white labor...once we introduce that class of labor Breckenridge will soon find a lower level than it has held for the last three years...If there is any property around here so poor that it will not pay to be worked by white men, it had better lie idle than introduce a kind of labor which will eventually drive out that which has made America what it is.

The story of Barney Ford, the first black prospector, is a well known example of traditional bigotry. In the 1860's a Negro did not have the legal right to hold title to mining property. However, a kindly Denver attorney offered to let Barney use his name on the claims Barney filed, in exchange for a share of the

Early car (1906 or '07) Cliff Peabody is seated in the right rear.

gold unearthed. Ford struck it rich in a little fork up French Gulch. Getting wind of this, the lawyer had the sheriff run Barney off. But the news of his discovery was out and rumors of fleeing Negroes and great riches resulted in the site being called Nigger Hill. Ford returned in the 1880 boom and became wildly successful. He achieved a position of prominence and respect. But residents waited until 1964 to rename Nigger Hill as Barney Ford Hill.

Class consciousness influenced the racial discrimination and separation of undesirables from the rest of society in Victorian Breckenridge. As social life advanced it became increasingly exclusive.

Members of the genteel class upheld the social graces and customs of the day and conducted themselves as gentlemen and ladies. Proper etiquette was strictly followed. In those days fashionable people arranged a social visit by the formality of calling cards. A lady sent the cards out in advance and then waited "at home" on certain afternoons to receive her guests. Men and women dressed in their Sunday best for these formal affairs. Elegant entertaining was very much "in." Members of the social

Picnicking in Victorian-age Breckenridge

set gave parties and luncheons. There the ladies demonstrated their culinary talents amidst the elaborate furnishings fashionable at the turn of the century. China cabinets displayed collections of exquisite cut glass, hand-painted china and fragile crystal wine goblets. Exclusive guest lists provided comment and gossip by the local newspaper, the *Summit County Journal:*

> We heard of a dainty little luncheon that was given on the Q.T. to a precious few one day this week - where the table was beautifully laid for six, with white damask, cut glass, hand painted china, and, oh, such a profusion of roses and hyacinths, and

the lunch served with the skill of an artist. We are not jealous that we were not there, not at all, but wish to let our friends know that society "do move" and will continue to move.

Social life flourished. Many of the social gatherings were white-glove events. Concerts, lectures, recitals and touring stage shows were commonplace. Dancing, however, was by far the favorite pastime for everyone. Community dances were held in any convenient place—the local schoolroom, courthouse, G.A.R. hall or barn might be cleared for the evening. These affairs drew the entire family and everyone came dressed in their best suit of clothes. A collection plate was passed to pay the local fiddler hired for the evening. Endless rounds of polkas, waltzes and square dances, and large bowls of punch and a table spread with cookies and cakes kept the guests going long into the night.

Several dances each year excelled in their elegance. The Firemen's Ball, the Masons' annual dance and the Redmen's masked ball were formal affairs. The gentlemen wore dark suits and the ladies donned fresh flowers and elaborate long gowns with bustles. Tight lacing of women's corsets was in style. The smaller a woman could squeeze her waistline, the more beautiful she was considered. Ladies sacrificed comfort for fashion.

In addition to the popular dances, social calendars were filled with sleigh rides, tobogganing and snowshoeing in the winter, and picnics in the summer. Card parties, strawberry socials and oyster suppers all made for a lively and enjoyable social life that brought people together. Life in this remote mountain town had achieved a refinement that would have surprised the early prospectors.

Cliff was a handsome young man who cut a graceful figure on the dance floor—a most eligible bachelor. But he thirsted for adventure. Ten generations of Peabodys before him had left their genetic imprint. The "Go West Young Man" spirit was in his blood. After finishing high school in Breckenridge, Cliff at 21 traveled to San Francisco. There he built ships. His biggest excitement was to witness the historic San Francisco earthquake and fire on April 19, 1906. The next day Cliff wrote a letter home to his mother describing the horrific event. This was published in the *Breckenridge Bulletin* on May 5, 1906:

Cliff Peabody Describes the Awful San Francisco Disaster

Under date of April 20th Clifton Peabody writes his mother, Mrs. A.D. Peabody, a lengthy description of the earthquake and fire in San Francisco, which he witnessed. We publish most of the letter as a matter of local interest here where the family is so well known:

San Francisco, Cal., April 20, 1906.

Dear Mother: Will try and tell you of the disaster. I was awakened by a rumble and jar of the house. Then there came a violent shaking of the house, and I looked for it to go over every second. Finally the quake ceased. We arose and looked out of the window down on the bay, and could only see the spray caused by the rocking of the bay. Grover, my roommate, said, "let's dress and go and see what it has done." We went out on the hill where we could see over the city. By this time, fire had broken out in six different places and one of the big gas tanks had exploded, the City Hall dome had fallen and was a total wreck; also the crematory chimney had collapsed.

After breakfast we went down Seventh street where the residence district was on fire. We could see thousands dragging trunks and moving things, children screaming and women carrying great loads. Firemen were helpless, as the earthquake had broken the water pipes. Saw one home where the whole front of the building had fallen out and the piano had been thrown into the middle of the street. Everywhere they were carrying out wounded and dead people. Saw one man wheeling a trunk in a baby buggy. Several times we were hemmed in by fire while trying to get to Market street where all the big buildings are. It is a good thing the disaster happened so early in the morning—later there would have been thousands killed by falling walls. Market street was full of fallen rock and brick. At this time there was no fire on Market. The dome of City Hall had crushed the rest of the building no doubt killing many prisoners in jail. Mechanics Pavilion, across from City Hall was turned into an emergency hospital and we watched them bring in the dead and wounded in automobiles, express wagons, patrols, ambulances, etc. We watched the Emporium, the largest store in California, burn, and five minutes later the Call building, fifteen stories high, was on fire. Fire was raging in every direction—the Examiner and Chronicle buildings were going. Then the soldiers drove us back. When we left, Market Mechanics Pavilion, where were so many wounded and dead, was on fire.

When we got home a girl who is stuck on Grover was there. Grover don't like her, so he went back to town. I went out and stayed a couple of hours, then went back. I sympathized with her before, and she had told me all her troubles and took on terribly. She finally went into hysterics and for two hours I had a time of it with her. Grover finally came back and we started to take her home. We had to walk about three miles and she had about three fits on the road. People would crowd around and throw water on her and us too. We both felt like fools. We finally got a carriage and got her home. She had been away from her mother all day and the city burning and her father out to sea. We thought we had seen the last of her for a week, anyway, but she came back next day.

We saw the Valencia hotel which had fallen into the earth. It was three stories high and only the top story stuck out of the ground. Many people were killed in it, and I think it burned the next day. Near it were cracks in the earth a foot wide all over the streets, and the streets had dropped several feet in places. Thousands of people camped on the hills with just a few blankets. We were on the go 19 hours that day.

We went back to Market street and to Chinatown the next day. The latter was a raging furnace of fire. In front of the Hall of Justice is a little park about a block square, and people were packed in there. We counted

30 dead bodies lying on the edge of this park and people camped right beside them.

At Kearney and Jackson streets we stayed and watched a fire. Saw a "Chink" come out of a burning house, run to the corner, then put on his socks, probably all he had saved.

We tried to get up to the house where Al White lives, but could not on account of the fire. Saw the Hopkins Institute of Art burn. Everywhere nothing but debris and ruins. Automobiles were abandoned and burned in the streets. No doubt hundreds perished who will never be known, especially in Chinatown.

About a mile below our house they gave out grub from freight cars, and I got one case (48 cans) of oysters and my room mate got a sack each of prunes and spice. We can get full of prunes once in our lives anyway.

The soldiers destroyed all the booze in all the saloons left.

The third day at 10 o'clock we saw a man lying dead on Market street with his pockets turned inside out. Later we saw eight or ten big beef steers partly covered with a fallen wall and had roasted in the fire.

It has been hard to get anything at the cars to-day. The soldiers guard them and one has to stand in line. One line was at least a half mile long. Some were carrying away dirty pieces of bacon, etc.

"Nothing but debris and ruins" remained after the San Francisco quake and fire, Cliff said.

The San Francisco earthquake and ensuing fire.

You cannot imaging the total wreck of a city like this is. Think of a city three times as large as Denver all in ruins except a few residence sections. One could put the whole of Denver into the burned district and have lots of space left. It is said 300,000 people are homeless here; Frisco had a population of nearly 400,000. Look at some old Bible picture of ancient ruins and you have Frisco as it is to-day, only there are miles and miles of ruins here.

We are thankful our house was not damaged and none of us hurt. I only hope you are as well at home as I am here.

Ever your loving kid,
—Cliff

After about a year in California, Cliff returned to his home town of Breckenridge. His boyhood pranks behind him, Cliff was a little older and wiser, but with a charm and mystique that made him attractive to the young ladies. Having seen some of the world he was ready to fall in love and settle down.

Elmer Clifton Peabody. Handsome young man and most eligible bachelor!

Halsey Victoria Rosedahl, Breckenridge's new school mistress.

One day in the late summer of 1909 a pretty young woman stepped down from the train in Breckenridge. The new school mistress had arrived. Halsey Victoria Rosedahl looked around at her new home high in the Colorado Rockies. How different from the flatlands of Kansas!

Who was this spunky young lady who traveled alone? Not a friend or family member accompanied her. How did she happen to choose this mining town as a place to live?

Gradually the townspeople came to know a little about Victoria, or Vic, as she was called. Four years earlier she had left the farming country of Horton, Kansas, and traveled West to live with her older sister who was married and living in Denver. Vic worked hard to pass the teacher's examination which she took in Ft. Morgan on Dec. 21, 1906. It gave her a certificate to teach the second grade. So, before she was 18 years of age, Vic taught her first school in the little ramshackle town of Roggen. This dirty railroad settlement on the Colorado prairie reminded Vic of western Kansas—dusty, flat and desolate.

Only much later do we learn how dreadful this experience was for her.

However Vic was able to save much of her $50 monthly salary which made it possible to enroll at Greeley, the Colorado State Normal School. One of the proudest days of her life was June 4, 1908, her graduation day. With degree in hand Victoria ventured further westward and taught a school year at Meeker, a little settlement in Colorado's northwest corner. The infamous Meeker massacre had taken place there 29 years earlier. Now, having accepted a teaching position in Breckenridge, a new chapter of her life began.

Other than these sketchy details, little was known about Vic. She rarely talked to anyone about her childhood, her parents, or what caused her to leave her home in the fertile farm country of northeastern Kansas. An air of mystery—or possibly shame—surrounded these earlier years.

Victoria was hired to teach in Breckenridge in 1909, the year the town opened its brand new school. This larger, brick school building replaced the two-story, frame schoolhouse built in 1882. Now an eleventh and twelfth grade could be added to the curriculum, and the school needed a new teacher. The frame, four-room schoolhouse with its elaborate gingerbread woodwork was actually Breckenridge's second school. The first school was a 20 by 25 foot one-room school house that children attended prior to 1882.

Interestingly, when early-day New England communities acquired civilization, churches came first. In the American West, however, schools were the priority and sprang up first. Schools served to socialize newcomers who spoke a variety of languages and who needed to polish their rough edges.

The following are two amusing letters written to the local newspaper by one such "rough-edged" citizen. At the time the town was discussing the question of building a larger school in order to replace the early one-room schoolhouse. It illustrates both the opposition to a new school and also the need for this civilizing element. Author Mark Feister records:

Daily Journal   Feb. 1, 1882

In your paper of yesterday I read a notis of a meeting for to bild a new school house. Now sir there is a nigger in the wood pile in that thing. I aint no profit or anything but you can put it down as a sure thing that is a put up job for somebodys benafit. I shall be at that meeting and opose all skeams. We have enuff schools now, if the room is to small bild a shed wing adition to it like Adamsons grociry. I am oposed to ecstravaganz and me and my friends will be on hand

you bet, you cant by us of for a glass of rot gut whisky neither. R.

Another letter followed the next day from the same gentleman

Mr. Editor—I see in to days paper you printed my lyttel note and you printed a lot of mistaks in it. I was in a saloon to-night and heard a lot of men laffing at it. Now sire that was a mean trick and I will remember you for it you may know how to spell better me but I have more money in bank than you have and it wasent learning that made it. I am oposed to this hyflightin fashun of stuffing childrun with so much education that they dont want to work. A good warm log school house was good enough for me and will do for my naburs childrun as well.

Dont go and spell this letter rong as you did the one you printed to-day or you will be sorry for it. Ime as good a man as you are and Ile make you no ot. Ime oposed to this school house swinddel and Ile be there to meeting don't you forget it. If you shute of yure mouth you will find some body to stop it.

Both the churches in the East and the one-room schoolhouses in the West tended to be of a similar white-frame construction. They both typically had long rectangular floor plans with windows on the side walls and a belfry above the entrance which was at one end. A pot-bellied stove supplied the warmth. And an outhouse always stood

Breckenridge's second schoolhouse, 1882. (The first was a one-room log cabin.)

nearby since there was no indoor plumbing.

Invariably few men gravitated to teaching because the salaries were so low. Most of the teachers were women. A teacher had many tasks to perform. Not only were they expected to teach the 3 R's to several grades at once, but they also served in the roles of janitor, nurse, surrogate mother and disciplinarian.

We hear stories about the harsh teachers of the early days who patrolled the classroom with switch in hand. "(Don't) spare the rod (or you will) spoil the child," went the famous saying. The phrase "toeing the line" originates from these early schools where the teacher drew a chalk line on the floor behind which the students stood at attention during reading and spelling recitals.

However, the challenges facing the young school mistress were extreme. Grama, (which is what I called Vic), later told us that many of her students were bigger than she. She was proud of her ability to maintain discipline with her students even though some of these strapping young men towered over her. Often these older students, unhappy that their parents insisted they attend school, would terrorize their teacher with unruly behavior and mischievous pranks. Many a teacher would leave before her term was up. Summit County rancher, Charlie Lund, once confessed that he and his classmates would go for "weeks on end" without a teacher. Presumably he and his pals made life so unpleasant for her that she felt forced to leave. The children then spent their school days playing and neglected to tell their parents that their teacher had long ago quit.

But Vic liked teaching. She loved English literature and poetry and took great pleasure in passing her enthusiasm on to others. By awakening a thirst for knowledge in her students, she hoped to open the doors of the world to these young people as she had for herself.

Wedding Day, Cliff and Vic

Cliff, the popular town boy, and Vic, the stranger from Kansas, quickly discovered one another. What fun they had. Picnics in the summer, tobogganing in the winter—and throughout the year dancing. They whirled and twirled around the dance floor, dancing the nights away. Such a handsome young couple. Vic with her tiny waistline, her delicate features and her sparkling blue eyes. And Cliff, so tall and good looking.

They were also drawn to each other on a deeper level. Cliff was attracted to her indomitable spirit. Although sometimes shy, even to the point of being self effacing, Vic was fiercely independent. She was soft and tender and yet could be feisty and outspoken. On the other hand, Vic was drawn to this adventuresome young man with boyish spirit. He showed a rare sensitivity and caring about her needs as a person. Cliff loved her passionately. And this touched something deep within Vic, a void that hungered to be filled.

As happens with lovers, plans emerged to marry and a wedding date was set. The following is a letter Cliff wrote to his beloved Vic 19 days before she was to become his wife. Vic had just completed teaching her second year of school at Breckenridge and was in Denver visiting her older sister, Annie. He addressed his letter to Miss H. Victoria Rosedahl, at 598 So. Lincoln St. Denver, Colorado. Cliff sounds fearful of losing Vic and apprehensive about her delaying the wedding.

Graduation day! Victoria Rosedahl with her class, Breckenridge, 1909-10.
(l. to r., back row:) Charles Brines, Will Hullender, Jack Brooks, Floyd Brinly, Clyde Oakley
and Victoria Rosedahl, teacher. front row: Etta Mc Clelland, Hilma Erickson, Ella
Howard, Pauline Hammel, Florence Tressler, Elizabeth Hardy, and Edna York.

Dillon, Colorado
June 11, 1911
My Dearest Love:

    I am going to write just a short note to night as it is quite late and tomorrow being Saturday the mail goes up and by good luck and delivery you should receive this Tuesday, there being no train on Sunday.

    Dearest you don't know, (perhaps you may if you feel the same as I do) how lonely it seems without you and for goodness don't postpone our marriage later than the 28th for every day seems a year. And what if something should take you away from me yet. I know it is foolish for me to think of it for you love me and I know there is nothing in the world could take me from you and you know I love you. Don't you dear? And it must not

Inside the one-room schoolhouse.

be longer than the 28th for I am going to be in Denver Monday, June 26th if the C & S can get me there. Besides we must be getting to California.

I don't care for a thing when I am away, or you are away from me, but it is grand to think that you are to be my wife and only three weeks, nineteen days to be exact. But think you are away off from me and in Denver while I am here on the ranch. Breckenridge would be a little better as I could get my mail oftener, and phone you if necessary. But think

how nice it is going to be when we can be together again dear.

When Clyde and I came down Wednesday we met Lily G. and Mrs. Knorr in front of Lund's ranch. They had been down visiting the school and you can't imagine how badly Lily's face was sun burned. She had on that little white hat and her face was almost a blister when I saw her and they were only halfway home then. I will bet she was afraid to smile by the time she got to B.

I met a fellow on the road to day who was coming up to the ranch. He

Breckenridge's new brick schoolhouse allowed students to graduate at the 12th grade level, not 10th as before.

is the man whom I had with me on the contract over in Clear Creek. He was over here a few days two years ago when I made a trip over, and he has been trying to get permission to settle on some land directly above those Ranger quarters (between Boulder Creek and Goulds) and will probably move over there to-morrow and make camp. If he settles there they will make good neighbors for the folks as he is about 50 and his wife about 40, and it would not be over a mile over there.

Dearest how glad I will be when this letter writing will be over for us and we can be together instead of miles apart. Nineteen more days how long but it does not seems so long that it was a whole year, with no definite time set. I know I must be patient and wait and bear in mind that you are also waiting.

Mother said to tell you she had your table cover almost finished. Goodness how we all miss you, the days seem so long when you are away.

I am going to close to night dearest love, and may your love ever be mine.

*Very affectionately, but impatiently
Yours Cliff*

Cliff and Vic, on their honeymoon trip to San Francisco, California (after their wedding, June 30, 1911).

In spite of Cliff's fears, their wedding day did come to pass. We know nothing more about this event. The ceremony was probably small and simple with only members of the immediate family present. Vic's older sister Annie and her husband, Frederick Strong, M.D. ("the doctor" as he was often referred to), would have been there. Charlotte, a sister five years older, whom Vic loved dearly, but with whom she also squabbled all her life, would surely have been there. (Lottie, as she was called, had followed her own dream and become a physician like Vic's brother-in-law with his emotional and financial help. She graduated in 1905 from the Denver Homeopathic College.) Also Roy probably helped to celebrate the day. Roy, five years younger than Vic was her favorite. Were there other siblings, parents, at the wedding? This remains a mystery.

It seems doubtful, from Cliff's letter, that any of his family traveled to Denver for the wedding. His parents and two older married sisters and their families all remained in Breckenridge.

After their honeymoon, Cliff and Vic remained in California. He worked on a gold dredge in Oroville. Gold dredging, also booming back home in Breckenridge, would soon reach its peak in Summit County's rich creeks and rivers.

Gold Dredging Had Its Glory Days in Cliff's Prime Years

In 1898 Ben Stanley Revett launched a form of placer mining new to Breckenridge: gold dredging. It made Summit County boom again. For a half century the floating dredge boats, like 80-foot mechanical dinosaurs, gobbled and chewed their way through Breckenridge's stream beds. Buckets on the dredge's revolving conveyor belt gouged and scooped up the gold-bearing gravel down to bedrock. After workers separated the gold from the mud, ooze and rocks, the dredge deposited huge mounds of waste rock in its wake.

A total of nine dredges scoured the river bottoms of the Blue River, Swan Valley and French Gulch with five working at one time in 1917 and 1918. In the midst of the Depression, when Breckenridge faced dire economic straits, the previously reluctant town fathers finally granted permission to the Tiger Alliance Company to dredge the streets and public lands of Breckenridge itself. The dredge ran night and day devouring the town. The racket of the screeching, clanging dredge was intense, but dredging did provide jobs. On October 15, 1942, a World War II war board ordered the dredges to cease operation because all available manpower and machinery were needed in the war effort. The environmental rape by these monster machines came to an end.

Today, the miles of gravel tailings, washed so clean that even weeds cannot grow between them, bear silent witness to the immensity of the operation and its devastating effects on the countryside.

Homesteading the lower Blue River ranch. Plowing the fields with a team of horses.

Early days on the Peabody Ranch, around 1919. E.C. Peabody, Jr. on right, with bicycle.

Elmer Clifton Peabody, Jr., Homesteading the Ranch

After the wedding Cliff and Vic left immediately for Yuba, California, their new home. Yuba, a little town near Oroville, is about 40 miles north of Sacramento. Here Cliff worked on the gold dredges. He had enjoyed his year spent in San Francisco a few years earlier and wanted to take his new bride back to the "golden state". However, after a few months, Vic became pregnant and "she could not take the heat" living in the Sacramento Valley. The distance from family and friends distressed her. So before their son, Elmer Clifton Peabody, Jr. was born on October 5, 1912, they had moved back to Breckenridge. For several years in Breckenridge, Cliff worked at the Wellington mine as a hoistman.

A few years earlier Cliff's parent's, Edwin and Almeda, had, with his help, homesteaded a small ranch a mile or so up Boulder Creek. The family called this the "Upper Ranch". Boulder Creek, a tributary of the Blue River, is located about 15 miles north of the town of Dillon. Two miles above the ranch's meadow site is beautiful Boulder Lake, surrounded by the rugged peaks of the Gore Range. Edwin and Almeda did not live on the Upper Ranch for long. In order to be granted title of a piece of land a homesteader had to develop it and occupy it for three years. After gaining title Edwin and Almeda returned to Breckenridge but held onto it for many years. They sold it in 1940, about the time Elmer Clifton, Jr. was married.

Sensing that profitable mining would not last forever, Cliff and Vic began to think about owning their own ranch. With Cliff's parents homesteading the Upper Ranch on Boulder Creek, they were drawn to the same area on the lower Blue. In 1915 they purchased the "Lower Ranch" from John Haff. This small 45-acre ranch is still located on the Blue River two miles north of Boulder Creek and one mile south of the little settlement of Slate Creek.

In spring, 1918, when Clifton was $5\frac{1}{2}$ years old, the family made the big move from Breckenridge to the ranch. Cliff quit work at the Wellington and began ranching. (Years later he again

Victoria R. Peabody and her new son, Elmer C. Peabody, Jr.

went back to mining, this time as the superintendent at the Wilfley mine in Kokomo.) Later in life Cliff and Vic also served as the county clerk and recorder, with their offices in the courthouse. Staunch Republicans, they were always very active in politics.

Life on the ranch meant hard work. Fields needed to be cleared and plowed, ditches dug, fences constructed. They built a house, barn and sheds of logs. For years there was no electricity or running water, and only an outhouse for a toilet. In time they dug a well which brought them clear, delicious water. The house, log like the rest of the buildings, consisted only of a kitchen and dining room downstairs and two bedrooms up.

Clifton had no brothers or sisters or nearby playmates so his animals became his best friends. He had a horse named Dot who "was a swell horse on the road, but a bitch to catch." There was a pig named Sarah, a cow named

Dutch Sadie and lots of chickens. "I had a dog named Bruno who was worthless for tricks but a wonderful watch dog."

Clifton's mother was devoted to him and determined that he would do well in life. That meant school! Years later she would look out the north window of the ranch down the long road to Slate Creek. Wistfully, she told me how her poor little tyke (my father) walked down the road by himself to the one-room schoolhouse. The winds could blow ferociously and the temperature plummet below zero, as her little six-year-old trudged the long mile through the snow. Clifton attended just the first and second grades there.

(This log schoolhouse was constructed about 1890. The frame building still standing at Slate Creek was not the schoolhouse but a community hall built as a 1936 Work Project of America effort. The hall served as a popular gathering place for local ranching families who turned out for square dancing every other weekend.)

Clifton's mother wanted her son to get a better education than she felt Slate Creek could offer. That meant Breckenridge. So for the next ten years he lived with his grandmother (who was still operating the Colorado House) until he graduated from high school (May, 1929, as class salutatorian.). During the summers he returned to the ranch. But the long journey was one not undertaken frequently. It took an entire day, by wagon, to reach the ranch from Breckenridge.

Clifton, a bright boy, did exceedingly well. He made his mother happy. She was proud of him when he entered the big university, the University of Colorado at Boulder. Not many pupils from Breckenridge went off to college in those days. And she was even prouder when he graduated in 1933, the youngest person ever to earn a degree from CU in engineering.

Not surprisingly, after graduating from college Clifton headed west. The "Go West, Young Man" spirit was alive in him too. Like his father before him, he went off to California, this time southern California.

An Independent Young Man

Clifton's mother always had high aspirations for him and strong opinions about how he should live his life. But Clifton had a need to find his own way and establish his own autonomy. Separating himself from his parents by a geographical distance of fifteen hundred miles, he felt removed from his parents' watchful eyes. Once in California he further sought to establish his individuality by choosing to live in a way quite different than his parents could ever approve.

As happens between parents and young people, news eventually trickled back home. They became concerned that all was not well with their only son. A first hand visit seemed in order. Unfortunately, Cliff's trip out to California to visit Clifton only served to confirm their suspicions. Alarmed and deeply distressed, they followed this

Ten year-old Elmer Clifton Peabody, Jr. at the ranch.

visit with a series of letters to Clifton imploring him to come to his senses. Their anxiety can be felt in the following two letters. They reached deep into their souls for the means to rescue him. For Cliff, who was a gentle, easy-going man, this meant giving him some strong fatherly advice. For Vic, a proud and private woman, this meant revealing to her son the dark secrets of her own youth.

The following letter was written from Cliff to his son shortly after visiting him in California. (I changed the woman's name to protect her anonymity.)

October 12, 1933

Dear Son:

I wrote to you after my arrival in Denver so there is nothing to write further about my trip.

The more I think about the opportunity that has opened for you to study airplane construction and aviation there the more I think you should avail yourself of every bit of time that you can spare as it is to be seen that the next big thing in transportation is further development in planes.

What you learn there may be the thing that will place you with the manufacturers of big planes, as it is only another form of mechanical engineering and your technical education along with some very practical training will just fit you for the time when the opportunity comes that you will be able to step in your place.

My trip there has more than ever awakened me to the fact that no matter how brilliant one may have passed through college they must have some outside influence to land anything and then it is very hard as you have seen as Senator Phipps has honestly tried to place you.

You are very young and no matter what knowledge you have gained at school wisdom will only come as you grow older and through contact with older people and through experience. Wisdom and knowledge are not synonymous terms as many suppose. One may have a thorough knowledge of a subject and at the same time be absolutely lacking in wisdom.

Your mother and I did not have any one to help and advise us as we went through life so what ever wisdom we acquired we had to do it by our self through hard knocks. As a consequence we tried to give you everything in our power we did not have and save you from the hard things we went through. One of the things you must learn is that you can never get any where without friends, the more the easier. Tolerance and patience coupled with courtesy and proper etiquette will do more to place you in high esteem with your superiors than any thing you can cultivate.

I was very much grieved and shocked when I learned of the clandestine affair you have been carrying on with Ethel. My grief is nothing to compare with that of your mother's. I can overlook the past but I can't a continuance of the same affair.

Men often have affairs of that kind but they seldom wish for those same girls or women to become their wives and mothers of their children. Nothing but sorrow and unhappiness ever comes of such unions. You could never look with pride at your wife as you would always have an undercurrent of thought that others knew your secret and doubt would always be in your mind. You may think you can get by with such things but the world is not much different now than it has been at all times past.

To be tied to any one who forced you to marry and you can't be forced as she is older than you and you were not twenty one at the time this was going on. In after life you would feel that you had been cheated out of your opportunity in life to have taken your rightful place in business and society. And by all means do not let any one cheat you in the game of life any more than you would in a business transaction.

As long as you are single we will help you until you are located, but if you allow yourself to be trapped into marriage with any one by such devices as this affair, do not look to us for any help as we are not going to welcome such a wife to our home, children or no children.

I have said we can over look the present affair but in the future you can do very well to stay clear and give yourself a chance to see some of the world and be some one of importance in a few years. But do not drag along with some one tied to you that can't help you in any particular. The world is full of girls whose family and parents are glad to have them marry good clean men of training even tho they are without much means of their own but who have plenty of their own and are willing to go the limit to help. It is as easy to love a girl with money as one without money, looks, and position.

Grover said he wanted you to stay there as he felt he could trust you to be with Florence and would look after her like a sister at the dances, and I know you can and will.

You probably feel resentful because this has been found out but I knew that something was worrying you because you could not sleep and were getting thin but I did not think it had gone so far. It is easy to forget and start everything new, school days are gone. Think of it as past.

This is the last time I am going to mention this affair and I shall expect you to conduct yourself as you would expect a son of your own to do. Only remember the dangers that may lay in your path and do not give too many liberties and you may avoid a like occurrence as people will take advantage of over confidence in them.

Remember we love you and have faith in you that you will justify the pride we have always felt and told people how wonderful you are and what you are going to do.

Love, Dad.

Vic Shares her Secret

(This was followed by Vic's letter to her son)

Breckenridge, Colorado
November 5, 1933
My dear Son,
Sunday night and a cold snowy evening it is. We are having a nice quiet day at home...Dad is sitting by the radio reading and I am in the mood to write so I think I shall get a lot of things off my chest that may interest you and they may just merely bore you, any way some things you should be told.

When you were in Colorado with me it did not seem necessary, but now it seems you should know a bit more clearly about things.

If anything happened to Dad or me or both the papers are in the tin boxes in the vault... The ranch, the lower one, is now in my name, but you should find a deed in the boxes... The ranch could always be a place of refuge anyway. This may sound goofy to you but I want you to know some thing about it. I am very adverse to any singing, prayers, services of any kind. If I could have my choice of a funeral I would ask that you or Dad close the lid and I want to be cremated, and the ashes put on Uncle Doctor and Aunt Annie's lot...

Son, I have often thought to myself how little we know, actually about the people we live with, and I have often had it in mind to talk a little bit to you of my own young life and perhaps you would see just why I have tried so hard to push you ahead. In my family there were quite a few of us, but there was always quite a little money, poorly applied or used, but my father was very well-to-do. He owned a lot of good Kansas farm land, several hundred acres and a lot of it bottom land, which was very rich. Herman and Annie were a lot older than Roy and I and they all were busy living their own lives and we got little or no attention. My mother was always sick. I never remember the time when she wasn't. She died when I was about ten a little

past. And in all my life Clifton I can never recall, my mother ever holding me in her arms or on her lap, kissing me, or loving me. I have no memory of any one ever caressing me, Ida, Annie, Lottie or none of them.

When I think of the forlorn little piece of humanity, that I was trundling to school, undernourished, probably dirty, and poorly clad fighting for myself like a little wild cat, trying to learn. I used to hunt for colored rocks and use the house, (it stood on the hill back of where it stands now), for my blackboard, and the schools that I taught and the dreams. I always had to wash the letters and numbers off.

How I hate Laura (Uncle Herman's wife) when I was about twelve I was staying with them and of course she begrudged Roy and I what we ate. They lived about two miles from the old home place and she would send me to the old home past the house where my mother died, to go back in the field and pull sun flowers. The corn looked like woods to me and I would be so scared I would cry and cry. She never gave me anything to eat to take along. We owned a big house in Horton, Kansas and after my mother died my father married again. Well there was dissension so he divided the property giving us children our mother's half.

I managed somehow to get to high school there and then I came to Denver and stayed with Aunt Annie. The Doctor was not particularly thrilled to have me but I worked hard to pass the Teacher's examination, I got a certificate in Weld County and taught my first school before I was eighteen. What an experience that was. I taught at Roggen. Had to live in the railroad station do all my own janitor work, cook, got head lice. If there had been any one in the world to care they never would have let me stay there over night but the $50 a month salary meant Greeley for me. I was just determined I was going to be something in the world. I got my Bachelor's degree in June, 1908. Not one member of my family was present, no one praised me, not a gift, not a thing the most of this time. Lottie was teaching and got her degree in medicine. She was always more popular than I with Aunt Annie and the Doctor. However even so things were none too easy for her. All the time I should have been getting a little money from the estate, but as an example I wrote once to Uncle Herman and asked for $100 that was due me and it was over a year before he sent it.

I taught a year in Meeker and then I came here. I taught here two years and the spring when your father and I married the schoolboard went to him and asked him if I wouldn't come back as I was an outstanding disciplinarian. You say what has all this to do with me? Only this Son, Dad grew up under conditions equally hard, in many ways worse. You know how Jesse, was given the help. Dad had to sleep in the coal shed to get away from the depraved morals of some of the boarders he was forced to sleep with and they never tried to help him. And with this handicap Dad and I have fought every step of the way and have no hesitation to meet the best in the state. What with your training and you, yourself there should be no limit to how far you can go, if you care to and try.

I hope you are not too much bored with this long, long story, but that I want you to get the most out of life.

I hope you will take up some reading. Have you ever read any of the Rubyiat of Omar? You should hear Dwight quote from it, you know how musical his voice is. It is like music when he says:
For in and out, above, about, below
Tis nothing but a Magic Shadow Show
Played in a box whose candle is the
Sun.
Round which we phantom Figures
Come and Go.

There is so much worthwhile literature. Did you ever read Macbeth? Richelieu?...

I wish you would visit with me a little bit in your letters. Do you wish you had gone East for this winter? Or are you satisfied with having gone West? Have you your camera? I would like a picture of the house you are staying in. Do you spend any time in the library? Have you met any one at all? Do you practice writing? Have you mingled at all in the festivities of the University. I listened in to the game Saturday and did not know whether I liked St. Mary's to win or not. I wanted the West to win but hated it to be Catholics.

I am sending the old watch, tape line and 35 cents from your own, plus some sox... This time I am letting Dad keep you supplied with money but if he neglects it tell me and I shall send some.

About your watch, I wish you would let us get you one for Christmas. You look at them and decide what kind you want. What do you say?

Well this is a long long letter, but I told you all this because if Dad and I could go as far as we have with the handicap we traveled under, you should have a lot of happiness and go a lot further than we did.

They held up the cafe next door to Olaf's this morning about six didn't get anything.
Lots of love,
Mother

Years later I discovered these letters tucked away inside a locked strong box. Vic's letter was a painful revelation about herself in the desperate hope of making a difference in her son's life. Only her son, who mattered more than life itself, could have brought about such an unprecedented opening up. After the letters were written they were hidden away and the contents never mentioned again. But for the fact that they weren't destroyed, I am grateful. They do help illuminate certain events and shed light upon the real person my grandmother was.

As Vic writes in her letter, her early life seemed to go from one painful experience of rejection to the next. Born the 10th of 12 children, little love or attention came her way. She had no memories of anyone holding her on their lap or hugging or kissing her. A week before her 11th birthday her mother died of TB. That same year her father remarried and moved to Chicago, deserting his children. Apparently this was not the first time he had abandoned a family. When he emigrated from Sweden, his first wife had also died and he left behind some children from that marriage.

After their mother died the oldest brother, Herman, wanted to keep the family together. So he took in the four youngest children. However, Laura, his wife, resented this obligation and treated them unkindly. Three years later, their oldest sister, Annie, invited them to come out to Denver to live with her and her husband—all except Vic. Why Vic wasn't invited also is not known. It wasn't simply her young age, since brother Roy was younger than she. It must have been a sad day in 1902 when the three Rosedahl children, Lottie, Otto and Roy were loaded up onto the buckboard and began the journey to Denver, leaving Vic behind. She stayed with Laura for another three lonely, miserable years—which she touches on in her letter. Finally she too went to Annie's in Denver to live, but she always felt unpopular with "The Doctor."

Vic's letter to her son was the first time she shared the story of her childhood with anyone (other than perhaps her husband.) A hard beginning for a young life. It left many scars. Never having been held and caressed, never having felt genuinely wanted by anyone, Vic felt basically unlovable and undeserving. Feeling unworthy of love was a source of great shame for Vic. As a result she kept the story of her childhood secret. She needed to hide her intrinsic wretchedness. This meant keeping secret the events that contributed to feeling such shame.

Sadly, Vic could not look back at her humble beginnings and feel proud of all she had accomplished. She was a college graduate at a time few women even went to college, a highly respected teacher, a loving wife and mother, and a caring friend to her neighbors. She was well respected in the Breckenridge community. Shame and secrecy kept her sense of unworthiness locked inside. Vic's outward success couldn't assuage her shame-filled interior. So it became terribly important that her son do well. She was determined to guide and encourage him as she wished she had been helped. Her pride revolved around his achieving success. Clifton felt the burden of his mother's needs.

An Unfortunate Choice

In spite of their valiant efforts, Cliff and Vic were not able to influence their son. Although he did end the "clandestine affair" with Ethel, he became entangled in another unfortunate rela-

tionship. While in California he met Gladys (not her real name) whom he married on September 12, 1935, in Denver. They lived in Leadville and he worked in the Climax Molybdenum mines on nearby Fremont Pass. But after only nine months Gladys left him and returned to California.

This entire phase of Clifton's life, his short marriage to a "lesser woman" (as Cliff referred to her in his letter) and subsequent divorce, disgraced his parents. They reacted to this shame in their customary way—by hiding it. Another skeleton in the closet. Another batch of papers in the strong box. Clifton's first wife and his divorce were never discussed again. Photographs didn't exist. They tried to erase the reality of this event from people's minds.

Years later when I discovered the locked strong box with the letters from Cliff and Vic, I also found packed away alongside them legal papers from Clifton's May 22, 1937, divorce hearing. Bitter accusations and denials were flung back and forth. He accused her of not getting up to prepare his breakfast, not packing his lunch bucket, and his having to help prepare the evening meal when he came home. She did not like to sweep the floor and was always nagging him to make more money. On the other hand, she accused Clifton of "drinking with (a friend) and laying around on the kitchen floor." A sad chapter had come to an end.

The Miller farm in Pierce, Nebraska, 1910. (left to right: Mother, Bertha holding baby Lenora, Arthur, Aunt Lena Schultz standing behind Frieda and Robert. Father, August Miller on the right.)

Lenora Miller (Peabody), A Nebraska Farm Girl

A year after his divorce, Clifton met a nice young woman from Nebraska, someone who met the approval of his parents. Lenora Anna Miller. They were married on February 12, 1939 in Denver. Lenora, like so many of my ancestors, was a farm girl who traveled West seeking a better life for herself. After high school graduation, she worked for eight years in the drugstore in the little town of Pierce, Nebraska. However, the prospects of finding a husband were diminishing and so off to the big city of Denver she went. Her older sister, Frieda, already worked there as a nurse at a TB sanitarium, and her two brothers, Art and Bob, soon followed.

Growing up on the farm had not been easy for Lenora. Her mother had been sick all of her childhood and spent a lot of time in bed. The children had a lot of work to do but received little maternal indulgence.

Lenora, too, told stories of walking the mile-and-a-half each way to school through blizzards and deep snow. (Perhaps everyone of that generation has similar tales.) Occasionally, however, they rode on the lumber wagon or a sled. Sometimes on the way to school they saw gypsies and horse traders. Frightened, they cut through the corn fields and came home the long way.

Lenora's sister, Frieda Miller (Stolte), tells the following story about growing up on the farm in Nebraska. I interviewed her on August 30, 1996. She was 90 years old, a lively, engaging and mentally sharp woman.

> Mother was born in Germany. She was about ten years old when she came to Nebraska. All of her brothers and sisters, except one, came over with her on the ship. Mother had one older sister who died of exposure coming over. Three days after they arrived here another sister died— probably also of exposure. My mother was deaf in Germany, but when she came over on the ship her ears popped from the salt water, and then she could hear after that.

> Mother always had a bad heart (rheumatic heart) and was not very strong. One year she missed school because of it. She'd have spells, and then survive and then all of a sudden get sick again.

Mother went through the fourth or fifth grade. Dad only went to the third grade in school. He was born in Davenport, Iowa. Mother and he met there in Iowa. When they got married she was eighteen, and then they moved out to the farm. She had us four kids there on the farm. Art was the oldest. Thirteen months later they had me. Fourteen months later they had Robert and then a four year span between Robert and Lenora, your mother.

Lenora had pneumonia when she was small maybe five or six. She was pampered a little bit because she was the baby and had been sick. In those days pneumonia was more serious than it is now. She was babied and spoiled. The four of us kids would have to walk a mile and a half to school. Sometimes we'd get started late. She was the youngest one and she didn't want to keep up with us. She hung on behind. We'd get quite a ways ahead of her and she'd start to cry and she'd always hold her breath and it'd scare us. She'd start to turn blue and we thought she was going to die. So then we'd have to walk back and get her. I guess we'd all spoil her because she was the youngest.

Dad and Mother's farm was 160 acres which was considered the average size for a farm. It was about three and a half miles outside of Pierce. We had a barn and a granary, a chicken house and hog house, and a pig pen—we had all these buildings up on the hill. And an old wind mill— we used to take our butter and milk and cream and put it in a big container and put a rope around the handle and lower it down to the bottom of the well to keep it cool.

There were two bedrooms upstairs and three rooms downstairs—a large kitchen, a parlor and one bedroom. No bath room facilities, just a back house out behind the house with two holes in it and a catalogue. We'd sit in it sometimes when we were supposed to do the dishes. We'd go and sit there and read the catalogue. It served both as reading material and toilet paper. It was kind of rough but it did the job. If we wanted to get out of doing any work or chores that mother would ask us to do, we'd run out to the back house.

We had quite a few hogs. Usually some of the neighbors got together and we'd do the butchering. And then we'd make our own sausages and everything and render the lard to get the fat from it. To butcher, they'd get the hog and tie its legs together and put it on its back and take a butcher knife and cut the neck and let the blood drain out. That's the way it died. It wasn't very pleasant to watch. Then they made the blood sausage. I don't know if you know what that is. My mother would have a big bowl and when the blood ran out of the neck, she let it run in that bowl. And then she put vinegar in so it wouldn't clot and make blood sausage from it. They put a lot of raisins in it and boiled it. And it was good stuff!

They'd also make liver sausage and smoked sausage because we had a smoke house. The neighbors would get together and help each other out and the kids would have a lot of fun. My mother killed the rooster for dinner. She'd take the head of the chicken and twist it and wring its neck. And that would kill it. I never cared about doing these things. For Thanksgiving we had a goose. I never saw a turkey until I came to Denver.

We made our own bread. I'd take a great big dish pan and I'd take it to where my mother was in bed and not able to get up. I'd add the flour and stir it and knead it besides her bedside so she could watch and show me how to do it.

Usually when we got home from school we had lot of chores to do. Mother had these heart spells, was sick a lot. So we had to take over a lot of things. One year she went to Pierce where she stayed all winter under a doctor's care. They decided she should be in town because it was horse and buggy days and the doctor couldn't come out to the farm easily. They took Lenora along because she was small, and I had to take over the household duties. I was about eleven or twelve. So that year I didn't get to go to school at all. I had to miss a whole year, but my brothers got to go to school.

I had to manage everything in the house. I did the cooking for my

Lenora Miller Peabody, 1928 high school photograph.

two brothers and father. Dad helped what he could in the winter but in spring he had outside work to do. We had some cows and I had to wash that separator. I had to do the clothes washing for the family in the old fashioned machine with the hand wringer. We had quite a few chickens so we had to gather the eggs and get them ready for Dad to take to town market. Gathering eggs is one job I hated to do because the old clucks always picked at you when you went to get the eggs. And then I'd throw cobs at them and the whole nest would be full of cobs. On Saturday we had to pick up the cobs down at the hog pen for fuel. We gave the corn to hogs to eat and then after they were through we'd start fires with them. They burn well.

I was about thirteen when we moved to town. We moved to Pierce because Dad couldn't take care of mother and the farm also. I had to take the eighth grade twice because of missing that one year. It seemed like the responsibility of all the work on the farm and the responsibility of raising all us kids was too much for her. Living in Pierce she kind of got better, she relaxed more.

All Dad could do was farm work. So he did odd jobs after mov-ing. He had a truck and did some trucking. Then he got some money from the farm. I think it was a hundred dollars an acre, or maybe less than that. So then we built a home in Pierce. Later on he went into the ice business. We had some rivers around Pierce. We didn't have refrigeration like they do now, so they got these big blocks of ice and he built a big building to store the ice blocks in and delivered ice around town. They packed the ice in saw dust to keep it from melting. Later when they started to have electric refrigeration that did away with the ice business. So he got a job at the high school as a janitor.

All of us kids eventually came to Denver. And then after Mother died Dad was lonely and came out to Denver too.

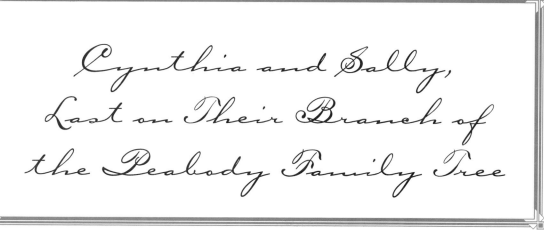

Cynthia and Sally, Last on Their Branch of the Peabody Family Tree

Clifton and Lenora made their first home in Denver, but shortly after their marriage Clifton was called away to join the wartime effort. He worked in Bridgeport, Connecticut, making ammunition for our troops to use in WW II.

In the midst of this war activity, their first child made her appearance. That was I, Cynthia Charlotte, born on June 18, 1941. I was named after Grama's sister, Charlotte Rosedahl Rader, M.D. (I think my family had high hopes I would one day follow in Aunt Lottie's footsteps and become a doctor.) Although Clifton could not come home to be with his young wife, his parents, Cliff and Vic, were there to help her. This began their important presence in my life. Another little girl,

The Wedding. Are we having fun yet?

Cindy and Daddy, getting a ride on Omar.

Sally Anne, followed three years later.

I was keenly aware of my father's and grandparents' disappointment that neither of us was a boy. My parents had no sons, and so with the addition of this last little twig, our particular branch would grow no more. An end had come to 11 generation of Peabodys.

Perhaps an unconscious motivation for writing this book has been to make known the lives of our ancestors for generations to come. I could not perpetuate the Peabody name, but I can carry forth the family story.

I grew up in Denver and spent a lot of time in Summit County at my grandparents' ranch. Eventually I became a clinical social worker and moved to California—like my father and grandfather. There I met the love of my life, Ted Anderson. When we mar-

ried on July 13, 1968, I became the instant mother of his sweet seven-year-old twins, Scott and Sandy. The four of us, plus golden retriever dog, reversing the flow of the preceding ten generations, journeyed eastward, back across the continent to Lexington, Massachusetts, where we made our home. Soon two more children, Karyn and Brett, joined the family.

The years came and went. Now, as a grandmother myself, I think back to the happy times spent with my grandparents at their ranch.

Elmer Clifton Peabody, Sr. with great Dane, Omar.

Childhood at the Ranch

There are all those early memories.
One cannot get another set.
　　—Willa Cather

It is another white knuckle drive to the ranch. The wind is howling, snow is coming down in sheets, and we are inching our way up and over Loveland Pass. Cars are stopped and strewn every which way as drivers put on chains or dig out of snow banks. We try to keep moving and hope the car ahead of us doesn't stop. If we lose our momentum we'll be stuck too. Then Daddy will have to get out, lie in the snow and struggle with putting chains on also.

Everyone is scared. My little sister, Sally, and I begin to bicker and cry, Mamma yells at us and Daddy shouts at her. We proceed in silence.

On one side the ground falls sharply away thousands of feet to the valley below. All we can see is swirling whiteness outside. Mamma rolls down her window so she can tell Daddy when we are getting too close to the edge. Guard rails are nonexistent and my imagination is full of frightening pictures of our car sliding off the road and tumbling over and over down the mountainside to the river far below.

In 1948 when I was seven years old, Loveland Pass was still a two-lane gravel road that snaked its way over the Continental Divide. It wasn't until 1973 that the Eisenhower tunnel was constructed. Travel in the wintertime over the high pass was often treacherous. Snowslides frequently buried the roadway and occasionally engulfed cars unfortunate enough to be in their path. We heard tales of runaway trucks losing their brakes, careening out of control down the highway, and ultimately crashing over the embankment to the valley below.

Throughout my childhood the four of us made the long drive from Denver to the ranch every other weekend. In the summertime, however, Sally and I stayed with Pags and Grama the entire time and didn't join our parents on their trips back and forth.

Descending from Loveland Pass we entered into the gorgeous Blue River valley, rimmed by the spectacular Ten Mile and Gore Ranges. I had arrived at heaven once again. We drove through the village of Dillon with its single main street and false-fronted buildings. (Today a dam and reservoir occupy the Dillon site.) Following the Blue River northward we passed many beautiful ranches nestled beneath the slopes of majestic Buffalo, Red, Keller and other

Gore Range peaks. Twelve miles later we rounded the last curve and my grandparents' Clover Meadow Ranch lay in the distance. We breathed a sigh of relief. We were home.

My worries stayed behind in Denver. I was a carefree child once again. My father had a lifelong struggle with alcoholism which he found especially difficult to control in the city. At the ranch he had less of a problem, and there we found it easier to pretend that drinking wasn't an issue. Our family had its own hard time dealing with it. We never talked about alcohol. At the ranch I felt secure, free from worry about him. I sometimes felt lonely there, because my only playmate was my sister. But the serenity and peace easily offset my lack of playmates.

Wintertime Fun

Grama was a plump, jolly woman who usually had a twinkle in her eye. She'd be bustling around the kitchen when we stomped in from the cold. Pags had shoveled a path through the snow drifts and helped us carry in all our bundles. The other family member waiting to greet us with great enthusiasm and tail wagging was our Great Dane, Lance. I was as happy to see him as any playmate.

Delicious aromas filled the house. Soon, steaming bowls were brought to the round oak table in the dining room. Split pea and ham soup, hot corn bread and honey, and bread pudding for dessert revived our spirits after the anxiety-laden trip.

We finished supper quite late, time for Sally and me to go to bed. The upstairs bedrooms were cold in the wintertime. So, to make crawling into our featherbeds more endurable, Grama heated up flat irons on the kitchen stove and wrapped them in newspapers and towels. She buried these under our quilts to add some warmth to the foot of our beds. It was still pretty chilly, though. I'd pull the covers over my head and start counting as I warmed the air with my breath. Usually I'd be sound asleep before I reached twenty.

The next morning I'd awaken to the smell and sound of bacon sizzling. Pags and Grama had been up since before dawn starting the fires and getting the house warmed up. While Grama cooked breakfast, Pags went to the barn to do the milking and outside chores.

A ranch breakfast was like none other. First came fruit or homemade rhubarb juice, and then a bowl of hot oatmeal. Grama topped this with brown sugar and a big dollop of butter or smothered the oatmeal with thick, thick cream. The cream was so thick it had to be spooned on. But this was only a beginning. The main course, pancakes and fried eggs and some kind of meat (bacon, sausage, or venison) followed. This was the typical breakfast, served every day of the week at the ranch. None of us thought about calories or knew about fat content in those days.

Then outside to play in the snow. Sometimes six-or-eight-foot high drifts

Cindy and Sally, winter-time fun at the ranch.

formed on the downwind side of the outbuildings. These were perfect for carving tunnels and caves. We also had fun skating and skiing, despite our rudimentary equipment. There were no ponds nearby, so we shoveled the snow off the ice on the irrigation ditches. Pags built a big bonfire and the family huddled around it while Sally and I made forays, skating up and down the frozen ditches.

Skiing then didn't resemble skiing today. Our skis were long, heavy and wooden. We wore a pair of galoshes and fit the toe under a laced webbing on the ski. A leather strap around the heel kept our galoshes attached. No quick release bindings! However, the heels of my feet could move freely around, not only up and down, but back and forth sideways too.

We did all our skiing on the gentle hills of the ranch meadows. We side-stepped up and then coasted down in a straight line, usually in the same track. When we drove back to Denver over Loveland Pass, I was fascinated watching the skiers at Arapaho Basin carving turns on the steep slopes. I found it such a mystery how they could make their skis turn. When I'd try to turn my ski, my foot would twist sideways but this had no effect at all upon the ski. The skis had a mind of their own, continuing in their own straight line. It wasn't until years later when I had better equipment that I solved the mystery of turning. Learning to handle those long, heavy skis was quite frustrating.

Christmas highlighted our winter. When we arrived at the ranch with our car packed full of mysterious boxes and bags, a glittering Christmas tree greeted us in the living room. Earlier in the day Pags had chopped down a blue spruce from an evergreen grove at the far end of the place. Grama had strings of popcorn and cranberries and gingerbread cookies all ready to decorate the tree.

The anticipation of presents on Christmas morning was as much fun as the actual opening of them. On Christmas Eve Sally and I snuggled together in Pags and Grama's bed and wondered what wonderful surprises were hidden inside the boxes with brightly colored paper and ribbons and bows. What would Santa bring? Actually I never believed in Santa Claus. My dad felt it was wrong to lie to his children, even to tell them a benign story about an old man flying through the air with a sleigh full of toys. So even as little children we were told Santa is the spirit of giving. I think I would have preferred him to lie about Santa.

In the morning we had to hold our excitement for a while longer. We opened our stockings, but the presents had to wait until Grama's bountiful breakfast was cooked, consumed and cleaned up. The wait seemed interminable. In addition to the typical ranch breakfast, a real delicacy was served. Calf brains! Grama served this special treat only on Thanksgiving, Christmas and Easter mornings. The brains were fried in butter and then scrambled with eggs. Yum! Years later I tried on several occasions to introduce my family to calf brains, but the dish was not a winner. (I enjoy them now only in my memories.) At long last the family gathered around the tree to open the presents.

At lunch we had oyster stew. Then came Christmas dinner, a duplicate of Thanksgiving—raw oysters in cocktail sauce, roasted turkey stuffed with giblet dressing and an oyster stuffing on the side. (Just as the early miners loved their oysters, my grandparents also considered them a special treat and served them in a variety of ways.) Mashed potatoes and gravy, sweet potatoes with toasted marshmallows, cranberries, peas, rolls, pumpkin, mincemeat and apple pies and homemade ice cream rounded out Grama's menu. The works! My mother and grandmother spent all day, and several days before that, in the kitchen preparing the feast. Grama set the Christmas table with her beautiful crystal and china for the occasion.

After dinner we sat around the table listening to Pags reminisce about the old days—how much a dozen of eggs or a pound of bacon cost or one of his many exploits as a young man. We had fun picturing him as a boy getting into mischief, tipping over out-houses, and playing tricks at Halloween. Grama said little about her own youth.

Carefree Summers

Summertime was my happiest time at the ranch. Instead of just the week-ends Sally and I stayed with Pags and Grama the entire summer. These were carefree days. I roamed the meadows, explored the outbuildings, and played down by the river. For days on end neither a comb nor brush would come near my hair. I wore the same raggedy clothes over and over. But I was happy. I didn't have to dress up or perform or "make nice" for anybody. That was reserved for Denver. At the ranch I could be myself, oblivious to the cares and demands of the real world.

Grama was like a mother to me. She took the burden of worry and family responsibility off my frail shoulders. I didn't feel as smiling or brave on my inside as I looked on the outside. At home in Denver my mother worked long evenings in a drug store. That left me to cook the dinner, supervise my sister and try to keep things running smoothly so as not to upset my father. I tiptoed around him. His alcohol problem dominated the household and made his behavior unpredictable and scary. At the ranch Grama was there to take care of me. I could be a child.

We had few toys at the ranch. The various sheds and outbuildings became my playground. Each one has its set of memories. I remember the barn. In addition to the cows and horses, a dozen or more cats made this home. We never knew the exact count of our cats at any one time because they multiplied like rabbits. These "mousers" (as Grama called them) performed a vital function for the ranch. Each day (or night, more accurately) the cats ambled out into the meadows and proudly

Cindy and Sally at the ranch. A couple of happy ragamuffins.

returned with their trophy—a fat, juicy field mouse. We never fed these cats except occasionally in the winter—they were completely self-supporting.

Above the cow barn was the loft where hay was stored after the fall mowing. Using a pitch fork, Pags dropped hay through a floor opening to the cows feeding in the stall below. Old leather harnesses, saddles and bridles hung by rusty nails on the huge log walls of the barn—dusty reminders of earlier days when Pags plowed the fields with a team of work horses.

Prim and proper Denver girls.

For our pleasure, Pags strapped an old saddle to a broken down tractor in the yard. I had hours of fun riding my makeshift horse across the range, lassoing cattle, and galloping down the trail in hot pursuit of robbers and bandits. Later on when I was older, I enjoyed putting a bridle on my real horse and riding bareback across the meadows.

In the cow barn I witnessed a most unusual, strangely exotic event—before I knew anything about the facts of life. One day as I was playing with the newest batch of kittens, I suddenly became aware of our cow lying on the floor and behaving in a most bizarre manner. She was breathing hard and struggling and in a lot of pain. At first I didn't know what was happening. I watched, transfixed. Slowly, and with considerable effort, she gave birth to a baby calf. It was an unreal experience at my tender age to see this enormous, wet blob gradually emerge from the cow's belly. He lay for a few minutes in a heap at his mother's feet—a huge, wet, slimy heap. Before long he began to move and with great difficulty struggled to his feet. Then he was a living, breathing calf.

When the little calf had outgrown his need for his mother, she needed to be milked—twice a day. That was not optional. Pags or Grama squatted on the three-legged stool, while various cats milled around hoping for a squirt aimed in their direction. The sounds at milking time are peaceful and intimate—the woosh, woosh, wooshing as streams of milk squirt against the sides of the bucket; mother cow contentedly munching away on her grain; the swishing of the cow's tail chasing away flies from her back; and Pags occasionally conversing with her, "So, boss... so, boss." Sometimes I begged him to let me try, but when I squeezed her teat I never got any milk.

After milking, Pags carried the buckets of warm milk into the pump house where the cream separator was located. He poured the milk into the top, and as I turned the crank, cream came out one spigot and milk came out the other. Also in the pump house was the well, which was our only source of water for the house.

Dressing Lance up—he was always such a good sport.

Pags and Grama were proud of making their own electricity. They did this for many years before power arrived at the ranches on the Blue from the Green Mountain Dam. When I was a child most of the ranches still used kerosene lamps for lighting. But my grandparents generated electricity with a wind charger. Batteries, found in the pump house, stored the electricity.

A long breezeway connected the pump house to the cellar house where steps led down to an underground room. The shelves in this cool cave-like room were packed with fruit and meat Grama had canned. Rows of glass jars also preserved pickles and tomatoes and other vegetables from her garden. Attached to the cellar house was a shed where wood, coal and ice were stored. Since we had no refrigeration other than an icebox to keep food cool, an ice truck delivered blocks of ice two or three times a year. These blocks lasted for months at a time. Pags buried the ice in sawdust in the shed to keep it from melting. He used big ice tongs to fish another block out of the sawdust when the ice had melted in the icebox.

Pags and Grama nicknamed one of the storage buildings the "Skunk House." I never grew tired of hearing Pags tell the story about a skunk who became disoriented and wandered into this shed one day. When the skunk discovered he was trapped, he did what all frightened skunks do—he sprayed everything. Pags had to take a bath in tomato juice and scrub himself for a long time to get rid of the odor. The smell never did leave the shed interior. To this day I think one could walk into the skunk house and still smell his presence.

Speaking of smells, a two-holer outhouse happened to be located next to the skunk house. Our family uses this outdoor bathroom even to the present day, even though indoor plumbing was installed years ago. As a little girl, I sat reading the pages from the 1920's magazines and calendars that decorated the walls. A strange thought popped into my head. Why didn't the hole in the outhouse ever fill up? For many decades the same outhouse has been used, but there's always room for more. To my knowledge no one has ever come to dig a new outhouse hole or shovel out this one. This bottomless pit was one of my childhood mysteries.

Walking down the little hill beyond the house, we come to a most unusual structure—a cyclone cellar. Years earlier, when homesteading the ranch, Pags dug out this small cave-like room from the hillside. He had hoped to help his young bride feel more secure living on the ranch miles from civilization. Grama was deathly afraid of tornadoes, and though they were unheard of in the Colorado mountains, she never got over her fear. Grama carefully instructed us that if a cyclone should suddenly descend, we must all run to this place of safety and take refuge until the storm had passed. Now, after learning more about her childhood growing up on the Kansas prairie, I can appreciate her anxiety.

The blacksmith shop was a short distance from the storm cellar. I liked watching Pags fire up the old forge and heat a piece of iron until it was fiery red hot. While it was hot and pliable he banged the iron out on the anvil until it took the shape he intended. Pags made all the shoes for his work horses this way.

Near the blacksmith shop was the pigpen which connected to the chicken house. Grama no longer had any pigs when I was a child, but she always had an abundance of chickens. Each spring time we brought a new batch of baby chicks from Denver. They required special care at first, needing warmth to survive. Though cute as little chicks, I didn't like them as grown hens. They could be mean. I hated the job of gathering eggs, but it had to be done every day. I was scared to reach my hand under an old hen sitting on her nest for fear she would peck me.

Our chickens had a good life. Unlike chickens these days who spend their entire lives cooped up in a little one by four foot wire cage producing eggs until it is time to be slaughtered, our chickens roamed free. They especially liked to wander up to the back door of the house. Grama had what we called the "slop bucket" into which she put all the food scraps and everything that nowadays we put down the garbage disposal. Every day she tossed out the contents of the slop bucket on the ground just outside the back door. This was a special treat for the chickens and they'd come scurrying from all around. They never knew how good they had it. At least, that is, until it came their turn for the cooking pot.

Cindy driving tractor to a family picnic at the camp grounds.

Whang-doodling the Rooster

Watching Pags "whang-doodle" the rooster was one of the week's most dramatic events. I don't remember how he caught the chicken, but once he had hold of its legs in one hand, he used his other hand to jam the chicken's neck between two big nails which were driven partway into a big stump. Then, still holding the legs, he'd grasp the handle of a heavy, sharp hand axe and bring it down upon the chicken's neck with a huge whack. The head went flying like the top of a carrot chopped off with a kitchen knife. Pags held tightly onto the legs of the headless chicken for several minutes as it flapped its wings in terrible spasms. Blood from the severed neck splattered everywhere. It was quite a horrific sight to witness as a little girl—but one I would not have missed.

Then Grama took over. She heated a big kettle of water on the wood stove and dunked the chicken into the boiling water for a couple of minutes. I disliked the job of pulling out the feathers and pin feathers. The smell of scalded chicken feathers disgusted me. But I had fun watching Grama clean out the innards. She identified the different body parts as she reached in and pulled out slimy handfuls of intestines, heart, liver, gizzard. Finally she had the chicken ready for the cooking pot. Getting a chicken from backyard to table every week was a production.

In fact, many of the activities necessary for daily existence were quite a production. Churning butter, for example. I sat for what seemed an eternity lifting the dasher stick up and down to agitate the cream in the churn. Finally, butter globules began to form, clump together and separate out from the liquid. Both my mother and grandmother delighted in buttermilk, the milky liquid remaining after the heavy cream had been transformed into butter. Buttermilk was their favorite beverage, probably because they both had been raised on a farm. I never shared their enthusiasm.

Grama maintained a large garden and raised all of her own vegetables—peas, green beans, zucchini, yellow squash, turnips, potatoes, onions, carrots, and tomatoes. Every summer she made valiant efforts to grow strawberries. But somehow the birds knew to come the day before we were ready to pick them. Eagerly Grama came to her garden to pick a big bowl full of strawberries, then with dismay realized that not a single red berry remained. She would exclaim, "Oh, piffle!" (a favorite expression of hers).

However, her rhubarb was bountiful. We had rhubarb sauce, rhubarb pie, rhubarb jam and, best of all, lots of rhubarb juice. Summit County has a short growing season due to its high altitude (9,000 feet), but Grama managed to feed her entire family from what the garden produced. Many of the root vegetables—potatoes, turnips, carrots and beets—kept for a long time down in the cellar, and Grama also canned a lot of fruit and vegetables which we used throughout the winter.

Weekly Chores

Life on the ranch followed a predictable routine. Monday was wash day. We pumped the wash water from the well in the pump house, lugged it into the kitchen and heated it on the wood stove. Then we carried it back to the pump house and filled the laundry tubs. The washing machine had a motorized agitator, but the wringer we turned by hand to feed the soapy clothes into the first rinse tub. We transferred the clothes into a second rinse tub with bluing in it, and from there into the clothes basket. Then we carried the wash out to the clothes reel and hung it up to dry—an all-day job.

Speaking of soap, Grama made all her own laundry soap. Like many pioneer women before her, she saved the ashes from the wood burning stove and poured hot water over them to make an alkali called potash. Then she boiled this potash in a big kettle with bacon drippings and grease leftover from cooking. This made big slabs of soap which she cut up into chunks. This soap cleaned well but was very harsh, and as I remember, had a terrible odor. We only used it for laundry.

Tuesday was ironing day. Before polyester and no-iron fabrics all material was cotton, linen or wool, and had to be ironed. Grama heated the heavy flat irons on the top of the kitchen wood stove and worked quickly to press the heavy material. When one iron cooled off she put it back on the stove to be heated again while she used another hot one. When I was quite young she let me iron the pillow cases and Pags' handkerchiefs. Later on she taught me how to iron shirts, trousers and dresses.

Wednesday was housecleaning day—dusting, wet and dry mopping the floors, changing the beds, and sparkling up the house. Grama took great pride in her beautiful home. The elegant French doors that opened into the spacious, attractive living room... the upright piano... the double set of couches on either side of the cheerful fireplace... the beautifully patterned carpet all represented prosperity and respectability to her. Several diplomas hung on the wall next to the piano. I can't begin to tell you the number of times Grama pointed these out to me (and to any visitor who stopped by). She told with pride that her son had graduated from CU, the youngest student at that time to receive a degree in Engineering.

One of Grama's proudest possessions was her dining room china cupboard. She and Pags purchased this early in their marriage. She loved showing off her fine crystal and china, her collection of souvenir spoons and plates from around the world. She especially liked to show us the small bowl Pags salvaged from the San Francisco earthquake and fire and brought home to his mother. Two or three times a year, Grama ironed her fine white linen table cloth and brought out her beautiful dishes to set the table for Thanksgiving or Christmas. Now, having discovered the humiliation she felt by her own emotionally impoverished beginnings, I understand her pride in these beautiful things.

The ranch thrived when Pags and Grama lived there. They maintained the house and out-buildings. Flowers bloomed in the garden, and the meadows and vegetable garden gave bountiful harvests. I feel sad and nostalgic when I see it now. The beautiful ranch of my childhood has fallen into disrepair and now is ramshackle and dilapidated. The house is filthy, the buildings are crumbling and the life has gone out of it.

But we're not ready to leave the 1950's yet...

Thursday we went to town—Dillon or Breckenridge—to shop and take care of business. Since this was a special day, Sally and I had our weekly bath and shampoo in the kitchen the night before. Grama filled a big metal tub with water she had heated on the kitchen stove. Sally and I took turns having our baths. Since there were only two of us, the water didn't get terribly dirty for the second one to take a bath. I think back to the large families of my ancestors. The children last in line to bathe had to climb into the dirty, cold water of six or eight siblings.

A trip to town meant Pags and Grama dressed up in their very best clothes. Grama pulled on her corset, hooked up her nylon stockings, smeared a dab of lipstick on her lips, and donned a pretty dress for the occasion. She always asked us if the seams of her nylons were straight. Pags looked handsome in his three-piece suit and dress hat.

Dillon, as I knew it in the '50's, was no longer a thriving town. It consisted of two parallel streets about five blocks

Five-cent candy bars and Classic comics highlighted the Peabody girls' visits to Old Dillon.

long. Located on Main Street were Lege's General Store, the City Market, the Dillon Drug and a gas station at the junction of US Highway 6 and Colorado 9. The school and church and some other random buildings were found on Back Street. But the predominant business establishments were the saloons and liquor stores—eight of these watering holes in a town of 80 residents! The Mint, the Antlers, the Arapaho Cafe and the Dillon Inn were popular with the local ranchers.

Breckenridge in the '50's was even more of a fading town. Except for a few die-hard saloons with their faithful patrons, nothing much was going on there. Many houses and stores stood empty, never dreaming that better times lay around the corner. Sometimes

Pags and Grama had business to take care of at the courthouse. They showed us the office where they both had worked when they served as the county clerk and recorder. What intrigued me most was a visit downstairs and peering in the jail, or the "hoosegow", as Pags called it.

While Pags and Grama stocked up on supplies and visited with old friends, Sally and I picked out our week's supply of five-cent candy bars. A special treat was a new Classic cartoon book to add to my collection. In those days many wonderful works of literature were re-written for children in the form of comic books. A wide assortment, including everything from A Tale of Two Cities to Huckleberry Finn, could be found. Before beginning the ride home we usually stopped for an ice cream cone—five cents bought a single scoop or ten cents a double dip. Driving north on Route 9, we passed many beautiful ranches on the Blue—the Rice's, the Lowe's, the Mumford's, the Hill's, the Knorr's, the Culbreath's, the Rouse's, the Smith's, the Marshall's and the Long's. Pags and Grama gossiped about how well each rancher's crops were growing, who had begun their haying, and how much of a yield they were getting.

Before we knew it, Friday had come and we were excited to see our parents again. The weekend flew by. No sooner had we kissed them hello, than Sunday arrived and we were kissing them good-bye as they headed back to Denver.

Along with this weekly routine lots of other chores had to be done. In those days much more was prepared from scratch. For meals Pags butchered chickens, pigs and cattle. We caught trout, baked bread, rolled out egg noo-dles, ground meat, shelled peas, churned butter, and canned vegetables, fruit and jam. All our cookies and pies, cakes and puddings were made from scratch. And, of course, we made our own ice cream in the hand-cranked freezer.

We even made our own "pop" (as we Westerners called it). First we poured root beer or ginger beer fla-vored liquid into clear glass bottles. A cartridge of CO_2 added the fizz, and then we sealed the bottles with a bottle-capper. We always thought it was more delicious than store-bought pop.

Each year Pags and Daddy went deer hunting and often came home with a deer or two strapped over their car fenders. I had little desire to kill such a beautiful creature myself, but Sally sometimes went hunting with them and shot her own deer. I did enjoy helping them skin and butcher the carcass. We wrapped the chops and steaks, and Daddy took them to a commercial freezer in Denver where they were stored until we were ready to use them.

A Sense of Wonder

Though I spent a lot of time help-ing Pags and Grama with the running of the ranch, (within my ability as an eight, ten or twelve-year old), when the chores were done, I was free to play and be lost in the fun or the wonder of the moment. I remember these carefree times the most.

I loved swinging with Grama in the hammock under the trees, watching the clouds float by. We played a special game in which clouds became animals or our imaginary friends. As we watched they dissolved or drifted away or trans-formed themselves into new and differ-ent shapes. At night Pags took us out to look at the stars and taught us some of the constellations—the Little and Big Dippers, the North Star, Cassiopeia. Sometimes we saw a shooting star. The night-time sky at the ranch, far away from the lights of civilization, was bril-liant, the stars dazzling.

Like the clouds drifting across the sky, a stream of happy memories still floats through my mind. The first time sleeping alone outside in a tent. Swinging from a rope in the hayloft and landing in the soft hay. Chasing butterflies in the meadow, floating imaginary boats down the ditch, collecting wild flowers by the river. More passing pictures—dressing up our big dog Lance in Pags' shirt and trousers, bob sledding with the family all piled high, playing baseball games in the backyard, hide and seek among the outbuildings, gin rummy around the dining room table.

Our grandparents believed it important that we knew how to swim (since they had never learned). Pags built a small concrete swimming pool in the front yard—an unheard of luxury in those days. He even rigged up a hot water boiler contraption to heat water for the pool. After splashing around in the water and practicing our swimming strokes, we sprawled out on our gentle Great Dane, Lance, and warmed ourselves in the hot sun. To further encourage our swimming, Pags and Grama took us on outings to hot springs swimming pools in the Colorado mountains. These pools, heated by underground springs, were Hot Sulphur, Steamboat, Princeton and, my favorite, Glenwood Hot Springs.

When we weren't swimming we were camping. Our campground was at the southern end of the ranch, nestled under a canopy of huge evergreen trees. The Blue River rushed by. I learned how to drive the tractor when I was ten years old and was given the proud honor of driving the family to the campground. We frequently packed up our cooking and camping gear, loaded the wagon and hooked it to the tractor. The whole family, including Lance, climbed aboard and headed off for a picnic or campout. While Grama and Mamma bustled around the fireplace cooking dinner, Pags and Daddy fished, Lance guarded the area from squirrels and chipmunks, and Sally and I built sand castles down by the river.

Sometimes we slept under the stars at the campground. We didn't own a sleeping bag in those days. Instead, Pags and Grama constructed a rudimentary bed with some old mattress springs on a plank. I remember it as lumpy and bumpy, but Sally and I, snuggling between Pags and Grama, felt warm and safe.

It was an adventure. We listened to the wind whispering in the pine trees and the eerie sound of coyotes howling in the darkness. Pags told us about finding Indian arrowheads years ago when he was plowing the meadow with a team of horses. Grama talked about the Ute Indian Chief Colorow and how frightened the women were when he looked at them through the windows of the miner's cabins. We talked about coyotes and bears, gophers and beavers. And Grama told us about the quaking aspens. Of all the trees in Colorado, she thought these were the most beautiful. She loved the spectacular colors of red, yellow and orange they turned in the fall. Grama told us the story about why the leaves quake, why they are in incessant motion. The story goes that as Jesus walked to his crucifixion he passed

Sally and Great Dane, Lance, after a swim.

under an aspen tree. It began to tremble in sympathy for him. Never in all the years since have the quaking aspens stopped trembling.

Both Pags and Grama instilled in me a sense of wonder of the natural world and a joy in exploring the outdoors. On many occasions they told us how millions of years ago this whole area was covered by an ocean. This was hard to imagine. But we found evidence for this on a steep hillside of shale just a mile south of the ranch. While Pags worked to clear beaver dams from the ditch, Sally and I scrambled and slid

around on the hillside. We collected snail shells and shale rocks which had the imprint of clam shells in them. Sally and I had to believe, as incredible as it seemed, that this high mountain country was once submerged under water. We also found another curiosity scattered around the hillside and imbedded in the shale: small perfectly round, iron-like rocks. Pags called them meteorites. I don't think this could be accurate, but what they are is still a mystery to me.

Because Pags was a miner I picked up his interest in rocks and minerals. He had been the mining superintendent at the Wilfley Mine for many years and sometimes enjoyed going back and reminiscing with his old cronies. The Wilfley, located 20 miles from Leadville, led its competitors in the rich silver lodes around Kokomo in Summit County's upper Ten Mile Canyon. Kokomo, diminished in size from its glory days, was abandoned in 1965 when Climax Molybdenum Company purchased its site. Kokomo is now entirely buried underneath the settling ponds of Climax. Nothing remains of the town today.

I still remember our visit to the Wilfley mine. When all the machinery was operating, what a loud clatter banging place it was! Our trip into the deep underground left a lasting impression on me. Pags bundled Sally and me up in warm clothes and the three of us climbed into the ore car. Wearing miner's lamps on our heads we entered the underground darkness. The ore car followed the winding tracks into blackness. It was dark, damp and spooky. If one were inclined towards claustrophobia, this would be the time to panic. I imagined the earth suddenly giving way and being buried under tons and tons of rock. The musty smell of the air, the dampness and dripping water, the fear of timbers caving in under the sheer weight of the earth pressing down—all made for an eerie feeling. But we children had fun, and an experience we never forgot.

One of Grama's pleasures was berry picking. All the old timers in the valley had their favorite patches which they never divulged to anyone. Officer's Gulch was one of her spots. But a hillside above Montezuma was Grama's most prized location. Here the rare, wild black currants were found. Her black currant jam was the best! Each time we went to Montezuma we also searched around the hillsides until we found a secret underground spring from which trickled a special kind of soda water. We filled our jugs, added a little lemon and sugar, and what a delicious drink we had!

Another favorite berry picking spot was up Boulder Creek. The remains of the old Peabody Ranch where Pags' parents had homesteaded in the early 1900's was located in a clearing about a mile and a half from the highway towards Boulder Lake A broken down old cabin still remained when I was a child, but now there is no sign of it. Berry picking, of course, really meant Grama picked while Sally and I played. I remember on one of those trips up Boulder Creek, when I was very young, I drifted away from Grama. When I looked up to find her, a big brown bear stood between me and Grama down the trail. I don't remember what happened next. He probably just ambled away. But after that Grama kept a closer watch over me.

A Ten-Year-Old's Ambitious Plan

What adventures we had! One summer day when I was about ten years old I dreamed up the scheme of hiking to the top of Ute Mountain with my little sister. Sally was only seven at the time and a willing follower of her big sister.

A few days earlier I had returned from my first time away at sleepover camp. There I'd had my first experience hiking and camping out overnight and I was eager to try my newly learned skills. I was freshly equipped with the knowledge of how to fold a two-blanket bed roll, build a teepee campfire, and cook s'mores and pigs-in-a-blanket hot dogs over the fire.

So Grama, participating in our enthusiasm, helped us roll our blankets and pack up some food, a flashlight and warm jackets. Thinking we would soon give up our childish fantasy, Pags and Grama waved good-bye to their two little granddaughters as they trundled off down the road.

We walked about half a mile and then left the road and began climbing the slopes of Ute. I had it all planned in my mind which route we would follow to get to the top. We were not following any trail, just the slope of the hill upwards. We trudged on and on, but felt weighted down by the knapsacks on our backs. After awhile we began to get tired and Sally started to cry. So we found a bare spot in the midst of the sagebrush and laid our bed rolls down and decided to have some lunch. A head of cattle were grazing and milling around. Did they wonder what these two little girls were doing in the middle of nowhere?

Sitting on our bed rolls, we opened up a can of sardines for lunch. We had just finished eating a package of dry chocolate pudding mix (our favorite treat as children) when over the hill came Pags! What was he doing here? Our surprise and pleasure quickly dissolved into fear when we realized he was mad! I had never seen him so furious. The only other time Pags had ever been angry at me was when he caught me chewing bubble gum in the barn. (He hated to see anyone chewing gum.) We were totally perplexed. This was so unlike our gentle, easygoing grandfather. We could not understand what we had done so wrong.

In about 30 seconds he whisked up all of our gear and marched us back down the hillside to where he had left the car. On the way back Pags scolded us for running away. He said if we were so unhappy spending the summer at the ranch he would drive us back to Denver tomorrow. I felt awful. I was disappointed to have our adventure cut short, and I was heartbroken that I had upset my grandparents. And I did not want to be taken back to Denver.

Pags and Grama were mortified that they had allowed their small granddaughters to venture off by themselves into the mountains. They felt they had risked our being trampled by a herd of wild cattle, gobbled up by coyotes at night, frozen to death in the cold mountain air or getting hopelessly lost in the wilderness. Search parties and newspaper headlines would proclaim to all of Summit County the negligence of these grandparents. I'm sure their imagination and guilt knew no bounds.

As a grandmother myself now, I can understand how responsible they felt

Elmer C. Peabody, Sr. accepting honorary key at Breckenridge Days, (circa 1955.)

and their devastation at what could have happened to us. But I still don't understand why they thought we were running away.

Once we finally reassured our grandparents that we did not intend to run away and we were happy at the ranch, the incident was forgotten. But all my life I dreamed of climbing to the top of Ute. In the summer of 1997 I finally accomplished this goal. From the summit the view of the Gore Range rising out of the west, with our ranch a little speck in the valley below, was truly spectacular. I am also certain that a seven and ten-year-old should not undertake this trek by themselves!

Independence Day

A high point in the summer was the 4th of July. Pags and Grama, proud to be Americans, cared deeply about their country. They were staunch Republicans and had always been active in county politics. In fact, in the 1950's Pags was honored to receive the Town Key at the Colorado Days in Breckenridge.

Every Independence Day, Pags raised our two American flags in the front yard. Then off to town the family went for excitement and celebration—the Dillon rodeo! We had fun sitting on the fence watching the steer roping and bucking broncos. Handsome cowboys swaggered around the rodeo grounds with their chaps and boots and spurs, cowboy hats pulled down over their rugged, sun-tanned faces. I was fascinated watching them chew and spit their tobacco. We didn't have cowboys like this at the ranch. When we went to the rodeo I felt like an outsider to the cowboy world, a city slicker. But one year I entered the greased pig contest and nearly came home with a little pig for my grandparents to raise—my claim to fame. After the rodeo ended we went back to the ranch for a picnic before setting off our own fireworks.

What I recall with the most happiness, however, was just being with my grandparents. Pags adored his two little granddaughters. His favorite song was "Beautiful Dreamer," and I knew I was his beautiful dreamer. Sometimes he put a record on the old wind up Victrola record player and we danced. I stood on his feet and we danced around and around the living room. I felt very grown up.

Most of all I liked snuggling on Grama's lap. I loved her soft plumpness. I called her my special pillow. Happiness was nestling into the soft folds of her lap and listening to her sing or read to me. I especially enjoyed The Wizard of Oz and Alice in Wonderland. When she read about the dreaded cyclone that swooped up Dorothy's house, I'm sure she was back on the farm again feeling the terror of her childhood. I don't know if she ever personally experienced a cyclone in Kansas, but the fear of one was deeply entrenched in her memories.

Grama's Bread Pudding

4 slices bread (homemade white or raisin bread)
4 cups whole milk
3/4 - 1 cup sugar
4 eggs
1 tsp. vanilla
cinnamon and nutmeg

Leftover bread that has dried out slightly works well. Butter the bread, sprinkle the slices with cinnamon and cut into 1" squares. Beat eggs, then add milk, sugar, and vanilla. Place bread cubes into buttered casserole dish. Pour egg mixture over the bread and let it soak for an hour or so. Sprinkle top with cinnamon and nutmeg. Bake at 350 for an hour and 15 minutes or until a knife inserted comes out clean.

Grama's Sauce for Bread Pudding or Cake

1 cup water
1/2 cup sugar
1/4 tsp. salt
2 level Tbs. corn starch
1 Tbs. butter
1 tsp. vanilla
cinnamon and nutmeg to taste

Gradually combine cornstarch with water, stirring until smooth. Add rest of ingredients and cook over a medium heat, stirring constantly until it comes to a boil and is clear and thickened. Serve over bread pudding or unfrosted cake.

Bittersweet Times

One of the songs I remember her singing was "Poor Babes Lost in the Woods." This tragic, hauntingly beautiful song was adapted from the story, *Babes in the Woods,* written in 1601 by

Rob Yarrington. It is the sad tale of two little children whose mother and father die, and they are entrusted to the care of their uncle. He wants to inherit the children's money, so he plots to have two ruffians murder them. These scoundrels quarrel, one kills the other, and then runs away leaving the children alone in the woods. They die of starvation and exposure. In the end the little robins of the forest bury their small bodies with strawberry leaves and all day long sing their sad song, "Poor babes in the woods, poor babes in the woods."

At the time I didn't know why this was such a favorite of hers, but now, knowing her better, I understand. This is the story of herself as a young, motherless child whose father abandoned her. She was frightened about getting lost in the tall cornfields of Kansas, the "woods"—and no one coming to find her. When I snuggled on her lap and she rubbed my back, gently saying to me, "My poor little baby," I didn't know why I needed comforting or what was poor about me. But I know now that she was talking to herself, the little girl within her. Grama was caressing me as she wished someone had comforted her as a child. There was a feeling of bittersweetness about Grama, an undertone of sadness even in our happy times together.

That same bit-

Babes in the Woods

Oh, don't you remember, a long time ago,
When two little babes, their names I don't know,
Were stolen away one bright summer day,
And lost in the woods, I've heard people say.

And when it was night, so sad was their plight,
The sun had gone down, the stars gave no light,
They sobbed and they sighed and bitterly cried,
Then the poor little babes, they lay down and died,

And when they were dead, the robins so red,
Brought strawberry leaves and over them spread,
And all the day long they sing their sad song,
"Poor babes in the woods, poor babes in the woods."

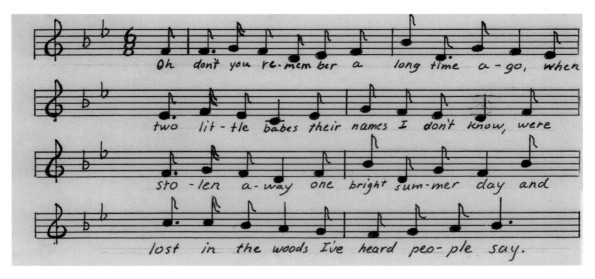

tersweetness even found its way into my life, affecting my love of driving. I'd driven the tractor since I was ten years old, and my dad taught me to drive the old Model A Ford car when I was 13. I welcomed any and every job that involved driving. With the tractor I hauled bottles and cans to the trash dump and pulled wagonloads of people to the picnic grounds. I moved lots of rocks and gravel and brush in the stoneboat, a tractor-drawn, flat sled we used, and once Grama allowed me to operate the mower at haying time. However, one task I had to perform with the tractor was a sad one.

One fateful morning in June I wandered into the barn and I stumbled over Lance's body. He had died the night before! This was the first time anyone important to me had ever died. Since I was alone at the ranch with Sally and Grama, it was up to me to find a way to bury him. With tears streaming down my face, I hooked the stoneboat to the tractor and drove it up to the barn. It took all three of us to lift his cold, lifeless body into the stoneboat. We dug his grave down by the stream in the lower meadow, and I cried with every shovelful of dirt. I didn't know it was possible to feel so sad.

Little did I know worse would come. Lance's death was an omen.

A year earlier, the doctor had diagnosed Pags with tuberculosis. Everyone presumed this resulted from his working down in the mines for years and breathing the toxic air. When he was taken away to a sanitarium in Denver to "recuperate" I didn't realize that I would never see my beloved Pags again. Summer was lonely without him. Pags and Grama wrote to each other daily, and Sally and I, not realizing the gravity of his condition, wrote more sporadically—I wish I'd written more.

A few weeks after we buried our dog, my carefree innocence came abruptly and forever to an end. One beautiful summer morning (July 31, 1956) while out in the yard collecting wildflowers, I looked up and saw my dad driving through the gate. What was he doing here? He never came up to the ranch in the middle of the week. I knew in an instant that something was dreadfully wrong. My Pags had died! I was not aware how sick he had been. I never had a chance to say good-bye. The next few days passed by in a fog. Our family felt broken, unable to be fixed. His death left a void in the family and an empty space in my heart.

Grama suffered the loss the hardest. Pags was the love of her life and their marriage was truly special. Grama was a survivor, however, and lived another 15 years, most of them on her own at the ranch. She did her best to continue the traditions she and Pags had begun.

When I was 16 and had my driver's license, our outings became more far-reaching—a ski trip to Aspen, a weekend at the Broadmoor Hotel in Colorado Springs, an airplane trip to San Francisco. We visited Uncle Roy and Aunt Rena in Colorado Springs and Aunt Lottie at the Colorado State

Hospital in Pueblo. (Charlotte Rader, M.D. was the physician at this mental hospital, which resembled the insane asylum in One Flew Over the Cuckoo's Nest.)

Readers may wonder, what about my parents? Where do they fit into this picture? My dad remained close to his mother all his life—and she to him. I had the impression that she worried about him and was unable to let go. My dad had made an abortive first attempt to leave home by moving to California and marrying a woman unacceptable to his parents. After that he had a hard time living his own life separate from them. Pleasing his mother mattered most.

This left my mother out in the cold. Although Pags treated her kindly and Grama was cordial, I don't believe my mother felt welcomed into the family or accepted by them. She didn't feel she "belonged" at the ranch. This thread ran through her life. As a little girl, the youngest child in her family, her siblings often left her behind. As a young woman, marrying into her husband's strongly connected family, she found it hard to find her place. She was the weak one, often excluded. It must have been daunting for her.

Grama acted as the matriarch. Family life revolved around her. Her strength and nurturing love had given me a lot, but also carried a cost. Grama loved and cared for me in ways my mother was less able to do. But her strong presence may also have diminished my mother's ability to mother me.

More of the bittersweet.

My grandparents gave me my roots and my wings. Family traditions and holidays celebrated, rich memories of childhood adventures all serve to ground me. Stories told and re-told about my Peabody ancestors are my roots. I feel a connectedness arching back over the generations to the early settlers of this country. Their pioneer spirit reverberates through our collective memories. Their courage in seeking their vision of a better life ripples through the generations.

My grandparents inspired me to venture into new territories. Our trips and outings gave me a sense of security in the larger world, a love of exploring and adventure. Their stories about magical clouds, ancient oceans and distant stars sparked my imagination. Grama was a free spirit and a "good sport." She and Sally, great Elvis Presley fans, listened to rock and roll music together. She was game for trying anything new and even tried dancing to the new fangled music of the '50's, hopping and jiggling around the dining room floor. Grama liked to laugh and be frivolous—not take herself too seriously.

Our family resembles many other families. We had our share of joy and success and also our share of shame and sorrow. As Anne Ellis wrote:

> If one stands trouble bravely, there is more happiness in looking back to trouble than there is in looking back to joy.

What Goes Around Comes Around

This we know: the earth does not belong to man, man belongs to the earth. All things are connected like the blood that unites us all. Man did not weave the web of life, he is merely a strand in it. Whatever he does to the web, he does to himself.

—Chief Seattle

Summit County has enjoyed three past mining booms: placer, lode and dredge. Now the mountain area is in the midst of its fourth boom, the pursuit of its famous white powder snow.

Several lazy decades drifted by after the dredges shut down in 1942. The mining industry had collapsed, and Breckenridge, Dillon and Frisco were rapidly on their way to becoming ghost towns. Debris from abandoned mines and dredge tailings littered the countryside.

Around Colorado, ski enthusiasm had spread slowly after Winter Park, Steamboat and Aspen opened in the 1930's. Only a handful of dedicated skiers, hauling their hickory and ash skis, regularly crossed the high mountain passes to reach these slopes. Arapahoe Basin, Summit County's first ski area, began its operation in 1946. In these early years a jeep and rope tow hauled skiers up for the price of $1 a ticket. Arapahoe's dazzling ski bowl, rimmed by the rocky spires of the Continental Divide, delighted the early-day, hard-core skiers.

Ignoring mountain terrain unrivaled in its potential for magnificent skiing, most people in Summit County contented themselves with ranching and shopkeeping. In fact, many of the locals resented the influx of the new breed from Denver and treated skiers with derision. After working outdoors all week, most cowboys and ranchers found little thrill in whizzing down snowy slopes only to stand in line again for half-an-hour to wait for a mechanical device to haul them back up. In the early days a cowboy viewed a skier as today's cross country skier regards a snowmobiler.

In time, enthusiasm for skiing spread to the Blue River valley. Businesses began to realize that skiers—prospectors for Summit County's white gold—could themselves be mined for huge profits. With the creation of the Breckenridge ski area in 1961, Summit County exploded into its skiing boom. Ten years later Keystone and Copper Mountain ski areas came into being, adding to the contagion.

Modern highways have made skiing more accessible. Since the completion of the Eisenhower Tunnel in 1973, the drive from Denver to Dillon is made in a trouble-free 60 minutes, passing under the massive peaks of the Continental Divide in a mere five minutes! No longer are travelers faced with raging storms over the 11,992 foot, unprotected gravel road of Loveland Pass.

Now throngs of exuberant people swarm to the mountain slopes in search of the white treasure. Ironically, this new boom in skiing happened almost exactly a hundred years after the magical gold dust first brought 1860's miners swarming to Breckenridge.

Breckenridge has undergone an enormous transformation in its short history. Prior to the prospectors' arrival, no white person, except for an occasional trapper or explorer, had ventured into Colorado's remote high mountain country. Not a wheel had rolled over its soil. In just a few short years the area was catapulted from a stone age culture that had existed for thousands of years into a highly advanced, technological society. Those pioneers who scaled the divide and viewed the Blue River valley for the first time would not recognize it today.

Our "progress" would shock the early pioneers. Four-lane freeways zoom travelers to high-rise condos with lightning speed. A staggering array of shopping malls, fancy restaurants, night clubs and souvenir shops greet the tourist. A plethora of snowboards, skis, sleds, and skates, sailboats, hang gliders, wind surfers, and sailplanes entertain the visitor. "He who dies with the most toys wins!" proclaims the bumper sticker. Ski slopes plaster the mountain sides as modern day prospectors seek out the white glitter with a frenzy. Their mottoes: "Conquer the slopes!" "Hurry up and relax!"

Not only our hectic pace but also our technology would astound the early pioneers. Automobiles have existed a mere 100 years. Technological progress since then has been astonishing. Just a few years ago Breckenridge residents communicated by hand-cranked telephones. Now, talking on a cellular phone, logging onto the Internet, faxing a letter to Paris, or receiving messages by satellite have become commonplace.

Many Endings

Eleven generations and 363 years have passed since the first Peabodys came to this country. Sadly, the long and interesting journey of my small branch of the family has ended. Though Sally and I have our own children and grandchildren, the family name was transmitted only to male descendants. Our father, Elmer Clifton Peabody, Jr., was the last twig on this particular branch of the Peabody family tree.

Along with this ending comes the end of another era—life close to the land. Ours is the last generation to have first-hand memories of the pioneer ways. No longer do settlers plow their fields with a team of work horses; milk their cows by hand; use kerosene lamps for lighting; talk on the telephone where the neighbors can listen in over the party line; "whang-doodle" the rooster for Sunday dinner; churn their own butter; use blocks of ice to keep food cool; make their own soap; wash clothes using a hand-turned wringer; or iron with flat irons heated on the wood burning stove. Now a simple flip of the switch saves hours of time doing laundry. A single stop at the grocery store provides all the food supplies that our grandmother spent days preparing.

Early day skiing at Breckenridge.

Sometimes we become nostalgic and romanticize these homespun ways. In reality, life was hard work. Our pioneer ancestors could not ignore these tasks. Activities of daily living took most of their time, and vacations were rare. Nowadays we may plant a vegetable garden or a patch of strawberries if we want to. We may can some jam or pickles if the spirit moves us. My grandparents did all this because they had to, not for fun.

We humans have gained enormous competence in the last century, beyond our ancestors' wildest imaginations. We've honed our skills at curing disease, living longer, building bigger houses and faster cars, computerizing home and business, launching flights into outer space and even cloning animals. The cascade of creative inventions and esoteric technology over the last century is amazing.

However, progress has cost us by alienating people from the natural world. Now most people live in cities, with minimal access to green and growing things, wild animals, natural light, the night sky and the cycle of the seasons. Over the last few centuries we have increasingly lost our intimate connection with Mother Earth. Civilization is astonishingly complex. As society has become increasingly elaborate, we have become more distant from our roots.

Al Gore illustrates how far we have separated ourselves from nature:

> Modern philosophy asks the famous question: "If a tree falls in the forest and no person is there to hear it, does it make a sound?" If robotic chain saws finally destroy all the rain forests on earth, and if the people who set them in motion are far enough away so that they don't hear the crash of the trees on the naked forest floor, does it matter? This rational, detached, scientific intellect, observing the world of which it is no longer a part, is too often arrogant, unfeeling, uncaring. And its consequences can be monstrous.

Our technology, designed to help us feel better and survive longer by controlling the outer environment, has left us estranged from our neighbors and Earth itself. The runaway cycle of things produced, consumed, discarded—with marketing and advertising creating the need for more and more things—has left in its wake piles of trash, energy depletion and continued human suffering. Caught up in the technological explosion, we have allowed life to become unbalanced. It is now time to see the importance of open spaces and wilderness areas. We need to rediscover our emotional connection with the natural world, to fall in love again with our precious planet.

Reconnecting with the Natural World

Like my ancestors, we too can still become enthralled with the earth in all its brilliance and awesome presence. Francis, while sailing on his small ship across the Atlantic, watched powerful storms descend. Benjamin, while hacking out a clearing to build a little cabin, contemplated the dense New England forest. And Almeda, while peering out her train window, saw the vast Midwestern plains stretch endlessly ahead and glimpsed the towering peaks of the Rocky Mountains from a stagecoach window. These pioneers witnessed the splendor of our planet.

Our materialistic, consumer-oriented society has captured our souls. The computerized, mechanistic world has dulled our senses. Modern travelers today surf the World Wide Web rather than hike on mountain trails or stroll down country roads. We are more entranced by a computer screen than awe-struck by the mystery of the earth's abundance. A web site is not a place. The gold-veined, mountain-spired, snow-blanketed, evergreen-dotted, sun-drenched, columbine-sprinkled landscape of Colorado is a place.

Developing an emotional connection with Earth may come from various sources. We can play on Earth. As it offers us mountains to ski, rivers to paddle, oceans to sail, and trails to hike, we feel a great joy with it.

We can develop a deeper knowledge of Earth. Understanding the story of our planet, its transformations over time and its spectacular geologic and biologic manifestations gives us an understanding of our amazing planet. Grasping the meaning of earth's roundness and its finite surface helps us appreciate our own vulnerability and the interdependence of all beings.

We can rediscover Earth through the unique perspective of our children. They have an innate fascination with nature. Through the eyes of a small child we can become entranced with nature in our own backyard—the magic of woods to explore and trees to climb, a stream where twig boats float, tall blades of grass where a little black ant lugs huge bundles. As children engage with the natural world they take their play very seriously. Sand castles to sculpt, salamanders to find, snowmen to build, leaves to collect, tree houses to build and frogs to catch—all are their important work.

Parents and grandparents have much to learn from children. Step into their world; see the wilderness through their eyes. A little fistful of dandelions is a precious gift; a carefully chosen rock is a magnificent specimen. A gently cradled little caterpillar is a wondrous creature to behold. Those of us who missed it in our own early years have another chance. Any young child can share the wisdom. All it

The moist scent of mown grass and its light feel in her hand fascinated three-year-old Cynthia Peabody.

takes is a willing adult open to the magic. Then we enter into a reverence for Earth.

We forge a spiritual bond with the world as we rediscover the splendor of the world around us and reconnect with trees, rocks, streams and mountains. We may return to the earth as a source of strength, of comfort and of serenity.

My Help is in the Mountain

My help is in the mountain
Where I take myself to heal
The earthly wounds
That people give to me.

I find a rock with sun on it
And a stream where the water runs gentle
And the trees which one by one give me company.

So I must stay for a long time
Until I have grown from the rock.
And the stream is running through me
And I cannot tell myself from one tall tree.
Then I know that nothing touches me
Nor makes me run away.
My help is in the mountain
That I take away with me.
—Nancy Wood

Mother Earth may not be just a figure of speech. We are told that one theory of how we got here is that Earth, rolling slowly through space, bathed in light and heat from the Sun, created mountains and trees, butterflies and rainbows, you and me. Mother Earth gave birth to all living and non-living things. We still need her, and she needs us to notice her and to care for her lovingly. If we lose our connection with Earth, we have abandoned her, our Ancestor of all ancestors.

New Beginnings

My pioneer ancestors who set out across the vast ocean and began life in the New World intrigue me as do the western settlers who headed across the plains to Colorado. Although separated in time by 200 years, both groups blazed trails to virgin territory. They journeyed into the uncharted wilderness of early New England; the dense, primeval forests of northern New York; the vast plains of the midwest; and the shimmering peaks of the Rocky Mountains.

Each group of pioneers faced the compelling question of how to survive on the frontier. As winter set in, how to keep warm in a rude hut in Plymouth, a log cabin in New York or a miner's shack in Colorado. How to hunt and fish and grow enough food to feed their large families. How to protect themselves from the threat of warring Indians whose land they occupied. And how to hold onto their own roots and cherished traditions from the past while adapting to the changing conditions of the present.

Our forerunners made hard choices to leave the familiar and the predictable. Holding onto a vision of a better future, they were willing to sacrifice and endure hardships. They faced the unknown terrain with resilience and courage.

A fresh start always waited beyond the frontier. "Virgin" territory demanded hard work and perseverance. The pristine wilderness on the western horizon beckoned those with dreams of a better life to pack up ship or wagon and head toward the setting sun.

We are grateful to our ancestors for their pioneering spirit. Their pursuing their dreams for a better life has given some of us a better life. But this has not been without cost. Our ancestors enabled themselves to move into new country, conscience-free, by defining it as uninhabited. It was "virgin" territory. No one lived there, so it was theirs for the taking. They created this illusion by dehumanizing other beings. The New England pioneer and the western settler alike viewed the Native Americans as sub-human. Whites deluded themselves that they were not taking away land from another person, since no person existed.

Life at the Clover Meadow Ranch clung to the old ways into the 1960's.

We have seen through our country's history a dehumanizing attitude—toward the Native Americans, the Chinese, the African American, women—and Earth itself. By denying that another being has feelings, needs, wants and desires like ourselves, we attempt to deify ourselves at other's expense. Our new "global awareness" is making the dehumanization of those unlike ourselves more difficult. Now we must face the impossibility of outward solutions to inward problems.

We live on a small planet whose size is constantly shrinking. The vast western expanse has vanished. What goes around comes around. We can't tar-and-feather an offender and "Warn" them out of town as the early pioneers did. We can't get rid of toxic waste by burying it in someone else's backyard. Dehumanizing our fellow human beings is not a solution. It is impossible to geographically cure our troubles by moving on to new, untrammeled land and starting over again. We have to make it work here.

We are at a unique place in history—a time of endings. As the 20th century ends, so does my branch of the Peabody family tree. Alongside these endings comes a threat to our earth-centered way of life. Many warn that technology running rampant, without regard for its devastating effects on our environment, could bring about an end to our life on this planet. Our existence is threatened by depleting the ozone layer, poisoning our water, deforesting our jungles, burning our rain forests, plundering the earth's resources and endangering the diversity of plants and wildlife.

Will we misuse technology to dehumanize ourselves and destroy our own lives as we misused our technical superiority and destroyed the Native American people? A stone age culture, the early humans of this country had lived in balance with the land and each other for thousands of years. But they were no match for the white settlers who invaded their territory wielding more powerful tools and weapons. Guns killed more in battle than bows and arrows. Locomotives chugged across the prairie enabling the slaughter of buffalo herds. Plows and white man's ways of farming were forced upon the native people. Like the buffalo that once roamed the endless plains, the Indians have retreated to an ever-diminishing piece of land. Some say that we, too, are careening headlong toward the same fate.

Every ending opens the door to a new beginning. As we begin the twenty-first century we enter a new age—the Information Age and the Ecological Age. We have the technology to connect instantly with people around the globe. Programs for preserving the earth's resources are proliferating. Let us use our incredible tools, our amazing intelligence and our concern for the natural world to help us connect with all of our diverse selves and to re-establish our loving connection with our precious planet earth.

The end of my Peabody name means change but not the end of this family's vigorous life and pioneering spirit. Peabody blood continues in families named Anderson and Storer and Richter and May and York and Gateley and Oakley and Wagner and Bawolski and Cook and Altland and Collard, and...and...

New lives begin. Interesting stories remain to tell.

Despite challenges presented by a new way of life in a New World, Francis and John Paybody didn't look back. Neither must we. Our new world is not "out there." It is within ourselves. And we have some pioneering to do.

Family Foundations

Origins of the Peabody Name

The Peabody name has its origins back in the ancient days of the Caesars when wild tribes roamed the British Isles. In the year 54 A.D. Nero became the Emperor of Rome as the result of treachery on the part of his mother, Agrippina. She was married to Emperor Claudius who also happened to be her uncle. Agrippina was determined that Nero, her son by her first marriage, should become the Emperor of Rome. So she had Claudius poisoned.

Eighteen-year-old Nero was a wasteful, self indulgent monarch. It was said that he never wore the same piece of clothing twice, and that he traveled with no less than a thousand baggage carts in his entourage. Nero soon became one of the most vile and depraved of monarchs, murdering anyone who stood in his way—even his wife, Octavia, and his own mother, Agrippina.

A few years earlier King Prasutagus of Briton, understanding Nero's greed, had willed half his land to the Roman emperor in hopes that ruthless Nero would be satisfied and leave the British alone. Those hopes were dashed. When Prasutagus died in 61 A.D. and his wife Boadicea became queen, Nero moved to take it all.

Boadicea resisted and the Emperor seized her land and whipped the queen in front of her court. Queen Boadicea possessed great strength of spirit and she refused to acquiesce. She called on her own people for support.

Down from the hills of what is now Norfolk came the bearded, brown-haired warrior, Boadie, a brave British chieftain. Boadie consulted with his queen and then sent messengers across the countryside. The people were ripe for rebellion and rallied against the hated Nero. By now Queen Boadicea had been publicly scourged and her two daughters raped by the Romans.

The outraged Britons prepared for battle. In the weeks that followed, Boadie and his men waged a massive rebellion, burying and pillaging Roman posts and killing some 70,000 Romans and Britons, proven sympathizers with Rome. But Nero's troops retaliated, quelling the rebellion with a force of 10,000 strong. In a decisive battle at today's Towcester, between London and Chester, the Britons were defeated and dispersed. Queen Boadicea took poison. Boadie fought fiercely striking down Romans time and again as men fell all around him. But the Britons made no match for the Romans' superior strength. Boadie managed to seize the helmet and armor from a Roman soldier and, with a handful of followers, fled into the mountains of Wales. Here they became crag dwellers, mountain men, who lived by preying upon the Romans in the lowlands below.

From one of his last Roman victims, Galbuta, Boadie took the special crest the Roman wore on his helmet. This emblem, granted to the soldier for some previous act of bravery, became a trophy preserved and handed down through the generations. These descendants of Boadie kept his name as a symbol of rank and honor. In the language they spoke boadie came to mean "man" and pea meant "mountain". So the leader was named Peabodie, or the "mountain man" and all his followers accepted this as their tribal name.

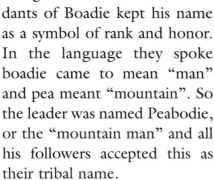

Later, in medieval times, a Peabodie joined the Knights of the Round Table, an honor bestowed by King Arthur himself.

The Peabody crest, which was the Roman coat of arms preserved through the years by Boadie's descendents, depicted a Roman eagle above a Roman casque, which decorated the top part of the shield. The upper half, done in red displayed two Roman suns. The lower half, done in blue and cut off by a crenellated line, was adorned with a sheaf of grain. Beneath all was the motto: Murus Airius Conscientia Sana

Selim Hobart Peabody, in his book, Peabody Genealogy, expresses a different viewpoint about the derivation of the name:

The oldest and most prevalent form previous to the settlement of New England was Paybody. Two common words, these syllables are, and perhaps they point back to a man or a succession of men in the fourteenth century (when surnames were crystallizing) who paid the servants, creditors and employees of barons, manufacturers or public officials. Body meant person or individual, pay-body would carry the same idea as pay-master or paying-teller. The name, if such be its origin, would be a memorial of ability and trustworthiness.

The Peabody name, along with its history, changed when transplanted from British soil. Originally the Peabody name was spelled Paybody, or sometimes Paybodie, Pabody, or Pabodie or Peboadie. The name itself was variously spelled in England even in the same parish or in the same document. Peabody, the spelling which now prevails in America, did not appear in English records. The spelling Peabody was first signed on this side of the Atlantic by Nathaniel Peabody of Topsfield, son of Francis, in 1715.

John Paybody, originator of the American branch of the Peabody family, was a native of the county of Leicester and of the portion in or immediately south of the city of Leicester, probably the little rural parish of Glen Magna or Great Glen.

Biographical Sketches

Each is given a bag of tools,
A shapeless mass,
A book of rules;
And each must make,
Ere life is flown,
A stumbling-block
Or a stepping stone.
—R.L.Sharpe in *The Peabody Influence*

Nathaniel Peabody (6), *{Jacob (5), Jacob (4), Jacob (3), Francis (2), John (1)}*
(February 18, 1741, Topsfield, MA—June 27, 1823) Physician, Congressional delegate and Revolutionary War leader

Like many young people of his day, Nathaniel had no formal education. From reading and writing to the practice of medicine, all his schooling came from his father, Dr. Jacob Peabody. Nathaniel then set up his medical practice in Plaistow, New Hampshire, and was following in his father's footsteps when the Revolutionary War broke out.

Of all the Peabodys who served in the war, Nathaniel is the most distinguished. After the battle in Lexington between the British and the Minutemen, Nathaniel resigned his royal commission as lieutenant colonel in the New Hampshire militia and joined the revolutionaries. He served in several important capacities. As a member of the Committee of Safety, Nathaniel considered secret measures to rid the warring colonies from spies. He was appointed Adjunct General of Militia of New Hampshire with the rank of colonel. He was selected as a Congressional delegate to the Continental Congress, and then elected chairman of the Medical Committee of Congress.

In 1780 Colonel Nathaniel Peabody played a crucial role in preventing the collapse of the colonies' effort to gain freedom from England. An ever worsening economic situation was bringing the fledgling nation to the brink of ruin. The economy failed to rally because of the British blockade and men's long absence from their farms. The treasury was empty. A spirit of discontent prevailed among the troops as they were unwilling to dress in rags and endure the torture of famine. The Revolution, so close to victory, verged on disaster. After learning that the starving, threadbare troops neared mutiny, Nathaniel and two other delegates visited George Washington and worked out a plan to alert the country and drum up supplies.

In 1793 Nathaniel's colleagues elected him Speaker of the New Hampshire State House of Representatives. The previous year he had received an honorary degree from Dartmouth College.

Despite these honors for his life of work promoting the greater good, Nathaniel was thrown in debtor's prison from time to time during his last years. His zeal for public office and habits of lavish spending diminished his fortune and made his creditors reluctant to forgive his debt. When he died, although he was theoretically still confined to debtor's prison, Nathaniel was so respected by the people of New Hampshire that he was allowed to live on his own.

Captain Joseph Peabody (6), *{Francis (5), Francis(4), Isaac (3), Francis (2), John (1)}*
(December 12, 1757, Middleton, MA—January 5, 1844) Wealthy merchant and privateer

Ninth of Deacon Francis' 12 children, Joseph educated himself by learning to read the Bible at home. As a 19-year-old during the Revolutionary War, Joseph stayed home and ran the family farm while his brother went off to war. Afterwards he decided he'd make his fortune as a sailor. He quite literally, did that. Joseph went to sea as a privateer for several years, and by 1791 had amassed a sizable amount of money—enough to come ashore and become a merchant ship owner. From small beginnings he built up a tremendous business. Eventually Joseph owned dozens of ships which sailed from the Salem harbor to ports around the world. This earned him a fortune in the Far East spice trade. He also accumulated his vast wealth with his fleet of privateers which captured and sank merchant ships of enemy countries (France, especially). By 1817 Joseph was the wealthiest merchant in the United States

Joseph, a stern man, maintained a reserve in his dealings with others. He kept to himself and devoted all his time and energy to his business. Peabody family biographer, Edwin P. Hoyt, likens him to Scrooge. He writes that one of Joseph's maxims was, "Make your company a rarity and people will value it. Men despise what they can easily have." Hoyt even tells about a countinghouse Joseph had:

> a huge loft of a room with an inner sanctum in which the Captain sat before the only fire while in the outer offices his clerks shivered at their high desks, poring over his bills of lading and making out his charges against those who bought from him.

However harshly the outside world judged Joseph, his children thought more kindly of him. His son, George, credited his father with having a "lofty moral tone" and "dignity of character." George acknowledged that although "he was hasty of temper, he was always right." His children's welfare and upbringing were important to Joseph. He saw to it that his sons received the finest education and that his daughters married well.

The Peabody Museum in Salem, Massachusetts was established in his honor.

Judge Oliver Peabody (6), *{Oliver (5), John (4), William (3), Francis (2), John (1)}*
(September 2, 1753, Andover, MA—December 28, 1844). Judge, senator

Oliver established a law practice in Exeter, New Hampshire, then earned appointment as judge and election to the State Senate. During his second term he was chosen President of the Senate and then later was selected as State Treasurer. Of the ten children of Judge Oliver and Frances Peabody, the third and fourth children were twin boys who led remarkable lives. The first twin, Oliver William Bourne was named for his father, and the second, William Bourne Oliver was named for his mother's father.

Rev. Oliver William Bourne Peabody (7), *{Oliver (6), Oliver (5), John (4), William (3), Francis (2), John (1)}*
(July 7, 1799, Exeter, NH—July 5, 1848) Lawyer, writer, minister

Oliver William Bourne felt the family pressure to follow in the footsteps of his father and become an attorney himself. So he attended Harvard Law School and for 11 years practiced law at Exeter, New Hampshire. He sat as a member of the state legislature from 1824 to 1831. But when his father died, Oliver left Exeter and his law practice and turned to the world of literature. He edited a set of Shakespeare's works, contributed many articles to the *North American Review* and to the *Library of American Biography*. Finally, he pursued his lifelong dream: he became a minister and was ordained by the Boston Ministerial Association. He became the pastor of the Unitarian church in Burlington, Vermont.

Rev. William Bourne Oliver Peabody (7),
{Oliver (6), Oliver (5), John (4), William (3), Francis (2), John (1)}
(July 7, 1799, Exeter, NH—May, 1847). Minister, writer

William Bourne Oliver was allowed to follow his own way after graduating with his twin brother from Harvard in 1816. He proceeded directly towards the ministry, graduating from Harvard Divinity School. William served as the Unitarian minister for 27 years in Springfield, Massachusetts. Like his brother, William also was an avid reader and literary figure of some prominence. William wrote essays, poetry, reviews for the *North American Review* and many other publications. A friend of Audobon he also wrote extensively about nature.

George Peabody (7), *{Thomas (6), David(5), David(4), John (3), Francis (2), John (1)}*
(February 18, 1795, South Danvers, MA—November 4, 1869) Merchant, financier, philanthropist

George ranks as the most celebrated of all the Peabodys. Born in South Danvers, which is now called Peabody, Massachusetts, he received only a rudimentary schooling because his family was poor. At the age of 11 George apprenticed in the village grocery store and then assisted his brother in a dry goods store At 16, after his father died, his self sufficiency and independence further developed. George rapidly worked his way up in the dry goods company becoming enormously successful. Everything he touched turned to gold. Within a few years George became a wealthy man. He moved into the international world of merchant banking, specializing in foreign exchange and American securities. In 1854 he took J. S. Morgan into partnership. George possessed a keen insight into financial matters earning him great respect as one of the foremost businessmen of the world.

But George was not content to simply sit home and count his money. As his wealth increased so did his sense of altruism and social obligation. George spent most of his vast fortune in philanthropy. He originated charitable foundations. First George bestowed upon his old hometown of Danvers a large and unexpected gift for the benefit of the immigrants and poor people. The town reciprocated his generosity by giving the name of Peabody to that portion of the town where he had been born.

Although he loved his native country, George resided permanently in London where he was extremely influential in preserving American-British friendship. In England he spent $2,500,000 for the erection of clean, comfortable housing for the hundreds of working poor. Among the many of his generous gifts were his donations to establish the Peabody Institute at Baltimore, MD; the Peabody Institute in Peabody, MA; the Peabody Museum of natural history and science at Yale; the Peabody Museum of archeology at Harvard; the Peabody Academy of Science in connection with the Essex Institute at Salem; and the Peabody Education Fund for promotion of education in the south.

George's generosity was appreciated and honored in London as well as in his native country. In 1869 the Prince of Wales unveiled a statue of him. When he refused to accept either a baronetcy or the Grand Cross of the Bath, Queen Victoria sent him an autographed letter of appreciation and a large miniature of herself. Following his death in 1869, his funeral was held in Westminster Abbey. A French and American navel vessel escorted his body back to this country and, after elaborate ceremonies, he was buried in Danvers, Massachusetts.

The Peabody Sisters of Salem

The three oldest daughters of Nathaniel and Elizabeth (Palmer) Peabody grew up to achieve considerable prominence in the literary and educational world. Their father, Nathaniel, practiced medicine and dentistry, and their mother, Elizabeth, conducted a private school where she educated all her children.

The Peabody sisters, Mary and Sophia, lived the words of literary great Ralph Waldo Emerson as quoted by biographer Megan Marshall. He addressed a women's rights convention in 1855 and earned applause from the feminists who agreed with Emerson's description of the exemplary qualities that 19th century women should possess. (They would sound condescending to today's woman!)

Man is the will, and Woman the sentiment...More vulnerable, more infirm, more mortal than men... [women] lose themselves eagerly in the glory of their husbands and children...Women are, by this and their social influence, the civilizers of mankind.

Mary and Sophia embodied these characteristics. Both were eager to lose themselves in the glory of their husbands, and, in fact, played an enormous behind-the-scenes role in the fame their husbands achieved.

Mary Tyler (Peabody) Mann (7), *{Nathaniel (6), Isaac (5), Matthew (4), Isaac (3), Francis (2), John (1)}* (November 16, 1806, Cambridge, MA—February 11, 1887) Educator, married the eminent educator, Horace Mann

From the time Mary first met Horace Mann, she felt she had discovered her destiny. Horace was brokenhearted from the death of his young wife, and her mission was to bring a smile to his face. For ten years Mary visited him, held his hand and offered support for his life project of reforming Massachusetts public schools. She never was certain of his love for her until he proposed a month before their wedding day. Mary was 37 years old when they married. She was old by 1800's standards, but not too old to give birth to three children to whom Mary devoted her life.

Horace went on to become an outspoken abolitionist and the first president of Antioch College. Mary believed that, rather than competing with men in the professions, woman's goal was to achieve a sense of power in her home as wife and mother. This domestic competence would compensate for her lack of political influence and respect in the larger world. Mary published her philosophy of domesticity in the popular *Christianity in the Kitchen: A Physiological Cookbook.*

Sophia Amelia (Peabody) Hawthorne (7), *{Nathaniel (6), Isaac (5), Matthew (4), Isaac (3), Francis (2), John (1)}*

(September 21, 1809, Salem, MA—February 26, 1871) Painter, married Nathaniel Hawthorne

Sophia was the frail, sickly sister who suffered debilitating headaches which lasted for days. (Now they would be called migraines.) She lived the first half of her life as an invalid. Sophia was an artist of considerable skill and found through painting an escape from suffering. Peabody biographer, Edwin Hoyt, writes that her mother made Sophia an invalid because she wanted desperately to keep Sophia at home. Her constant conversation informed Sophia how sick she was, much too weak to venture into the world.

When Elizabeth introduced Sophia to Nathaniel Hawthorne, Sophia was entranced with this man who looked like Lord Byron—and he with her, this pale delicate girl. It was love at first sight. According to biographer, Megan Marshall, Nathaniel later told Elizabeth, "She is a flower to be worn in no man's bosom, but was lent from Heaven to show the possibilities of the human soul."

Their romance, like Mary and Horace's was a long, secret courtship. Secret because Sophia's mother was determined that her daughter never marry. They kept their engagement from her for a long time. Hawthorne's mother and sister were equally opposed to his marrying, fearing that distraction by a wife would end his creative writing career. To the contrary, Sophia was the light of his life and inspired him to write many of his finest works. Hawthorne demonstrated brilliance in his insight into human nature.

When she married Nathaniel, Sophia's health improved dramatically. The day after their wedding the young couple rode to their new home at the 'old Manse' in Concord. Megan Marshall reports the following words Sophia wrote to her mother. "Every step the horses took, I felt better and not the least tired. My husband looked upon me as upon a mirage which would suddenly disappear. It seemed miraculous that I was so well." She was an invalid no more.

Next, mother Peabody insisted she must never have a child—that her health would not permit it. However, Sophia removed from her mother's power, had not just one but three children. Her life centered around her home. After her marriage Sophia became less interested in her painting career. Love, not art, replaced her illness.

Elizabeth Palmer Peabody (7), *{Nathaniel (6), Isaac (5), Matthew (4), Isaac (3), Francis (2), John (1)}*
(May 16, 1804, Billerica—January 3, 1894) Teacher, writer, lecturer, founder of the public kindergarten in America

Elizabeth opened her first private school at the age of 16 and began a life of teaching. She was invited to join the Transcendental Club, an elite group of literary figures. These literary giants—William Ellery Channing, Bronson Alcott, Ralph Waldo Emerson—became her lifelong friends. Possessing a brilliant mind and an outspoken personality, Elizabeth could compete with the best in the world of ideas. Elizabeth introduced Nathaniel Hawthorne to these Boston friends and also to her sister, Sophia.

In 1839 Elizabeth opened a bookshop in Boston which became a gathering place for transcendental reformers, liberal clergymen and Harvard professors. She set up a printing press in the back room and published three of Hawthorne's books, several of Margaret Fuller's translations from German and Emerson's literary journal, *The Dial.*

Her most notable achievement was establishing the kindergarten in American schools. The innovative German kindergarten begun by Friedrich Froebel inspired her, and she traveled abroad to study his method and philosophy. In 1860 she opened the country's first kindergarten in Boston. Elizabeth promoted the idea, "Children should be led to discover everything...when their minds are in the ease of spontaneous play."

Indefatigable, Elizabeth wrote, translated and printed dozens of books on education as well as voicing her opinions on numerous speaking tours. In addition to promoting the kindergarten, Elizabeth campaigned for abolition. Twice she visited President Lincoln urging emancipation for the slaves.

Elizabeth had several romantic attractions, including both Nathaniel Hawthorne and Horace Mann before they met and fell in love with her sisters. None of her male friends materialized into a marriage partner, however. Elizabeth may have preferred to devote her life to her career rather than to marriage. And she may have come across in a way which made her less attractive to potential suitors than her more "feminine" younger sisters. Elizabeth was a dynamo. She had a brilliant mind, a forthright personality and a robust physique. According to Marshall, she once begged Horace Mann to tell her if he thought that "thro' earnestness—enthusiasm—or any other innocent cause even—I was ever betrayed into an overbearing—intrusive—masculine manner." He answered no, but like all the others, after a brief infatuation, drew back from Elizabeth. In 19th century New England intelligent women were admired, but still expected to appear, in Emerson's words, "more vulnerable, more affirm, more mortal than men."

Rev. Ephraim Peabody (8), *{Ephraim (7), Ephraim (6), Thomas (5). Ephraim (4), William (3), Francis (2), John (1)}*
(March 22, 1809, Wilton, NH—July 5, 1856) Minister, abolitionist

Ephraim grew up a farm boy, then went off to Bowdoin College and later studied for the ministry. An ardent foe of slavery, he spoke with such gusto that he was asked to be the pastor of King's Chapel in Boston in 1846. In an attempt to prevent the slavery issue from dividing the nation, Ephraim contended that the slavery decision belonged to the individual states. He believed that as long as Northern states agitated against slavery they frightened the South and delayed the southern states arriving at their own decision to liberate the blacks.

Ephraim believed the blacks should be set free and sent away—back to Africa, or to Mexico or even a Caribbean island. He feared (like nearly everyone at that time) that intermarriage between blacks and whites would create a "third race," inferior to both white and Negro. In addition, he believed, they needed to be sent away because in America they could "never rise above the firm lines of caste, even if set free."

The Reverend Ephraim gained respect as a man of good common sense and purity of character. His thoughts received much credence. Perhaps it is fortunate that Ephraim died at an early age before the North and South became embattled in bitter war and the slavery question was resolved.

Rev. Andrew Preston Peabody (8),
{Andrew (7), Andrew (6), Zerubabel (5), Joseph (4), Joseph (3), Francis (2), John (1)}
(March 19, 1811, Beverly, MA—March 10, 1893) Author, minister, educator

Andrew became the Peabody family's most prodigious author. He published 190 books over his lifetime, 120 of which were written in his last 20 years of life. Regarded as a child genius, he began to read at the age of three. Andrew was only 12 when he passed with distinction the entrance requirements to Harvard College. But his teachers and guardians considered him "too immature" and delayed his entrance for a year. During this time he continued in private instruction and gained further ground. When he enrolled at Harvard at the age of 13, he entered as a member of the junior class. In 1826 Andrew graduated, the second youngest ever before 1900 to graduate from Harvard.

Andrew obtained a teaching post in Middleton, Massachusetts as his first job after college. As a shy, 15-year-old Andrew found it difficult instructing students older than himself and who delighted in giving him a hard time. This first teaching experience stands out as the only unsuccessful venture in his life. As an escape from teaching Andrew decided to follow the path of so many other Peabodys and enter the Unitarian ministry. He graduated from Harvard Divinity School and took over the congregation in Portsmouth, New Hampshire in 1833.

For years Andrew served as their minister as well as traveling, lecturing and writing prolifically. Andrew had an enormous appetite for work. He bought the *North American Review* and became the editor-in-chief. He served 40 years as a trustee for Phillips Exeter Academy and 18 as chairman of the board. He was the first to propose a graduate school for Harvard. Andrew held countless other positions and achievements too numerous to list. His dazzling literary career included books written on history, biography, archeology, moral philosophy, theology, travel, poetry, art, science and literature.

Andrew's association with Harvard deepened in 1852 when he was chosen as Preacher to Harvard University and Plummer Professor of Christian morals. For 21 years he taught at Harvard. Just as the scope of his writing was broad, the classes he taught covered a wide range—ethics, logic, political economy, astronomy, Hebrew and forensics. In addition to his teaching responsibilities he conducted daily prayer services, preached two sermons on Sunday and tended to the ministerial needs of the students. Twice, in 1862 and 1868, he served as acting president of Harvard. Andrew, well liked and often referred to as "Old Doc" or "Dear Old Doctor Peabody," truly cared about the students and helped soften the harsh discipline that still marked Harvard.

At the age of 70 he retired from Harvard but continued preaching, lecturing and writing at the same prodigious rate. In spite of Andrew's vast range of interests and astonishing production of literary works, he made no significant contribution to any one field. Likewise, he lacked eloquence as a preacher or inspiration as a teacher. Yet he emerged as one of the most beloved of all the professors at Harvard. Students, when asked who had the most beneficent influence upon them, often named Andrew Peabody. Thus, he earned his nickname, the College Saint.

When he died, Harvard placed a marble bust of him in Gore Hall, named a building after him, commissioned a portrait, and put up a bronze tablet in his honor on the wall of Appleton Chapel.

Robert Swain Peabody (9), *{Ephraim (8), Ephraim (7), Ephraim (6), Thomas (5), Ephraim (4), William (3), Francis (9), John (1)}*
(February 22, 1845, New Bedford, MA—September 23, 1917) Architect

Robert Swain Peabody was only 11 in 1856 when his father, Rev. Ephraim Peabody, the misguided abolitionist minister of King's Chapel, died. In time he, like so many other Peabodys, entered Harvard College. Here he developed a keen mind and a strong body. Robert rowed on the eight that swept its field in the Eastern Rowing Championships. Because of his high marks and popularity, his class chose him Chief Marshal on Class Day.

After graduation in 1866, Robert headed for Paris where he could pursue his dream—architecture. France had at that time entered a period of architectural brilliance and the arts were flourishing. Robert enrolled in the Ecoles des Beaux-Arts in Paris where he steeped himself in the study of great buildings. Finishing his studies, Robert returned with his fine artistic ability enhanced by a brilliant memory for what he had seen and drawn in Europe. But he lacked business knowledge and the practical experience of dealing in the real world with contractors and clients, so he joined forces with John G. Stearns, also a Harvard graduate. Together, their partnership conquered the world of architecture. In time theirs became one of the leading architectural firms in America.

They designed such landmarks as Mathews Hall and Hemenway Gymnasium at Harvard; the Customs House Tower; the Exchange Building and the Telephone Building in Boston; the Groton School for Endicott Peabody; the granite State House at Concord, New Hampshire; and the Union League Club in New York. In Colorado he built the lodge house on top of Pikes Peak and the Antlers Hotel in Colorado Springs, in its day the finest resort hotel in the country.

Robert Swain Peabody was known for his Italian Renaissance style, one he admired and brought back from his student days in Europe. Great honor came to him during his lifetime. He was elected many times as president of the Boston Society of Architects and was an overseer at Harvard for 11 years. Robert played a prominent role in the beautification of American cities. In Boston he worked towards rejuvenating city buildings without destroying old landmarks, and he strongly supported the turn of the century effort to beautify Washington D.C.

His monument is in King's Chapel, Boston.

Selim Hobart Peabody (9) *{(Charles Hobart (8), John (7), Stephen (6), William (5), Stephen (4), William (3), Francis (2), John (1)}*
(August 20, 1852, Rockingham, VT—May 26, 1903) Educator

As the son of a Congregational minister, Selim grew up in a strict, repressive Puritan household. Selim suffered a miserable childhood. At school the bullies taunted him as the preacher's son. Then his father died. A wealthy suitor of his mother provided the means for him to attend Boson Latin School for a year. But when his mother married a poor deacon, he was sent out to work for a farmer in exchange for board and clothing. The farmer's wife treated him horribly, dressing him in rags and feeding him only salt pork and salt cod, milk and potatoes. He had to sleep above an unheated woodshed where his hands and feet became frostbitten during the cold winter. After a year he left and worked as a carpenter's apprentice, developed tuberculosis, and took a job binding shoes.

Selim was a survivor. He decided his health had closed the door to many occupations, so he needed to educate himself and become a professional man. Selim wanted to become a teacher, most definitely not a minister like his father. He scraped together the means to attend the University of Vermont and graduated third in his class in 1852.

Over the years Selim taught at or served as the principal, superintendent or president of a number of high schools and universities in Vermont, Pennsylvania, Wisconsin, Illinois and Massachusetts. In recognition of his success, he was elected president of the Wisconsin Teacher's Association in 1836. As spokesman for this organization, he lobbied long and hard for a state supported normal school and the establishment of teacher's institutes.

In 1891 Selim retired from his illustrious teaching career and became a specialist in international expositions—the World's Colombian Exposition (1891); the World's Fair at Paris (1899); the Pan-American Exposition in Buffalo (1901); and the South Carolina Interstate and West Indies Exposition at Charleston (1902). He died while working on the Louisiana Purchase Exposition (1902).

For many years Selim's labor of love was gathering information and compiling the materials for a Peabody family history. The family is indebted to him for his comprehensive *Peabody Genealogy* which was edited by Charles Pope and published in 1909 after Selim's death. This monumental work gives a complete listing of all the descendants of Francis and William Peabody from 1635 to 1897.

Josephine Preston Peabody (10) *{Charles (9), Francis (8), Allen (7), Francis (6), Bimsley (5), Francis (4), Isaac (3), Francis (2), John (1)}*
(May 30, 1874, Brooklyn, NY—December 4, 1922) Poet, dramatist

Another Peabody literary light, Josephine was educated at Boston Girls' Latin school and at Radcliffe College (1894-1906). After her father died when she was 10 years old, she became an omnivorous reader and later a creative writer. Her first volume of poetry, *The Wayfarers*, was published in 1898. Numerous other poems and plays followed: *Fortune and Men's Eyes; Marlowe; The Singing Leaves;* and *Pan, A Choric Idyl*

In 1906 Josephine married Lionel Simeon Marks, of the engineering department at Harvard University. Her happiness as a wife and mother contributed to her artistic development. In 1909 Josephine's play, *The Piper*, won the Stratford Play Competition against 350 competitors. Alongside her successful career, Josephine developed a growing concern for labor conditions, expressed in *The Singing Man*. She also was active in the women's suffrage movement and joined the Women's Party. Her last two works, *Song for the Pilgrim Women* for the Plymouth Pageant and *Portrait of Mrs. W* were published a few months before her death.

The Song of the Pilgrim Women

After the nights and days,
Our hearts pour out their praise,
O Father, who hast led us here,
Over the dim sea-ways.
The dread sea-ways.

Earth, Earth, she bloometh!—
The water-brook it hummeth.—
And ah, when April cometh—
(Run, lads, run)
Hey-ho, land at last:—
Hey-ho, the Sun!
Our strength was like to fail,
Even as a shuddering sail—
Trembling upon our lips,
Thy hand upheld us who went down,
Down to the sea in ships!
Down to the sea in ships.

And some day, from our sowing,
Midsummer overflowing:—
Ways of brightness, for our feet unknowing!
(All, all unknowing).

Thistle-down, for spinning, O!
Bless the good beginning!

O, fold us in Thy keeping:
Hold us above our weeping,—
Us, and our young, young children,
Thou Unsleeping!
(Unsleeping, unsleeping)

Bring all your boughs for burning:
Run, lad, run!
Boughs of fir—
And juniper—
Breathing in the Sun.

Forgive our blind amaze
Through all these blindfold days.
Thou knowest.—Thou wilt see
Beyond our poor discerning.
All of our treasury
We offer here to Thee:—
We, the unreturning.
(Unreturning)

Endicott Peabody (9), *{Samuel Endicott (8),*
Francis (7), Joseph (6), Francis (5), Francis (4),
Isaac (3), Francis (2), John (1)}
(May 20, 1857, Salem, MA—1940) Minister, educator

A Bostonian educated in England, Endicott became an Episcopal minister. In 1882, he was asked to take over the church in Tombstone, Arizona. He served here as a frontier preacher in the midst of gunfighters and desperadoes, miners and drunken cowboys. Endicott rose to the challenge of life in the rough and tough West. People liked him and were able to tolerate his English ways.

But after a couple of years Endicott became homesick for the East and returned to Massachusetts. Despite his father's objection, in 1886 he married his true love, first cousin, Fanny Peabody.

Endicott went on to found the Groton School for boys which developed into a highly respected institution. The announced purpose of the school was "to cultivate manly, Christian character, having regard to moral and physical as well as intellectual development." Endicott's dream was to exert an influence on the world through these boys, by instilling in them a capacity for leadership and service.

His dream was most certainly realized. Hundreds of famous Americans in many fields graduated from Groton. When Franklin Roosevelt, a Groton graduate, became engaged to Eleanor, Franklin wrote Endicott and asked him to be sure to come to the wedding. Despite his occasional churlishness, both former members of the faculty and former students kept in contact with their old mentor.

Endicott served Groton as headmaster for over 50 years.

Endicott Peabody (11), *{Malcolm (10), Endicott (9), Samuel Endicott (8), Francis (7), Joseph (6), Francis (5), Francis (4), Isaac (3), Francis (2), John (1)}*
(1920—1998) Politician, Governor

Endicott Peabody, the grandson of Endicott who originated the Groton School, not only shared his grandfather's name, but also the Peabody family character—an ironbound conscience and a will to do public good.

Endicott's father, Malcolm Peabody, became a minister and pastored his own church, Grace Church in Lawrence, Massachusetts before his appointment as Episcopal Bishop in central New York. Young Endicott went to Groton to study under his grandfather. He excelled both in sports and in his studies. At Harvard he played varsity hockey, tennis and football and was chosen All American guard. But Chubs, as his buddies nicknamed him, focused not only on sports. He had grown up in the Groton tradition of a well-rounded man. He joined Harvard's theater group, the Hasty Pudding Club. His classmates elected him to Harvard's student council and as second marshal of his graduating class.

Endicott's graduation coincided with World War II and he went off to war, serving as a commissioned officer in the Navy Submarine Corps. He not only emerged from battle unscathed but with several decorations as well—the Silver Star and a Presidential Unit Citation for bravery under fire.

After the war Endicott decided to become a politician so he returned to Harvard to earn his law degree in 1948. Active in politics, he campaigned for Harry S. Truman and later for Adlai Stevenson, both presidential candidates. Endicott himself enjoyed moderate success in his bids for public office. Twice he lost the Democratic nomination for Massachusetts Attorney General. He did serve a two-year term as Governor of Massachusetts beginning in 1963, but was unsuccessful in subsequent attempts to win election. Some say that his independence in politics and failure to lean on the old Democratic machine cost him success.

Mary Parkman Peabody
(July 24, 1891, Boston—February 6, 1981)

Mary Parkman Peabody was a Peabody by marriage, not by birth. She met her future husband, who was then a missionary in the Philippines, on a round the world cruise after her college graduation. In 1916 she married Rev. Malcolm E. Peabody, the son of Endicott, Groton School founder.

Mary's first claim to fame came as the mother of both Massachusetts Governor Endicott Peabody and Marietta Peabody Tree, U.S. delegate to the United Nations Trusteeship Council in 1964-65. Her second claim arose from the social activism for civil rights and antiwar causes that marked her aging years.

Mary had lived a relatively sheltered, privileged life as the mother of five children and wife of central New York's Episcopal Bishop. But she had always been interested in community work and social causes. So in 1964, at the age of 72, she responded to Martin Luther King's request and left the comfort of her home in Boston's Back Bay and traveled to St. Augustine, Florida. Here she led a sit-in by blacks and whites at the racially segregated dining room of a motel. Police standing by with tear gas, elecric cattle prods and leashed police dogs confronted the protesters. They arrested Mary and threw her in jail with 116 other activists. As she was taken away, she declared, "We need some old people in this thing. We are just what they say we are—do-gooders."

Word flashed across the nation's air waves that the mother of the Governor of Massachusetts had been locked up after a sit-in. In response, Endicott told a news conference, "I can only express admiration for her courage, sincerity and determination."

After the turmoil ended, Mary, a tall, white-haired woman wearing sensible shoes and a simple print dress, spoke in her cultured Brahmin accent: "Really, it was quite an attractive jail. It was clean and whitewashed, and there were the loveliest yellow and orange flowers planted along the sidewalks. Next door in the other cell there were 50 Negro women. Our food was passed to us under the bars. There weren't enough utensils, so we ate our hominy grits with our fingers. But we managed nicely."

After her jail stay in Florida, Mary became active in antiwar protests during the Vietnam War. She marched to protest nuclear weapons in the 1960's and 70's. Mary's friends regarded her as a woman of deeply independent spirit and strong character. She only grew stronger as she grew older.

Francis Peabody used this mallet to close the gates of the old Peabody grist mill in Topsfield, Massachusetts. The metal band on the mallet's handle has an inscription indicating that the band was fashioned from the original gate hinge.

The Last Will and Testament of John Paybody

In and upon the sixteenth of July in the yeare of our Lord 1649 I John Paybody of Duxburrow in the Collonie of New Plymouth, plantor, being in perfect health and sound in memory, God be blessed for it, doe ordaine and make this my Last Will and Testament in manner and forme as followeth:

Imprimis I bequeth my soule to God that gave it hopeing to be saved by the Merritt of Christ my blessed Savior and Redeemer; as for my wordly goods as followeth;

Item I give and bequeth unto Thomas, my eldest sonne one shilling.

Item I give and bequeth unto ffrancis Paybody, my second son, one shilling.

Item I give unto William Paybody, my youngest son, one shilling.

Item I give and bequeth unto Annis Rouse, my daughter, one shilling.

Item I give and bequeth unto John Rouse, the son of John Rouse, my lands att Carswell in Marshfield after my wife's decease.

Item I give unto John Paybody, the son of William, my lott of land att the New Plantation [Bridgewater]

Item I give and bequeath all the Rest of my goods that are known to be mine, living and dead, unto my wife, Isabell Paybody, whom I make my sole Exequitrix of this my Last Will and Testament;

Memorandum all these legacyes before sett downe are to be payed by William Paybody, my youngest son, when they shalbe demanded.

John Paybody

John ffernesyde
Boston in New England
the 27th of Aprill 1667

Mr. John ffernesyde came before mee under written and deposed that by order of John Paybody above written and mentioned: hee wrote what is above written and Read it to the said John Paybody on the day of the date thereof and declared the same to be his Last Will and that when hee soe did hee was of a sound disposing mind to his best knowlidg and alsoe subscribed his name thereunto John ffernesyde as a witness:

As Attesteth Edward Rawson
Recorder

The Last Will & Testament of William Pabodie

The Last Will & Testament of William Pabodie of Little Compton in the County of Bristoll being aged and weakly, but of perfect understanding, as at other times, blessed be God for it, for the settling & continueing peace in my family and amongst my children after my decease do order my estate in the world as followeth—

Impimis that my Body after it be Dead have Decent buriall & all funerall charges be Defrayed out of my estate....

Item that all my Lawful Debts be fully & clearely and truely payed out of my estate as soon after my Death as Conveniently Can....

Item I give unto my beloved wife all my houseing and lands in that part of y town of Little Compton aforsd called the three quarters of a mile square the land being the one halfe of fourteen eleven acre lotts of land lyeing all of them in said three quarters of a mile square the Dwelling house being the East end of said house (the one halfe of sd fourteen eleven acre lotts of land. I gave formerly unto my son William Pabodie as may appear by a Deed of Gift unto him under my hand and Seal) Dureing the time of her widowhood: but if she Marry againe then I give her the Third part only Dureing her life. Allso I give unto my sd wife all my household stuff beds and beding puter brass Iron Tinn wood—except onely one sett of Green Curtaines which I have given unto my Daughter Lidea Greenill after my wives Decease Together with the vallens thereunto belonging Allso I give unto my wife what cattle or beast of any sort or kind shall be found mine at my Death Together allso with all Bills due unto me at my death and what money shall be found mine at my Death Provided she Marry not againe and allso Rest contented with this my bequest to her in this my last will & Testament But if my wife shall see cause to claime her Thirds of my house and lands that was mine at Duxbury which I sold unto Samuel Bartlett and make use thereof then my will is my son William Pabodie shall have the whole use of houseing & lands at Little Compton & pay Samuel Bartlett fifty shillings by the year Dureing the time his mother makes use of her thirds at Duxbury...

Item my will further is that if my wife will not be Contented with her thirds at Little Compton onely nor with her thirds at Duxbury onely but shall claime her Thirds in both places or Marry Againe then my will is that I do hereby make Voide all my Bequest to her before Mentioned in this my last will & Testament and that she shall have onely such part of my estate as the law provides when the Husband. Dyes Intestate, and my bequest in this my last will & Testament in what its more than the law Request as aforesaid shall goe to make up the Damage any person shall sustain by her Refusall...

Item I give to my son William Pabodie after his Mothers death that part of my house and land in Little Compton which I have bequeathed unto his mother dureing her life to him & his heirs for ever with all the Appurtenances...

Item I give unto my son William Pabodie one Quarter part of a four & Twenty acre lott of land in Little Compton the Eighth in number among the four & Twenty acre lotts in Little Compton to him his heires and assigns for ever...

Item I give unto my son William Pabodie all my books not otherwise Disposed of before my Death and all my tools Axes hoes augurs saws Chaines hooks plows Irons. Crow &c.

Item I give unto my three Gransons Namely Stephen Southworth the naturall son of my daughter Rebecca now Deceased and the naturall sons of my said son William Pabodie Namely John Pabodie & William Pabodie as followeth, whereas there are certain lands belonging unto me the Testator Lyeing in or about a place called Wesbanange westward of the town of Providence in Rhod Iland Jurisdiction in New England not as yet bound out nor Divided namely one whole share I purchased of Philip Taber as may appear by Deeds under the hand & seale of sd Taber bearing date November the 12th 1685. and one other share in sd. Land in the same

Country Purchased by my son in law William ffoabs of Shuball Painter as may appear by a Deed under his hand and seal bearing date March the 8th, 1682, but assigned over by the said William ffobes unto my son in law Icabod Wiswell and my self the Testator as may appear by an assignment on the back side said Deed Now I give unto my three Gransons before named vix Stephen Southworth John Pabody and William Pabodie one third part of that whole share of land bought of Phillip Taber the other two third parts haveing formerly sold unto my two sons in law namely Edward Southworth & William ffobes allso I give two third parts of my halfe share of what was said Suball Painters the other third part of said half share I sold unto my said son in law Edward Southworth now I say the one third part of my share I bought of Phillip Tabor & two third parts of that half share that I bought that was Suball Painters I give unto my said three Gransons namely Stephen Southworth John Pabodie & William Pabodie by an equal Division to them and their heirs for ever.

Item   I give unto my naturall Daughter Mary one shilling & to my naturall Daughter Mercey one shilling and unto my naturall Daughter Martha one shilling and unto my naturall Daughter Priscilla one shilling & unto my Naturall Daughter Ruth one shilling and unto my naturall Daughter Sarah one shilling & unto my naturall Daughter Hannah one shilling & to my naturall Daughter Lidia one shilling and to the heires of my naturall Daughter Elizabeth one shilling and unto the heirs of my naturall Daughter Rebeccah one shilling.

Lastly I constitute and appoint mty beloved wife & my son William Pabodie sole executors of this my last will and Testament—Desireing my beloved friends:

William Pabodie

Signed and sealed in the presence of these witnesses May 13th: 1707

John Woodman

Peter Taylor

Samuel Wilbore

An Inventory of the goods and estate of the Late Deceased Mr William Pabodie who dyed the 13th day of December 1707:

	POUNDS	SHILLINGS	PENCE
Itt: To 70 acres of land at 4':10:p acre is	315	00	00
Itt: To six acres of land	006	00	00
Itt: To a share of land in Purchase called Washganaug in Rhoad Island Collony (the value not known)			
Itt: To a Dwelling house & halfe the Barn	30	00	00
Itt: To one Mare & her yearling being a Mare	6	00	00
Itt: To one cow and a young Calfe both at	3	00	00
Itt: To Sundry books	6	00	00
Itt: To 2 feather beds and the furniture belonging to them	14	00	00
Itt: To 4 basons & 3 platters & 3 porringers all	1	11	00
Itt: To a tankard and a pint pott and a boal cup and one plate	10	00	
Itt: To 2 old chamber potts & an old bed pan & 2 cups and some old puter	12	00	
Itt: To 2 Iron potts & one iron kettles	1	00	00
Itt: To an old Brass pan & 2 little Kettles & 2 skillitss	1	05	00
Itt: To 2 Trammels & a spit & a pair of tons& a fire slice all	01	00	
Itt: To a pr of An Irons 14" to an old Driping pan & to an old skimer 2 Turning potts & gratter	17	06	
Itt: To a warming pan & 2 earthen potts	08	06	
Itt: To 4 Trayes & 3 Keelers & a cheese fatt	10	00	

Itt: To 3 Chests two of them being smale and nine

other chaires   1   04   00

Itt: To old Tooles & an old saddle & bridle all

     1   17   00

Itt: To 2 pair of pinchers & 2 hammers & 4 awles
& 6 fishing hookes & lines

     1   07   00

Itt: To 2 old plow Chaines & a iron barr & a pair
of old plough shares

     1   01   00

Itt: To a pair of Cupples and a halfe peck all

      02   06

Itt: To one duz of Napkins & 2 Table cloaths & a
looking Glass   1   18   00

Itt: To a grid iron & an old sword

     1   18   00

Itt: To a pair of marking irons & a smale pewter bot-
tle & Cow bell 03   06

Itt: To a Churn and a Runlett & two Glasss bottled

     06   00

Itt: To powder & shott & flints all

     05   00

Itt: To Cash   02   10   00

Itt: To al his wearing apparill both lining & woolen

     10   00   00

Itt: To more found since one pitch forke is

     407   14   00

We whose names are underwritten being choosen by M William Pabodie son to y Dec M Pabodie to Inventory the estate of the Dec M Pabodie have as above written prised it according to the best of our understanding witness our hands y 30th day of December: 1707

    John Palmer
    Edward Richmond

Bristol Ss // in Little Compton feb 27; 1707 M Elizabeth Pabodie & her son William Pabodie executors of the Last will and Testament of M William Pabodie late of Little Compton Deceased Appered before Natha Byfield Esq Judge of Probate of wills & within the County of Britol And made Oath that the Inventory on the other side is the whole of the estate the said Dec Dyed seized of & is come to their knowledge and when they know of more they will Reveal it & bring it to the Reg.

    N Byfield
   John Cary Reg
     entered March 3rd: 1707
     by John Cary Recorder

William Pabodie, Executor, presented the account of his administration Sept. 13, 1709; showing that he had paid each of the heirs their cash legacies and had paid the expenses of the funeral, which included one shilling for the roge, six shillings for digging the grave, three shillings for the coffin, twelve shillingts for 3 gallons of rum and 13 shillings for the grave stones, beside paying the doctor two pounds and three shillings (Bristol Co. Records, Vol. 2, pp. 193-5, 268.)

Children (dates in original "style," the year beginning March 25):

i.   John, b. Oct. 4, 1645; sold his grandfather's legacy in 1668; d. Nov.17,1669. The coroner's jury found that "hee riding on the road, his horse carried him underneath the bow of a tree, violently forceing his head unto the body thereof, broke his skull, which wee doe judge was the cause of his death." (Plym Col. Rec.)

ii.   Elizabeth, b. April 24, 1647; m. John Rogers.

iii.   Mary, b. Aug. 7, 1648; m. Nov. 16, 1669, Edward Southworth

iv.   Mercy, b. Jan 2, 1649

v.   Martha, b. Jan 2, 1649; m. Samuel Seabury (Mayflower Desc.)

vi.   Priscilla, b. Jan. 15, 1653

vii   Sarah, b. Aug. 1656; m. Nov. 10, 1681, John Coe; he d. Dec. 10, 1728, and she m. (2) Oct. 7, 1731, Casear Church. She d. Aug. 27, 1740.

viii.   Ruth, b. June 17, 1658.

ix.   Rebecca, b. Oct. 15, 1660; m. William Southworth; she d. Dec. 3, 1702

x.   Hannah, b. Oct. 15, 1662; m. Oct. 2, 1683, Samuel Bartlett.

xi.   William, b. Nov. 24, 1664, at Duxbury; m. first Judith, b. in 1669, d. July 26, 1714. He married second Elizabeth___. He m. third Mrs. Mary (Morgan) Starr. He d. Sept. 17, 1744.

xii.   Lydia, b. April 3, 1667; m. Daniel Grinnell.

The Last Will and Testament of Francis Pebody

The Last Will & Testament of Lieut: Francis Pebody of Topsfield in y county of Es[sex] [in] New England: I Francis Pebody taking into consideration the uncertainty of my life and certainty of my death being of perfect understanding & memory have seen good to m[ake] such a disposall of the temporall estate which God of his grace hath given me in this w[orld] as followeth,—

Impr. I committ my immortall soul into the hands of God & my body to a decent buriall [when] God shall take me out of this world

Secundo I give to my son John Pebody & Joseph Pebody all that tract of Land which I bought of marchant Joseph Juett of Rowly which Land lyeth in Boxford, I give to my son J.... two thirds of y aforesaid tract of Land & to my son Joseph y other third which I give to them & to their Heirs for ever & moreover I do give to them both in c[ountrey] pay (not mony) five pounds to each of them, y is five pounds apiece, besides what I have already given them.

Item, I do give to my son William Pebody all that Land which I bought of John Tod Sen [of] Rowly & of John Perley (excepting one hundred acres) which land I do give to him & his Heirs for ever, moreover I do give to him five pounds besides what he hath [...] me already, which I do this rather on consideration of his being (by y providence of God) deprived of y use of one of his arms, w five pounds is to be paid as is above specified.

Item I do give to my son in Law Daniell Wood That hundred acres of Land which is above excepted to my son William & is already in part possessed by my son in [law] Daniel Wood which said Land I do give to him & to his Heirs for ever it be[ing] in consideration of what I was oblidged to do for him when come to age & pro[vided] y he shall be satisfyed therewith on y account & give a discharge thereof to such [...] shall concern Which Land I have already promised & do purpose forthwith to [give] him a deed of in a way of firm conveyance in which deed I shall bound...Limit y aforesaid hundred acres accordingly

Item I do give to my son Isaac Pebody all the land y I do now live upon which I bou[ght] of Mr Simons & my will is y my son Isaac shall have all y said Land which lyeth on [ye] south side of y brook running through the said farm both upland & meadow so bo[unded] I give to my son Isaac Pebody together w my dwelling house & housing, orchard, mill, millyard w all y I bought of William Evans & moreover I give to my son Isaac from [the] bridge all y meadow downward on y north east side of y brook which runneth through...Tho: Dormans meadow: as also I do give to my son Isaac a Rod & half of upland... to y aforesaid meadow all along for y bringing of his hay from time to time which afore[named] Land I do give to my son Isaac & to his Heirs forever, together w seventy acres of Land... y south side of y River, neer to y dwelling of Joseph Town Jun, Also I give to my son [Isaac] that bed with the furniture thereunto belonging which he now hath y improvement [of] & this I would have noted, That I have given y more to my son Isaac on consideration [of] y providence of God disinabling him by y loss of one of his Leggs.

Item I do give to my Grand child Jacob Pebody (y son of my son Jacob Pebody deceased) y h[ouse] which his father dwelt in together with all y upland on y side of y brook y is on...North side of y aforesaid brook, as also all y meadow on y same side of y brook...y bridge & so upward, my will is y in case my said Grandchild Jacob Pebody do [live] to y age of twenty one years then he shall have as is above said to injoy himselfe..his Heirs for ever, But in Case y said Jacob live not to y age y then any of my other[...] shall have liberty to have y land & house abovesaid provided y he or they shall [...] to my grandchildren Kezia & Mercy Pebody y children of my son Jacob Pebody deceased an hundred and twenty pounds in common currant pay (not silver) notwithstanding... is abovesaid in case y said Jacob should have issue before he should arrive at y aforesaid age y y said Land shall be at y disposall of y abovesaid Jacob Pebody together [...] aforesaid. Also I do give to my grandchildren Kezia and Mercy Pebody y children of [my] son Jacob deceased I do give to each of them Thirty acres of Land apiece, provided th[at] [they] shall live to y age of eighteen years, which Threescore acres of Land Lyeth on y south s[ide] of y River in y south-west Division beyond m Endicotts farm in y place called y stick[y] meadow which Land abovesaid I bought part of Deacon Tho Perkins about thirty [acres] & about thirty more which I bought of Daniell Dorman, but in Case of neither of y chi[ldren] Kezia or Mercy shall live to y age of eighteen y then y abovesaid Thirty acres apiece shall return to my next & immediate children to be equally divided amongst them [but] in Case one of y said grandchildren live to y age & not y other that then y whole Threescore acres shall fall to y surviver of them.

Item I give to my son Nathaniell Pebody together with my Grandchild Samson How a[ll] that four hundred acres which I bought of m Stephen Sewall Lying in Rowly village called Box-ford which land lyeth near Bradford & was formerly m Nelsons of Rowly. My will is y my son Nathaniell shall have three hundred & Samson How y other hundred acres which for quantity and quality y aforesaid Samson How shall have y said Hundred acres provided y y said Samson How shall be at my despose till y age of twenty[one] years. But in Case my son Nathaniell shall dye without Lawfull Issue that they y above said three hundred acres shall fall to my other children by equall devision, his widdow notwithstanding injoying y benefit thereof during life & as to his moveable estate which he is already in possession of I leave it all to be at his y is my son Natheniells despose here is to be understood y what shall be left undesposed of by my son Nathaniell at his death of his three hundred acres shall be for y use of his widdow during her life as abovesaid y is y life of her widdowhood.

I do reserve for Mary my wife y South End of my house for her Use to live in as also y New Cellar as also y Use of two milch Cows which she shall choose out of my milch kine, Also my will is y my son Isaac shall pay to my wife Mary yearly twenty bushells of Indian Corne, four bushells of wheat, four of rye & six of malt, also y my wife have liberty to keep two or three swine, as also yearly half a dozen pounds of wool, also my will is y my wife shall have pasture for her cowes with my son Isaacs as also y my son Isaac shall provide fodder for them in y winter. As also my wife shall have Liberty for an horse to ride on as she shall have occasion. Also my will is y in Case my wife shall marry again y then all y priviledges abovesaid shall cease, but during her widdowhood she shal also have (as benefit by my orchard) yearly a barrell of Cidar as also som apples as her occasions either in the summer or winter shall require, More-over my wife shall have y use & despose of two beds together with needful firewood provided for her for which end she shall have y use of such of my oxen as shall be needfull. Also I do order y Samson How shall live with my wife till he shall come to y age of twenty one years & be at her Command to be help-full to her on all accounts as she shall have occasion & in case Samson How shall be taken away by his father before he shall have served as abovesaid y then my wife shall have that hundred acres of land above-said (given Conditionally to y said Samson) to pro-vide for herself such help as shall be necessary. & in Case my wife shall dy before y said Samson How shall arrive at y aforesaid term of years y then he shall be at my wives despse to whom she shall see good & in case y said Samson will not comply with such despose y then y said hundred acres of land intended for him shall be at my wives despose

Item I give to my daughter Lydia Perley five pounds besides what she hath already had of my

I do give to my daughter Mary Death five pounds besides what she hath had already

I do give to my daughter Sarah How five pounds besides what she hath had already

I do give to my daughter Hephzibah Ray five pounds besides what she hath had already all which Legacies ordered to my Children I do appoint to be paid in common currant pay as is before specified to others of my children

Note y what Legacies I do here give in my will shall be paid by executors out of my estate which I do leave in my son Isaac hands & to my wives, as corn or Cattell & my debts & funerall expences being discharged.

And finaly. I do appoint, Consititute & ordain my wife Mary to be an executrix together with my son John Pebody & Isaac Pebody as executors of this my last will & testament & in Case after Legacies paid there by any estate left to be devided y it shall be desposed of in a way of division as my execetrix together w executors shall see good.

That what is here above written is y last will & Testament of y abovesaid Francis Pebody appears by his own hand & seal y day & Date here mentioned as also by y testimony of y witnesses hereunto subscribed

It is to noted y notwithstanding what is abovesaid concerning mty son Nathaniells three hundred acres returning to his brethren in Case of his dying wout lawfull Issue, It is to be understood by y three hundred acres what he shall not see Cause to despose of before his death I hereby notwithstanding what hath been said giving him full power in Case he see good to despose of it either in part or whole not knowing but divine providence may necessitate him thereunto, otherwise what is above written to be of full force as is expressed.

The above said premises were signed & sealed & declared to be my last will & Testament of y said Francis Pebody y twentieth day of January in y year of our Lord one thousand six hundred Ninety & five or six, in presence of us
Joseph Capen
Thomas Baker
Ephraim Dorman Sen

This will was proved August 7, 1698; in due time the following Inventory was made and filed:

The Inventory of y estate of ffrancis Pebody made this 20th May—1698—

	POUNDS	SHILLINGS	PENCE
two oxen; at: 7 pounds. three Cowes. at: 9 pounds, 15 shillings. three young cattell at: 6 pounds	23	00	00
sheep. 4 pounds—one mare and Colt—1 pound 10 shillings	05	10	00
chaines axes wegges— and chisells; and other iron tooles	02	04	00
wearing cloaths	02	04	00
Beds and beding 12 pounds napkins table cloths and other linnen at 5 pounds 9 shillings	17	09	00
chests, tables, chaiers, and other lunber	05	15	06
peuter, and brass ware	05	12	00
Iron ware, as pots, kettles, tramells:&c.	02	05	00
New cloth home made	02	11	00
ten bus: of malt, 1 pound 15 shillings Indian Corne, eight bus: 1 pound 4 shillings. six bushells barley — 1 pound 1 shilling	04	00	00
ffour Swine	02	00	00
Land given to his son John Pebody	200	00	00
Land to Joseph Pebody	100	00	00
Land to William Pebody	100	00	00
Land to Nathaniel Pebody	150	00	00
Land to Samson Howe	050	00	00

Land to Kezia & Marcie Pebody

| | 050 | 00 | 00 |

Land and house to Jacob Pebody

| | 160 | 00 | 00 |

the homestead to Isaac Pebody. as upland, meddow, dwelling house and one barne, and mill

| | 400 | 00 | 00 |

| Sillver mony | 044 | 15 | 00 |
| totall summ: | 1327 | 05 | 06 |

William Howlett
Daniel Redington
Ephraim: Willds

[On the reverse of the foregoing]

Topsfeild y 3oth of September 1698
An addition to the inventory of the estate of ffrancis Pebody as doth apear on the other side of this paper

tow oxen att	09	00	00
nine books	00	13	00
two Cowes	05	00	00
two oxen	08	00	00

two lining spining wheels

| | 00 | 06 | 00 |

two wolen spining wheels

| | 00 | 06 | 00 |

given to y widow two beds with the furniture

| | 19 | 00 | 00 |

eight yards of woll Cloath

| | 01 | 12 | 00 |

| six cushens | 00 | 06 | 00 |

bed and beding given to Isaac

| | 03 | 10 | 00 |

Daniel Redington
Ephraim Willdes
Joseph Byxbe

Children:

i.   Lydia, bapt. Aug. 30, 1640; m. July 8, 1667, Thomas Perley.

ii.   John, b. about 1642 at Hampton N.H.; m. (first) Hannah Andrews Nov. 23, 1665; she d. Dec. 25, 1700. m. (second) Sarah Mosely, Nov. 26, 1703. He d. July 5, 1720.

iii.   Joseph, b. about 1644 at Hampton N.H.; m. (first) Bethiah Bridges Oct. 26, 1668; m. (second) Mary Wheeler Jan. 4, 1714, Will dated Mar 20, 1721.

iv.   William, b. about 1646 at Hampton N.H.;m. (first) Mary Brown Dec. 8, 1680; M. (second) Hannah Hale Aug. 14, 1684. He d. March 6, 1699.

v.   Isaac, b. about 1648 at Hampton, N.H.; m. Sarah Estes. He signed his name "Isaac Peabody," to his will, Oct. 21, 1726. He d. 1727

vi.   Sarah, b. about 1650; m. at Ipswich March 26, 1678, Abraham How. Son Samson How mentioned in her father's will.

vii.   Hepsibah, b. about 1652; m. April 10, 1678, Daniel Rea of Salem Village (Danvers)

viii.   Mary, b. about 1656; m. 910 John Death, of Framingham; m. (2) Samuel Eames

ix.   Ruth, b. May 22, 1658; not mentioned in her father's will.

x.   Damaris, b. June 21, d. Dec. 19, 1660.

xi.   Samuel, b. June 4, 1662; d. Sept. 13, 1667 age 5.

xii.   Jacob, b. July 28, 1664 at Topsfield; m. Abigail Towne Jan 12, 1686. d. Nov. 24, 1689. age 25.

xiii.   Hannah, b. May 8, 1668;

xiv.   Nathaniel, b. July 20, 1669; m. Frances. Died in 1715, leaving no children.

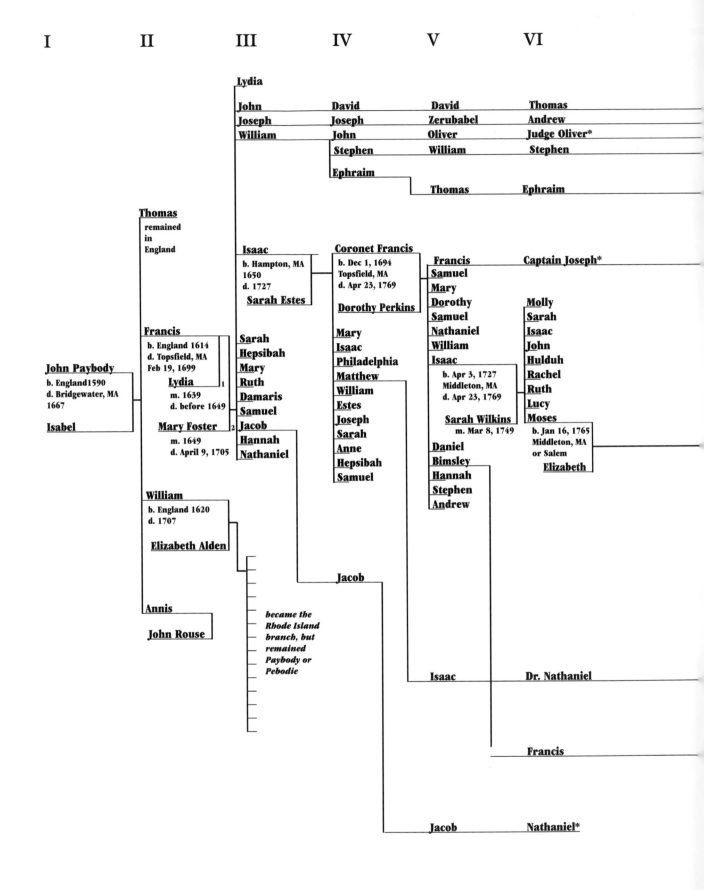

I	II	III	IV	V	VI

Lydia

John — **David** — **David** — **Thomas**

Joseph — **Joseph** — **Zerubabel** — **Andrew**

William — **John** — **Oliver** — **Judge Oliver***

Stephen — **William** — **Stephen**

Ephraim

Thomas — **Ephraim**

Thomas
remained
in
England

Isaac
b. Hampton, MA
1650
d. 1727
Sarah Estes

Coronet Francis
b. Dec 1, 1694
Topsfield, MA
d. Apr 23, 1769

Dorothy Perkins

Francis — **Captain Joseph***
Samuel
Mary
Dorothy
Samuel
Nathaniel
William
Isaac
b. Apr 3, 1727
Middleton, MA
d. Apr 23, 1769
Sarah Wilkins
m. Mar 8, 1749

Molly
Sarah
Isaac
John
Hulduh
Rachel
Ruth
Lucy
Moses
b. Jan 16, 1765
Middleton, MA
or Salem
Elizabeth

Francis
b. England 1614
d. Topsfield, MA
Feb 19, 1699
Lydia   1
m. 1639
d. before 1649
Mary Foster   2
m. 1649
d. April 9, 1705

Sarah
Hepsibah
Mary
Ruth
Damaris
Samuel
Jacob
Hannah
Nathaniel

Mary
Isaac
Philadelphia
Matthew
William
Estes
Joseph
Sarah
Anne
Hepsibah
Samuel

Daniel
Bimsley
Hannah
Stephen
Andrew

John Paybody
b. England1590
d. Bridgewater, MA
1667
Isabel

William
b. England 1620
d. 1707
Elizabeth Alden

Annis
John Rouse

*became the
Rhode Island
branch, but
remained
Paybody or
Pebodie*

Jacob

Isaac — **Dr. Nathaniel**

Francis

Jacob — **Nathaniel***

THE PEABODY FAMILY TREE

VII	VIII	IX	X	XI	XII	XIII

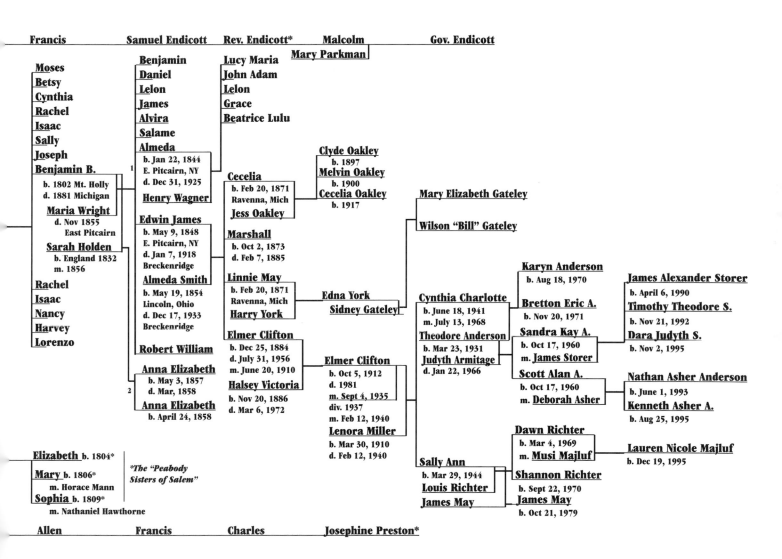

George*
Andrew   Andrew Preston*
Oliver William Bourne*
William Bourne Oliver*
John   Charles Hobart   Selim Hobart*

Ephraim   Rev. Ephraim*   Robert Swain*

Francis   Samuel Endicott   Rev. Endicott*   Malcolm   Gov. Endicott
    Benjamin   Lucy Maria   Mary Parkman

Moses
Betsy
Cynthia
Rachel
Isaac
Sally
Joseph
Benjamin B.
   b. 1802 Mt. Holly
   d. 1881 Michigan
   Maria Wright
    d. Nov 1855
    East Pitcairn
   Sarah Holden
    b. England 1832
    m. 1856
Rachel
Isaac
Nancy
Harvey
Lorenzo

Benjamin
Daniel
Lelon
James
Alvira
Salame
Almeda
   b. Jan 22, 1844
   E. Pitcairn, NY
   d. Dec 31, 1925
   Henry Wagner
Edwin James
   b. May 9, 1848
   E. Pitcairn, NY
   d. Jan 7, 1918
   Breckenridge
   Almeda Smith
   b. May 19, 1854
   Lincoln, Ohio
   d. Dec 17, 1933
   Breckenridge
Robert William
Anna Elizabeth
   b. May 3, 1857
   d. Mar, 1858
Anna Elizabeth
   b. April 24, 1858

Lucy Maria
John Adam
Lelon
Grace
Beatrice Lulu

Cecelia
   b. Feb 20, 1871
   Ravenna, Mich
   Jess Oakley

Marshall
   b. Oct 2, 1873
   d. Feb 7, 1885

Linnie May
   b. Feb 20, 1871
   Ravenna, Mich
   Harry York

Elmer Clifton
   b. Dec 25, 1884
   d. July 31, 1956
   m. June 20, 1910
   Halsey Victoria
   b. Nov 20, 1886
   d. Mar 6, 1972

Clyde Oakley
   b. 1897
Melvin Oakley
   b. 1900
Cecelia Oakley
   b. 1917

Edna York
Sidney Gateley

Elmer Clifton
   b. Oct 5, 1912
   d. 1981
   m. Sept 4, 1935
   div. 1937
   m. Feb 12, 1940
   Lenora Miller
   b. Mar 30, 1910
   d. Feb 12, 1940

Mary Elizabeth Gateley

Wilson "Bill" Gateley

Cynthia Charlotte
   b. June 18, 1941
   m. July 13, 1968
Theodore Anderson
   b. Mar 23, 1931
Judyth Armitage
   d. Jan 22, 1966

Sally Ann
   b. Mar 29, 1944
Louis Richter
James May

Karyn Anderson
   b. Aug 18, 1970
Bretton Eric A.
   b. Nov 20, 1971
Sandra Kay A.
   b. Oct 17, 1960
   m. James Storer
Scott Alan A.
   b. Oct 17, 1960
   m. Deborah Asher

Dawn Richter
   b. Mar 4, 1969
   m. Musi Majluf
Shannon Richter
   b. Sept 22, 1970
James May
   b. Oct 21, 1979

James Alexander Storer
   b. April 6, 1990
Timothy Theodore S.
   b. Nov 21, 1992
Dara Judyth S.
   b. Nov 2, 1995

Nathan Asher Anderson
   b. June 1, 1993
Kenneth Asher A.
   b. Aug 25, 1995

Lauren Nicole Majluf
   b. Dec 19, 1995

Elizabeth b. 1804*
Mary b. 1806*
   m. Horace Mann
Sophia b. 1809*
   m. Nathaniel Hawthorne

*The "Peabody
Sisters of Salem"

Allen   Francis   Charles   Josephine Preston*

*** See Biographical Sketches of these family members
in *Family Foundations*, beginning on page 203**

Author Cynthia Peabody Anderson at ruins of the old stone wall on the site of Francis Peabody's 1660 farm and grist mill in Topsfield, Massachusetts.

Bibliography

Books

Alderson, Nannie T. and Helena Huntington Smith. *A Bride Goes West*. Lincoln, Nebraska: University of Nebraska Press, 1942. Reprinted by Bison Books, 1969.

Aldrich, John K. *Ghosts of Summit County*. Lakewood, Colorado: Centennial Graphics, 1986.

Armitage, Susan and Elizabeth Jameson. *The Women's West*. Norman, Oklahoma: The University of Oklahoma Press, 1987.

Backus, Harriet Fish. *Tomboy Bride, A woman's personal account of life in mining camps of the West*. Boulder: Pruett Publishing Company, 1969.

Baker, George P. *The Pilgrim Spirit: A Pageant in Celebration of the Tercentenary of the Landing of the Pilgrims at Plymouth, Massachusetts, December 21, 1620*. Boston: Marshall Jones Company, 1921.

Bandelier, Adolf. *The Delight Makers*. Orlando Florida: Harcourt Brace Jovanovich Publishers, 1971.

Beyer, Earl. "Ship Passenger List".

Bird, Isabella. *A Lady's Life in the Mountains*. Norman, Oklahoma: University of Oklahoma Press, 1960.

Brackstone, Sir William. *Commentaries on the Laws of England*. Oxford: Clarendon Press.

Bradford, William. *Of Plymouth Plantation, 1620-1647*. Edited by Samuel Eliot Morison, New York, 1952.

Brewer, Professor William H. *Rocky Mountain Letters 1869*. Gunnison, Colorado: James D. Houston, Publisher, 1992.

Brown, Robert L. *Ghost Towns of the Colorado Rockies*. Caldwell, Idaho: The Caxton Printers, Ltd., 1968.

Campbell, Joseph. *The Power of Myth*. New York: Prarie Publishing Company, 1988.

Carson, Rachel. *The Sense of Wonder*. New York: Harper and Row, Publishers, 1956.

Cutter, William Richard. *Genealogical and Family History of Northern New York, Vol.1* New York: Lewis Historical Publishing Company, 1910.

Dorset, Phyllis Flanders. *Colorado's Gold and Silver Rush, The New Eldorado*. New York: The Macmillan Company, 1970.

Ellis, Anne. *The Life of an Ordinary Woman*. Boston: Houghton Mifflin Company, 1929.

Endicott, C. M. *Genealogy of the Peabody Family with a Partial Record of the Rhode Island Branch*. Revised by William S. Peabody. Boston: David Clapp and Son, 1867.

Farrell, Ned. *Colorado, The Rocky Mountain Gem, as it is in 1868*. Published, 1869.

Felt, Joseph B. *History of Ipswich, Essex and Hamilton* (Ipswich, Massachusetts: Clamshell Press, 1834), edited Cambridge, Massachusetts, 1966.

Fiester, Mark. *Blasted, Beloved, Breckenridge*. Boulder: Pruett Publishing Company, 1973.

Gill, Crispin. *Mayflower Remembered, A History of the Plymouth Pilgrims*. New York: Taplinger Publishing Company, 1970.

Gilliland, Mary Ellen. *Breckenridge!* Silverthorne, Colorado: Alpenrose Press, 1988.

Gilliland, Mary Ellen. *Summit, A Gold Rush History of Summit County, Colorado*. Siverthorne, Colorado: Alpenrose Press, 1980.

Gore, Al. *Earth in the Balance*. Boston: Houghton Mifflin Company, 1992.

Greven, Philip. *The Protestant Temperament, Patterns of child-rearing, religious experience, and the self in early America*. New York: Meridian Book, 1977.

Harris, John. *Saga of the Pilgrims from Europe to the New World*. Chester, Connecticut: The Globe Pequot Press, 1983.

Hawke, David Freeman. *Everyday Life in Early America*. New York: Harper and Row Publisher, 1988.

Hill, Frances. *Delusion of Satan: The Full Story of the Salem Witch Trials*. New York: Doubleday, 1995.

Hoffman Leonore and Margo Culley, (editors). *Women's Personal Narratives, Essays in Criticism and Pedagogy.* New York: The Modern Language Association of America, 1985.

Hough, Franklin B. A.M. M.D. *History of St. Lawrence and Franklin Counties, New York, from the Earliest Period to the Present Time.* Originally reprinted by St. Lawrence County Historical Association.

Hoyt, Edwin P. *The Peabody Influence, How a great New England family helped to build America.* New York: Dodd, Mead and Company, 1968.

Leach, Douglas Edward. *Flintlock and Tomahawk — New England in King Philip's War.* New York: 1958, republished in paperback, 1966.

Leach, Douglas Edward. *The Northern Colonial Frontier, 1607-1763.* Holt, Rinehart and Winston, Incorporated, 1966.

Lockridge, Kenneth A. *A New England Town, The First Hundred Years.* New York: Norton and Company, 1970.

Luchetti, Cathy and Carol Olwell. *Women of the West.* Berkeley, California: Antelope Island Press, 1982.

Malone, Dumas. (editor) *Dictionary of American Biography VII.* New York: Charles Scribner and Sons, 1934, copyright renewed, 1962.

Merk, Frederick. *History of the Westward Movement.* Alfred A. Knopf, Incorporated., New York: Random House, 1978.

Merriam, Sidney A. *Ancestry of Franklin M. Peabody.* 1929. Boston Public Library, Book no. 4433.341.

Mourt's Relation: A Journal of the Pilgrims at Plymouth. edited by Dwight B. Heath from the original printing of 1622. New York: Corinth Books, 1963.

Peabody, Andrew P. *A Manual of Moral Philosophy.* New York: American Book Company, 1873.

Peabody, Selim Hobart. *Peabody Genealogy.* Edited by Charles Henry Pope, Boston: Charles H. Pope, publisher, 1909.

Peavy, Linda and Ursula Smith. *Frontier Women.* New York: Barnes and Noble Books, 1996.

Pettengill, Samuel B. *The Yankee Pioneers, A Saga of Courage.* Rutland, Vermont: Charles E. Tuttle Company, 1971.

Pettit, Jan. *Utes, The Mountain People.* Boulder, Colorado: Johnson Books, 1990.

Pritchard, Sandra F. *Roadside Summit, Part II, The Human Landscape.* A Summit Historical Society Publication, 1992.

Robbins, Roland Wells. *Pilgrim John Alden's Progress, Archaeological Excavations in Duxbury.* Plymouth, Massachusetts: The Pilgrim Society, 1969.

Robinson, Enders A. *The Devil Discovered, Salem Witchcraft, 1692.* New York: Hippocrene Books, Inc., 1991.

Roszak, Theodore. The Voice of the Earth. New York: Simon and Schuster, 1992.

Rutman, Darrell B. *Husbandmen of Plymouth, Farms and Villages in the Old Colony, 1620-1692.* Boston: Beacon Press, 1967.

Rollins, Alden M. *Vermont Warnings Out. Vol I, Northern Vermont and Vol. 2, Southern Vermont,* Camden Maine: Picton Press, 1995.

Schlissel, Lillian. *Women's Diaries of the Westward Journey.* New York: Schocken Books, 1982.

Simmons, Virginia McConnell. *Bayou Salado, The Story of South Park.* Colorado Springs, Colorado: Century One Press, 1966.

Singing the Living Tradition. The Unitarian Universalist Association, Boston: Beacon Press, 1993, #552.

Smedley, William. *Across the Plains, An 1862 Journey from Omaha to Oregon.* Boulder: Johnson Books, 1994.

Stewart, Elinore Pruitt. *Letters of a Woman Homesteader.* Lincoln, Nebraska: University of Nebraska Press, 1961.

Stratton, Eugene Aubrey, FASG. *Plymouth Colony, Its History and People, 1620-1691.* Salt Lake City, Utah: Ancestry Publishing Company, 1986.

Stratton Joanna. *Voices from the Kansas Frontier.* New York: Simon and Schuster, 1981.

Sprague, Marshall. *Colorado, A Bicentennial History.* W. W. Norton and Company, 1976.

Story of the Great American West. Pleasantville, New York: Reader's Digest Association, 1977.

Tepper, Michael. *Passengers to America; a Consolidation.* Genealogical Publishing Company, 1978. (p. 16, 17).

Thacher, James, M.D.A.A.S. *History of the Town of Plymouth from its First Settlement in 1620 to the Present Time with a concise History of the Aborigines of New England and their Wars with the English.* Originally published 1832, Yarmouthport: Parnassus Imprints, 3rd edition, 1972.

Tharp, Louise Hall. *The Peabody Sisters of Salem*. New York: Book-of-the-Month Club, Inc. 1980.

Ulrich, Laurel Thatcher. *Good Wives, Image and Reality in the Lives of Women in Northern New England, 1650 - 1750*. New York: Vintage Books, 1980.

Usher, Robert G. *The Pilgrims and their History*. Macmillan Company, 1918. reprinted by Corner House Publishing Corporation, 1984.

Vance, Randolf. *Ozark Folksongs*. Columbia, Missouri: State Historical Society, vol. 1., 1946-50.

Waldman, Carl. *Who Was Who in Native American History: Indians and non-Indians from early contacts through 1900*. New York: Facts on File, 1989.

Wentworth, Dorothy. *The Alden Family in the Alden House*. Published by the Duxbury Rural and Historical Society, 1980.

Wentworth, Dorothy. *Settlement and Growth of Duxbury, 1628-1870*. Published by the Duxbury Rural and Historical Society, 1975.

Whitehill, Walter Muir. *Captain Joseph Peabody, A Record of his Ships and of his Family*. Salem, Massachusetts: Peabody Museum, 1962.

Wilkie, Richard W. and Jack Teger, (editors). *Historical Atlas of Massachusetts*, Amherst, Massachusetts: University of Massachusetts Press, 1991.

Windsor, Justin. *History of the Town of Duxbury*. Boston: Crosby and Nichols, 1849.

Wolle, Muriel Sibell. *Stampede to Timberline*. Denver: Sage Books, 1949.

Women as Tall as our Mountains, Mini-biographies of Summit County Women. Summit County Colorado: Project of PEO, Chapter FU, 1976.

Ziner, Feenie. *The Pilgrims and Plymouth Colony*, by the editors of American Heritage, Mahwah, New Jersey: published by Troll Associates, 1961.

Newspapers and Periodicals

Crossen, Forest. "Jimmie Jones Recalls Early Days of Placer Mining in South Park", *The Denver Post*, August 27, 1953.

Fairplay Flume, April 15, 1898.

Gilsinger, Jane. "Slaghts, a forgotten Platte Canyon townsite", *Park County Republican and Fairplay Flume*, March 27, 1998, p. 17.

"History: Slate Creek Hall and Town", *Voices, A Summit Historical Society Publication*, December, 1997.

Korell, Jason H. "Elizabeth Peabody founded kindergartens", *The Lexington Minuteman*, December 22, 1977.

MacPherson, Myra. "Genteel dissension among 3 generations of Peabody Women", *The Boston Globe*, May 5, 1979.

Marshall, Megan. "Three Sisters who Showed the Way", *American Heritage*, September-October, 1987. p. 58-66.

McFadden, Robert D. "Mary Peabody, 89, Civil Rights Activist", *The New York Times*, February 7, 1981.

"One room schools offer a rare look into America's past", *Voices, A Summit Historical Society Publication*, vol. VI, No. 1, ed. 2., Spring , 1991.

Ourada, Patricia K. "The Chinese in Colorado", *The Colorado Magazine*, p. 273-84.

Peabody, Elmer C. "Reminiscences of the Good Old Days," *Summit County Journal*, Aug. 7 - Sept 4, 1953.

Peabody, Elmer C. "Cliff Peabody Describes the Awful San Francisco Disaster", *Breckenridge Bulletin*, May 5, 1906.

Peabody, Elmer C. "E. C. Peabody Gives Personal Account of the Big Snow - As Told to His Granddaughters", *The Summit County Journal*, six installments: March 26, April 2, 9, 16, 23, 39, 1954.

Rocky Mountain News. News about Lelon Peabody on Gold Run, July 17, 1868.

"Who is Fort Mary B.'s Namesake?", *Voices, A Summit Historical Society Publication*, June, 1998.

Records and Deeds

Early History of Town of Duxbury, Town Records, Duxbury Rural and Historical Society, Duxbury, Massachusetts.

Fish, Henry. Early Town Records of Duxbury. Unpublished manuscript, Duxbury Rural and Historical Society, Duxbury, Massachusetts, 1923.

Pulsifer, David (editor). Plymouth Colony Records, Deeds, Vol. I, Boston, 1861.

Dumas Malone, editor. *Dictionary of American Biography, VII*. New York: Charles Scribner Sons, 1934, copyright renewed 1962.

Photography Credits

Please note:

AC indicates Author's Collection;

CHS indicates Colorado Historical Society; DPL indicates Denver Public Library, Western History Collection;

SHS indicates Summit County, Colorado Historical Society.

ii-iii, Pioneer couple, Kansas Historical Society.
iv. Peabody family, AC.
vi. Wagon train, CHS.
2. Elmer Clifton Peabody, Sr., AC.
3. Victoria Rosedahl Peabody, AC.
6. Plymouth Plantation, winter, AC.
7. Alden proposing, AC.
9. John Alden House, Duxbury Historical Society.
15. Alden House kitchen, Duxbury Historical Society.
17. Millstone, AC.
22. Pilgrim in garden, AC.
25. Pilgrim woman in doorway, AC.
27. 1621 work activity, AC.
31. 1621 dinner, AC.
42. Wampanoag Indians, Suzanne Kreiter, The Boston Globe.
49. Logging, St. Lawrence County, New York Historical Society.
51. Erecting a log cabin, Idaho Historical Society.
53. East Pitcairn cabin, St. Lawrence, New York Historical Society.
55. Seminary, St. Lawrence, New York Historical Society.
56. Deer hunter, AC.
58. Floating logs, St. Lawrence, New York His- torical Society.
61. Market Street wagon train, DPL.
63. Gold panning, Quandary Antiques.
64. Two miners, AC.
65. Jessie Mill ruins, AC.

69. Stagecoaches, CHS.
71. Ute encampment, CHS.
73. Wagon train, CHS.
75. Wagon en route to mine camp, CHS.
77. 1860's Breckenridge, DPL.
79. Burros hauling lumber, SHS.
80. Chief Colorow, CHS.
83. Buffalo shoot, Kansas Historical Society.
85. Buffalo hides, Kansas Historical Society.
87. Ute family, CHS.
95. Covered wagon, Kansas Historical Society.
98. Peabody women, Bill Gateley Collection.
102. Lunch at the placer mine, California Historical Society.
109. Derailment on Boreas Pass, SHS.
110. Locomotive, Quandary Antiques.
112. Peabody family, AC.
114. Extension and Jumbo, AC.
115. Breckenridge ore mill, SHS.
117. a. Burros on ridge, CHS.
    b. Breckenridge mine, Quandary Antiques.
118. Wagon train, Breckenridge, DPL.
119. E.C. Peabody, AC.
120. Cliff's wagon and team, AC. (Also on cover).
123. Big Snow Winter, Breckenridge, DPL.
125. Big Snow, 1898-99, DPL.
127. Big Snow, Boreas Pass summit, Quandary Antiques.
131. 1890's parlour, SHS.
135. a. The Colorado House, Quandary Antiques. b. Fatty's Restaurant, AC.
136. Almeda Smith Peabody, AC.
139. Early car, AC.
140. Victorian picnic, AC.
143. a. "Nothing but ruins," AC.
    b. Earthquake, AC.
144. Elmer Clifton Peabody and Halsey Victoria Rosedahl, AC.
147. 1882 schoolhouse, AC.
149. Graduation day, CHS.

Order Extra Copies of *Pioneer Voices* Today!

- *A book to intrigue Breckenridge and Summit County, Colorado enthusiasts*
- *A collector's item for readers who love Colorado's past*
- *A "find" for Plymouth, Massachusetts fans and colonial history buffs*
- *Fresh insight on female pioneers for women readers*
- *A new dimension in the family saga for Peabody descendants*

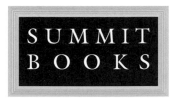

Mail Order To:
SUMMIT BOOKS
3 Currier Court
Lexington, MA 02420

I would like to order:

____copies of *Pioneer Voices* @ 22.95 $_____

Tax (Massachusetts residents only add $1.15/copy) $_____

Shipping and handling @ $3 per book $_____

TOTAL ENCLOSED $_____

Please mail **Pioneer Voices** to the address below:

Name_____

Address_____

City_____State_____Zip_____